The Political Economy of Environmental Justice

The Political Economy of Environmental Justice

Edited by H. Spencer Banzhaf

Stanford Economics and Finance
An Imprint of Stanford University Press
Stanford, California

Stanford University Press
Stanford, California

Special discounts for bulk quantities of Stanford Economics and Finance are available to corporations, professional associations, and other organizations. For details and discount information, contact the special sales department of Stanford University Press.
Tel: (650) 736-1782, Fax: (650) 736-1784

Printed in the United States of America on acid-free, archival-quality paper

Library of Congress Cataloging-in-Publication Data

The political economy of environmental justice / edited by H. Spencer Banzhaf.
    pages cm
  Includes bibliographical references and index.
  ISBN 978-0-8047-8061-2 (alk. paper)
    1. Environmental economics—United States.   2. Environmental justice—Economic aspects—United States.   3. Environmental policy—Economic aspects—United States.   I. Banzhaf, H. Spencer, 1969– editor of compilation.
  HC110.E5P655 2012
  333.70973—dc23
                                                                    2012000733

Typeset by Newgen in 10/14 Minion

For Kerry,
with thanks

Contents

Acknowledgments

THIS BOOK had its genesis at two points in time. The first was a conversation sometime in the spring or summer of 2001, when Randy Walsh and I took a break from the grind of finishing our dissertations and set out from our shared office—always hot and stuffy—for a walk in Duke Gardens. We reflected on the issue of "environmental gentrification," a notion we were just coming to terms with, and plotted a research agenda for testing it empirically and fleshing out its implications for environmental justice. That was a good day, as I hope this book helps affirm. For a decade of stimulating conversation, productive teamwork, and friendship, I'm deeply grateful to Randy.

The second origin of this book was the summer of 2007, when, with the generous support of the Searle Freedom Trust, I spent two wonderful months at the Property and Environment Research Center (PERC) developing this topic. The conversations I had there and subsequently with Terry Anderson, Dan Benjamin, Roger Meiners, and many others visiting PERC were tremendously helpful and productive. Momentum continued to build and culminated in a Lone Mountain Forum, organized by PERC with generous support from the Earhart Foundation in the fall of 2008. The chapters in this volume came directly out of that forum. For helping make it such a success, I am especially grateful to Monica Guenther and Colleen Lane of PERC, who put in countless hours and other resources. I also thank Vicki Been, Bob Deacon, and Jason Johnston for taking part in the forum and offering many constructive suggestions.

Not the least contribution to this book came from my family, especially my wife, Melissa. I thank her for her understanding on more than one occasion when I spent a late night at work or went on the road while completing it, and for all her love and support.

Contributor Biographies

Terry L. Anderson is the executive director of the Property and Environment Research Center in Bozeman, Montana. He is also a senior fellow at the Hoover Institution at Stanford University and professor emeritus at Montana State University. He has published widely on property rights, especially as they relate to environmental policy.

H. Spencer Banzhaf is an associate professor of economics at Georgia State University. He received his PhD in economics from Duke University in 2001. His research focuses on environmental economics and policy analysis. More narrowly, much of his work studies the interactions among local environmental amenities, local real estate markets, and the demographic composition and structure of cities. His work has been published in journals such as the *American Economic Review, Journal of Environmental Economics and Management, Journal of Urban Economics*, and *History of Political Economy*. He is a research associate at the National Bureau of Economic Research and a senior research fellow at the Property and Environment Research Center.

Trudy Ann Cameron is the Raymond F. Mikesell Professor of Environmental and Resource Economics in the Department of Economics at the University of Oregon. She specializes in methods for the valuation of environmental health-risk reductions for regulatory benefit-cost analysis, with additional interests in measurement of the social benefits of climate change mitigation and the distributional consequences of different environmental policies, among other topics. She is a past president of the Association of Environmental and Resource Economists and a current member of the board of directors of the Society for Benefit-Cost Analysis.

Graham Crawford received a BS in economics and a master's degree in business administration from the University of Oregon. He spent five years working as a research analyst for the economic consulting firm ECONorthwest. He currently holds the position of principal cost analyst and manages an overseas business unit that provides financial oversight of logistics support services and infrastructure development projects.

Brooks Depro is a senior economist in RTI's Social, Statistical, and Environmental Sciences Division. Since 1997, he has conducted and managed regulatory impact analyses for the US Environmental Protection Agency. He also continues to study how changes in environmental quality influence the residential location decisions and the length of residential stay. He received his PhD from North Carolina State University in 2009.

Wayne B. Gray holds the John T. Croteau Chair in Economics at Clark University. He is also the director of the Boston Census Research Data Center and a research associate at the National Bureau of Economic Research. His research focuses on the effectiveness and economic impact of government regulation of environmental and workplace hazards.

Robin R. Jenkins is an economist with the US Environmental Protection Agency's National Center for Environmental Economics. Her work focuses on the economics of municipal solid waste, hazardous waste, and contaminated site cleanup. Recent projects include examining the Superfund Emergency Response and Removal Program and developing a handbook addressing the benefits, costs, and impacts of land cleanup and reuse. She received her PhD in economics from the University of Maryland.

Kelly B. Maguire is an economist with the US Environmental Protection Agency. Her research focuses on issues of environmental justice and valuing mortality risk reductions from environmental policy. She received a BA in economics from the University of Rochester in 1991 and a PhD in economics from Georgia State University in 1999.

Ian McConnaha is currently pursuing a law degree at the University of California at Berkeley, where he is focusing on environmental and natural resources law. He has a particular interest in land use issues and has conducted research on demographic changes resulting from environmental policy choices. Prior to law school, he obtained a bachelor's degree in economics from the University of Oregon and a master's degree in statistics from Columbia University.

Eleanor McCormick graduated from Smith College in 2006. She was on the staff of Resources for the Future, a think tank based in Washington, DC, from 2006 to 2008. In 2011, she completed her master's of divinity degree at Yale University and is currently serving as the community life director of the United Congregational Church of Bridgeport, Connecticut, and is the executive director of Norma F. Pfriem Urban Outreach Initiatives, Inc., also in Bridgeport.

Douglas S. Noonan is an associate professor in the School of Public Policy at the Georgia Institute of Technology. He applies microeconomic and policy analytic approaches to urban environmental topics (e.g., brownfield remediation, greenspace, air pollution). He is co–contributing editor of *Managing the Commons*. Since receiving his PhD from the University of Chicago in 2002, his research has been published in various economics and policy journals and has been funded by the National Science Foundation and the US Environmental Protection Agency, among others.

Ronald J. Shadbegian is an economist with the US Environmental Protection Agency's National Center for Environmental Economics. He has recently published "Location Decisions of U.S. Polluting Plants: Theory, Empirical Evidence, and Consequences" (with Ann Wolverton) in the *International Review of Environmental and Resource Economics* (2010) and "Environmental Justice: Do Poor and Minority Populations Face More Hazards?" (with Wayne Gray and Ann Wolverton) in *The Oxford Handbook of the Economics of Poverty* (2012).

Joshua Sidon is an economist with the Bureau of Land Management's National Operations Center in Denver, Colorado. He received his PhD in economics from the University of Colorado in 2006. He has expertise in National Environmental Policy Act (NEPA) analysis, process, and documentation; housing market research; and analysis of environmental policies and regulations.

Christopher Timmins is an associate professor of economics and of the Nicholas School of the Environment at Duke University. He is also a research associate at the National Bureau of Economic Research. He received his BSFS in international economics from Georgetown University in 1991 and his PhD in economics from Stanford University in 1997. His work has appeared in *Econometrica*, *Economic Journal*, *Journal of Environmental Economics and Management*, and *Journal of Urban Economics*, among others.

Jacob Vigdor is a professor of public policy and economics at Duke University and a faculty research fellow at the National Bureau of Economic Research. He earned a BS from Cornell University in 1994 and a PhD in economics from Harvard University in 1999. His work has appeared in the *Journal of Political Economy*, *Review of Economics and Statistics*, and *Journal of Law and Economics*. It also has been featured in the *New York Times*, *U.S. News & World Report*, *The Economist*, *Washington Post*, *USA Today*, and *National Review Online*.

Randall Walsh is an associate professor of economics at the University of Pittsburgh and a research associate at the National Bureau of Economic Research. He holds a PhD from Duke University and a BA from the University of New Hampshire. He is co-editor of the journal *Economic Inquiry* and a member of the Allegheny County Health Department's Air Toxics Advisory Committee. His research has been funded by the National Institutes of Health and the National Science Foundation and has appeared in such journals as the *American Economic Review*, *Review of Economic Studies*, and *International Economic Review*.

Ann Wolverton is an economist at the National Center for Environmental Economics at the US Environmental Protection Agency. She has twice served as a senior economist at the Council of Economic Advisers, in 2006–2007 and again in 2009–2010. She received her PhD in economics from the University of Texas at Austin in 1999.

The Political Economy of Environmental Justice

1 The Political Economy of Environmental Justice

An Introduction

H. Spencer Banzhaf

Introduction

Since the landmark studies by the US General Accounting Office (GAO; 1983) and the United Church of Christ (1987), the environmental justice literature has consistently shown that poor and minority households systematically live in more polluted neighborhoods. This correlation appears to be quite robust to the type of pollution considered: for example, the poor live closer to hazardous waste facilities, landfills, and other locally undesirable land uses (LULUs); they live closer to large air polluters; and they live in communities with higher concentrations of air pollutants.[1] The correlation is also robust to the statistical methods employed by researchers.[2] In short, the correlation qualifies as a "stylized fact" as much as anything in social science.

This finding of a disproportionate environmental burden borne by the poor and people of color has led to the introduction of several "environmental justice acts" in Congress (although none have passed) and to President Bill Clinton's Executive Order 12898. Still in force, the order requires nondiscrimination in federal environmental programs and focuses federal resources, such as the Brownfields Program of the US Environmental Protection Agency (EPA), on low-income and minority communities. More recently, the EPA has launched a number of initiatives to incorporate environmental justice considerations into its rule making.

In addition to such top-down initiatives, the environmental justice findings have fed grassroots activist movements. Sometimes with help from national leaders of the environmental justice movement, local stakeholders have sought more involvement in permitting polluting facilities and in making other environmental plans.[3] They also have filed lawsuits against governments for discriminatory environmental enforcement and against polluters for environmental nuisances. For example, in one prominent case, local activists forced California's South Coast Air Quality Management District to settle a suit over the geographic distribution of trades under its Regional Clean Air Incentives Market (RECLAIM) pollution trading program.[4]

Evaluating claims of discrimination and injustice requires an understanding of the social causes lying behind the correlation between pollution and demographics. So does evaluating the efficacy of any policy remedies. Economic models can provide important insights into these issues. These include economic models of discrimination, of local public goods and real estate markets, of firms' profit maximization, and of political organization and lobbying. Generally speaking, these models have tended to "push back" the locus of injustice from firms' individual decisions, such as where to locate and how to operate, to the more fundamental issue of the distribution of income and wealth and the ways in which markets allocate goods—including environmental amenities— to households. This point has been made well both by critics and by participants in the environmental justice movement, and has been discussed fruitfully by such authors as Vicki Been (1993, 1994), Lynn Blais (1996), Sheila Foster (1998), and Laura Pulido (2000), among others.

Despite the importance of the question, we do not really understand *which* socioeconomic forces lie behind the observed correlations. Moreover, the full implication of these various economic models for the distributional impacts of potential policy *remedies* for environmental injustice has not been well understood, either. Yet if the ultimate social goal is actually to improve the welfare of disadvantaged groups, as well as to describe social processes, understanding the distributional effects of environmental policies is crucial. These distributional effects will, in turn, depend on the social process generating the observed pattern in the distribution of pollution. Consequently, the social forces driving the poor's exposure to pollution represent a critical lacuna in our understanding.

The Lone Mountain Forum

For this reason, we felt it was time to revisit environmental justice questions, with a concentrated effort to flesh out the economic and social dynamics lying behind the observed correlation between pollution and demographics. The opportunity to make that effort came with a Lone Mountain Forum, organized by the Property and Environment Research Center (PERC). The forum was made possible with generous support from the Earhart Foundation.

The authors of the chapters included in this volume gathered in Big Sky, Montana, in October 2008. The authors were all economists, but our group also contained a mix of additional economists and legal scholars, who joined us in the dialogue.[5] Additionally, the group included scholars long engaged in the environmental justice literature as well as others who were new to it and brought fresh perspectives.

One thing we did *not* try to do was to revisit the question of whether there is a correlation between pollution and the presence of poor or minority households. Granting the presence of at least a simple correlation, we came rather to discuss questions about the economic forces lying behind it, seeking to gain insights from both theoretical models and empirical analyses. We also wanted to explore the *implications* of these insights for public policy.

The chapters in this volume are the fruits of that meeting. While they all come from the perspective of economists, our hope is that they will be of use to all participants in environmental justice conversations, including legal scholars, sociologists, geographers, philosophers, and historians, whether in academia, government, business, or community organizations.

These research questions and their intended audience motivated the title of the collected volume, *The Political Economy of Environmental Justice*. The term "political economy" conveys the discipline of economics lying at the heart of the volume, of course, but it has numerous additional shades of meaning beyond simply "economics." It can mean the economic analysis of politics and public choice, including interest group politics, regulation, and redistribution. It can mean simply wedding economics to public policy. And it has an older, archaic meaning growing out of its roots in moral philosophy, as the more comprehensive study of societies and states in all their economic, political, legal, historical, and moral aspects. All of these meanings are packed into this term, which serves as part of the volume's title.

Economic Models of Environmental Justice

Economists' perspective on environmental justice issues was articulated first and best by James Hamilton (1995). Hamilton identified three broad categories of explanations for environmental justice correlations: pure discrimination, economic efficiency, and political action. Promoting some of his subcategories and adding another, I consider these in six categories.

The first category is "pure discrimination." Following the model of Becker (1957), this notion is that firms may have a differential preference for sheltering whites from pollution or even a perverse desire to harm minorities. Essentially, firms act to achieve a set of objectives, which includes not only profits but also discriminatory preferences for environmental outcomes on different demographic groups. Firms would thus make production decisions that harm minorities even if it is not in their own profit-maximizing interests, paying a price in foregone profits to indulge their discriminatory tastes. Believing firms focus solely on profits, economists tend to be skeptical of this explanation.

A second interpretation, known as "coming to the nuisance," essentially reverses the causality. Firms site their facilities and make other production decisions for numerous reasons, and local demographics may be a negligible factor. If they do emit pollution in any given location, for whatever reason, however, it will make that location less attractive to residents. Wealthier households, in particular, with more opportunities, will move out, lowering demand for housing in the area. Consequently, local land and housing prices will fall. Poorer households may actually move in, prioritizing the low housing costs despite the disamenity of the pollution. This process was well articulated by Vicki Been in a series of influential articles (1993, 1994, 1997), as well as by Hamilton (1995) and Blais (1996). Banzhaf and Walsh (2008) and Banzhaf, Sidon, and Walsh (see Chapter 4) confirm this intuition in a formal economic model in the style of Tiebout (1956), whereby households choose neighborhoods in which to live based on local amenities and costs (including property prices and tax rates).

In this way, the demographics might follow the spatial distribution of the pollution. As long as there is some pollution, it must have a spatial distribution, and so somebody will be nearest to it. As emphasized by Charles Tiebout himself, these models suggest that ultimately the spatial distribution of pollution is economically efficient. The term "efficient" is a linguistic minefield, which can lead to substantial misunderstanding between economists and others. To economists, it means simply that households with the highest values for a cleaner environment—those with the highest willingness to pay, in economists' jargon—do, in fact, avoid it in the end. Conversely, those with the lowest willingness to pay for a cleaner environment—those least willing to sacrifice other goods like housing, food, or entertainment—are the ones living nearest the pollution.

If people's values for avoiding pollution differ because of differences in family makeup (e.g., the presence of children or the elderly), physical sensitivity to pollution (e.g., having asthma), or similarly formed preferences, then the allocation would seem quite sensible indeed. However, these values also proceed from people's ability to pay, based on their income. This raises additional questions about the nature of injustice but pushes those questions back to the underlying distribution of income itself as the more fundamental issue. That is, the question turns to why particular groups or individuals are poor in the first place and hence unable to acquire some of the good things in life—a clean environment included.

A third, and closely related, interpretation is that the geographic pattern of local environmental nuisances arises from negotiations between firms and local stakeholders, whereby firms compensate communities for hosting unwanted facilities (Hamilton 1993, 1995). As Ronald Coase (1960) famously argued, such negotiations would arise when the right to pollute (or to be free of pollution) is clearly defined and when the costs of negotiation and transacting compensatory payments are low.

Coase (1960) pointed out that when property rights are well defined, they also become tradable. Specifying the right to pollute—or to be free from pollution—allows pollution, too, to be traded. Coase suggested, for example, that negotiations could arise over factory smoke. If factories have a right to pollute, local residents may pay them not to pollute. If local residents have a right to be free from pollution, factories might compensate them to accept some pollution. In the same way as can happen through land markets, environmental quality will again be highest near those who value it most highly, and lowest near those who are prepared—for whatever reason—to sacrifice fewer other goods to obtain it.

In this Coasian world, other things equal, firms would locate in neighborhoods that are willing to accept lower payments as compensation. Like the Tiebout model, the Coasian model implies that the spatial distribution of pollution is economically efficient but again only conditional upon the existing distribution of income. The primary difference between the two models is that Coase's is a story of firms choosing a location based on their negotiations with local residents, whereas Tiebout's is a story of households choosing a location based on its existing amenities and prices.

Fourth, firms may seek out areas with weaker political resistance to their polluting activities. If local residents must use costly political action to fend off unwanted pollution, then the level of their political resistance is likely to be proportionate to their willingness to pay to avoid pollution. In this way, political wrangling can be, for all practical purposes, a special form of the pricing mechanism operating through the Coasian process, and so, too, the outcome might be efficient in the same way—again, conditional on the existing income distribution (Becker 1983).[6] Those with the highest willingness to pay to avoid pollution invest the most in pollution-resisting activism; meanwhile, firms seek to avoid paying the political cost of trying to overcome such activism and so avoid those communities.

However, the strength or weakness of a community's political opposition may not, in fact, be proportionate to its desire to avoid pollution. Some communities may have better access to the halls of power than others. Others may be better organized politically or, in Coasian language, may face lower transaction costs of coming together to negotiate with (or oppose) polluting firms. Hamilton (1993, 1995), for example, found that communities with lower voter turnout were more likely to see local firms expand their processing of hazardous wastes (see also Brooks and Sethi 1997; Arora and Cason 1999). From this perspective, environmental justice activists who provide legal advice and facilitate local capacity building in poor neighborhoods are achieving two ends: they are serving the poor while helping these social processes to function more efficiently, lowering Coasian transaction costs.

A fifth interpretation is that firms, while not reacting so much to local demographics per se, are attracted to other factors that happen to be spatially correlated with the demographic composition of neighborhoods. Examples of such factors might include low wages, low land prices, access to transportation corridors, and proximity to suppliers or to other similar firms (because of so-called agglomeration economies). Wolverton (2009; see also Chapter 8) finds that such factors do appear to be one of the main drivers behind firms' location decisions. Some of these factors, like low wages, might, in fact, be demographic characteristics. Other factors might be correlated with demographics indirectly through Tiebout-like processes. For example, nearby transportation corridors may be an attractive amenity to firms but a disamenity to households, one that drives away the richer residents. Or the age of a community's housing stock might well be tied historically to the development of nearby manufacturing, and it may be the life cycle of the housing stock that drives the observed correlations. Research by Rosenthal (2008) and Brueckner and Rosenthal (2009) shows that a community's population tends to grow poorer over time along with the age of the housing stock, until the community reaches a period of redevelopment and renewal. Further exploration of this so-called filtering model in the environmental justice context would be fruitful.

A sixth and final interpretation focuses attention not so much on firms as on government—and its failure to enforce environmental standards and regulations equitably. Governments might, for example, enforce such provisions more rigorously in areas with higher levels of political support for the current administration. But they need not be intentionally discriminatory for such outcomes to arise. Government enforcement agencies may find it easier or even more efficient to react to complaints from local citizens. But as with the "squeaky wheel that gets the grease," those agencies would be more likely to respond to better organized, better connected, and otherwise more politically powerful citizens (see McCubbins and Schwartz 1984; Hamilton and Viscusi 1999). If environmental justice communities are more poorly organized or politically connected, this dynamic would give rise to the observed environmental justice correlations. (If so, this might also be a further reason that firms would be attracted to areas with less political power.)

Why "Why" Matters

No doubt, others would be able to offer additional explanations, but these are the ones most likely to occur to most economists. Even the very act of listing them can help overcome a common misunderstanding between economists and others about the idea of "environmental justice" or "environmental racism." When an economist hears these terms, he typically thinks in terms of the first model described above, the story of pure discrimination, in which firms sacrifice profits in order to steer pollution toward less valued groups. Interpreting "discrimination" or "injustice" through the lens of this particular model, economists and many social scientists have tended to subject environmental justice correlations to various controls (e.g., multivariate regression). If the correlation between pollution and poor and minority populations disappears when controlling for other factors, such as education, land values, or voter turnout, then economists often conclude that there is no environmental justice concern. Indeed, they too often conclude that environmental justice advocates and researchers from other disciplines are simply naïve.

In fact, if we economists would spend a little more time reviewing the environmental justice literature, we would realize that very few people have ever made the suggestion that firms' tastes for something like "pure discrimination" are responsible for the observed correlations. Most are well aware of the socio-economic processes involved. Indeed, many scholars (e.g., Bullard 1990; Foster 1998; Pulido 2000) have articulated nuanced conceptual frameworks for interpreting environmental justice questions, frameworks that exhibit a grasp of the economic issues that might surprise some economists.

From the point of view of many of these alternative frameworks, the fact that market and/or political forces lead to the observed correlations between pollution and demographics does not render the question of an "injustice" moot. Indeed, consider the EPA's definition of environmental justice:

> Environmental Justice is the fair treatment and meaningful involvement of all people regardless of race, color, national origin, or income with respect to the development, implementation, and enforcement of environmental laws, regulations, and policies. EPA has this goal for all communities and persons across this Nation. It will be achieved when everyone enjoys the same degree of protection from environmental and health hazards and equal access to the decision-making process to have a healthy environment in which to live, learn, and work. (EPA 2010)

Bryant (1995) defines it this way:

> [Environmental justice] refers to those cultural norms and values, rules, regulations, behaviors, policies, and decisions to support sustainable communities, where people can interact with confidence that their environment is safe, nurturing, and productive. Environmental justice is served when people can realize their highest potential, without experiencing the "isms." Environmental justice is supported by decent paying and safe jobs; quality schools and recreation; decent housing and adequate health care; democratic decision-making and personal empowerment; and communities free of violence, drugs, and poverty. These are communities where both cultural and biological diversity are respected and highly revered and where distributive justice prevails. (p. 6)

Of the two, Bryant's is clearly the more holistic, encompassing a wide range of issues only indirectly connected to the natural environment. But the key point is that both definitions encompass notions of procedural justice and distributive justice, while neither focuses on the question of the *intent* of polluters.[7]

Beyond clarifying the vocabulary of "discrimination," understanding which of these explanations are the most significant is important for three additional reasons. First, it colors the interpretation of the injustice in the distribution of pollution. Second, it has implications for the efficacy of policies designed to reverse environmental justice correlations. And third, it has implications for the actual welfare effects on the poor of cleaning up their neighborhoods.

If the correlation between pollution and minority and poor populations results from intentional discrimination by government agencies, it would violate the equal protection clause of the Constitution and possibly Title VI of the Civil Rights Act of 1964 (which prevents discrimination by agencies receiving federal funds).[8] Even if there were no discriminatory intent, there would still be a question about the justice in the agencies' procedures as well as concerns about distributive justice.

If the observed correlations are a consequence of "coming to the nuisance" and similar socioeconomic processes mediated through real estate markets and housing decisions, however, then the correlation between pollution and demographics appears not so much a cause of an unequal distribution as a result. In this case, there is still a question of distributive injustice, but the locus of that injustice lies in the underlying distribution of income rather than in the distribution of environmental quality.

The environmental justice literature, by and large, has acknowledged the potential role played by market dynamics while arguing that such processes do not undermine the normative significance of the injustice of disproportionate environmental burdens. Be that as it may, it does not follow that understanding such social processes is irrelevant. However unfair the distribution of income, markets provide an effective opportunity for individuals and groups to enhance their welfare, *given their limited resources*. It follows that if market-based processes (such as Tieboutian allocations mediated through real estate markets and Coasian bargaining over pollution itself) are important, then undermining the market outcomes may undermine the efforts of even the most disadvantaged groups to better themselves. Focusing on the root problem—poverty—by redistributing income is likely to be a more effective way to improve the welfare of the poor than improving environmental quality.

For example, a Tiebout process of "coming to the nuisance" would undermine the efficacy of any policies designed to reverse the correlation through the targeting of firm behavior. As pointed out by Been (1993), as long as some areas are more polluted than others, migration might always reestablish the correlation. Perhaps more importantly and more surprisingly, the process would have important and counterintuitive implications for household welfare. For instance, Sieg et al. (2004) and Walsh (2007) find that targeting dirty, poor neighborhoods for cleanup with the intention of helping the local residents can be counterproductive. The reason is that residents who live in dirtier communities tend to place a high priority on low-cost housing relative to the environment, presumably because they cannot afford to sacrifice such necessities given their limited finances. In contrast, new residents who move in following a cleanup have a higher willingness to pay for environmental quality. As they move in, they bid property values up by their own higher willingness to pay. Thus, cleaning up the environment may increase housing costs for the poor by more than their willingness to pay. Moreover, as they generally rent their housing, poor residents stand to lose from these increased housing costs, while landlords reap the benefit. Sieg et al. (2004) refer to this effect as "environmental gentrification." Such perverse distributional effects are not only a concern of the academic literature: they have emerged as a top concern of grassroots movements as well, as expressed in a recent report from the National Environmental Justice Advisory Council (NEJAC; 2006). This issue of environmental gentrification is discussed in more detail in Chapters 2 and 3.

Role of Housing Discrimination

One theme in the economic approach to environmental justice that has emerged is the importance of market processes in allocating pollution, as a more subtle yet more realistic process than pure discrimination in production decisions. But this begs the question, what about discrimination in those mediating markets, especially the real estate market?

The question pushes the logic back one step, but many of the principles are the same. The most overt possibility here is pure discrimination in the housing market. In this case, pure discrimination is, on the face of it, more plausible, although discriminating sellers or real estate agents must still pay a price for their discrimination in the form of foregone customers. Nevertheless, historically, pure discrimination in the housing market has taken the form of neighborhood covenants and the refusal to sell or rent to individuals of color. But there is an indirect version of discrimination here as well. A more subtle form of discrimination is the decision of individuals to live (or not live) in a neighborhood based on its demographic composition. For example, segregation will arise if whites prefer to live with other whites, as evidenced in processes such as "white flight." Importantly, the converse does not necessarily follow: the existence of segregation does not necessarily imply such indirect discrimination. It could follow, for example, from the Tiebout process and interracial differences in willingness to pay for public goods (McGuire 1974).

Cutler, Glaeser, and Vigdor (1999), in their fascinating historical study of segregation in the United States from 1890 to 1990, found that the pattern of housing costs for blacks and whites suggests that pure discrimination marked the rise of segregation in the first two-thirds of the 20th century but that the more implicit form, based on individual residential choices, was more salient by 1980.[9] Card, Mas, and Rothstein (2008), for example, estimate that in most cities, whites begin to flee neighborhoods when minorities comprise 5 to 20 percent of the population. These estimates are consistent with survey findings about whites' tolerance for minority neighbors. Blacks, on the other hand, state that they prefer a 50–50 mix of racial composition (Farley et al. 1978; Farley and Krysan 2002).

Such housing market behavior can magnify the consequences of the Tiebout model for environmental justice. As shown by Schelling (1971, 1972), even when everybody prefers some integration, such preferences can result in a "tipping point" at which communities become quite segregated. When combined with the Tiebout model, it is not surprising that whites enjoy the high-amenity areas (see Becker and Murphy 2000; Banzhaf and Walsh 2010; see also Chapter 4). These areas have higher land values not only because of their environmental amenities but also because the white majority values them simply because they are whiter. This white premium becomes yet another force driving minorities to more polluted communities: they must not only join white communities to obtain high levels of public goods and risk being the "odd man out," but they must also pay extra for the privilege (Ford 1994). Consistent with these hypotheses, Depro and Timmins (see Chapter 5) find preliminary evidence that minorities face a higher opportunity cost of obtaining clean air than do whites.

Advancing the Ball

The chapters in this volume all speak to one or more of these issues, either testing various economic theories of environmental justice correlations, working out hypotheses about their respective implications for public policy, or testing those derived hypotheses. In some cases, the chapters make use of an online appendix, at http://www.sup.org/environmentaljustice, where additional details about the data and empirical findings can be found. Each chapter references the appendix where appropriate.

A plurality of the chapters explores various aspects of Tiebout's hypothesis that real estate markets mediate the exposure of demographic groups to pollution. Reviewing the evidence, Eleanor McCormick and I find substantial support for this mechanism (Chapter 2). We also find evidence of the effects of gentrification on prices. Brooks Depro and Christopher Timmins (Chapter 5) provide additional evidence of Tiebout's process in a detailed study of households' responses to ozone improvements. Whites appear to be more likely to move up to low-ozone neighborhoods than are blacks or Hispanics.

On the other hand, in Chapter 6, Trudy Ann Cameron, Graham Crawford, and Ian McConnaha do not find such systematic patterns in their examination of the evolving demographics around Superfund sites. They point out that white males tend to view environmental risks as smaller, so minority and female-headed households may be *less* likely to "move to the nuisance." Moreover, they point out that observing these patterns in the data over time is complicated by the changing perceptions of risks as some contaminated sites are either cleaned up or, alternatively, permanently stigmatized.

Other chapters exploring the issue provide additional nuance to our understanding of gentrification. Jacob Vigdor (Chapter 3) points out that if environmental justice communities have many vacant houses, then the excess housing supply may be more than sufficient to absorb the increase in demand following cleanup, so investments in environmental justice communities may not trigger price increases. Similarly, Douglas Noonan (Chapter 7) points out that many projects involve redevelopment. If the increased supply from the new development balances the increased demand from the improved amenities, then there will not be any price effect. Neither author finds evidence of price appreciation in the applications they consider, cleanup of Superfund sites in the former case and a brownfield-to-greenfield project in the latter. Finally, in Chapter 4, Joshua Sidon, Randall Walsh, and I consider the case in which households sort on the demographic composition of the community as well as amenities like the local environment. Such preferences reinforce the observed environmental justice correlations but also dampen gentrification effects.

Ann Wolverton (Chapter 8) offers what may be the strongest analysis of firm locational choice in this literature. She finds that when firms site their polluting facilities, they prioritize factors that likely lower their operating costs and locate in areas with lower wages, with good access to transportation, and with existing activity in their industry. After controlling for these factors, the racial composition and income of communities do not appear to factor in their locational decisions.

There thus seems to be substantial evidence for the second hypothesis for observed environmental justice correlations discussed above (mediation through land markets) and the fifth (profit-maximizing locational choices by firms). However, progress is not made only by verifying ideas. Eliminating hypotheses is just as useful. In Chapter 9, Ronald Shadbegian and Wayne Gray consider the sixth hypothesis, discrimination by governments. They test for variation in states' pollution enforcement activity based on local demographics and find no connection (with the exception that liberal areas get more enforcement and conservative areas less). Similarly, in Chapter 10, Robin Jenkins and Kelly Maguire find no connection between state taxes on hazardous wastes and local demographics.

This still leaves at least two important economic theories that were not explored by the authors in this volume. One is Coase's theory of compensatory transactions for pollution. There is some evidence that Coasian processes are functioning in local pollution markets. For example, in their study of the largest solid waste landfills in the United States, Jenkins, Maguire, and Morgan (2004) find that about half of the landfill owners provide compensation to communities, with payments averaging about $1.5 million in 1996, and in one case $20 million. Forty-six percent made regular cash payments, and 36 percent made miscellaneous in-kind payments in the form of wells, parks, firehouses, and so on. Thus, although not universal and although probably hampered by high transaction costs, Coase's mechanism appears to be working, at least to some extent.

The second hypothesis that this volume does not directly address is the role of political power and local interest groups in firms' pollution decisions. As noted previously, polluting firms may avoid communities that are better organized and have more political power, and Hamilton (1993, 1995) presented evidence on the importance of these factors, as measured by voter turnout. Since Hamilton's seminal work on this topic, new developments in the political economy have opened up potentially new lines of inquiry. For example, Alesina, Baqir, and Easterly (1999) have hypothesized that areas with more demographic heterogeneity will have the hardest time assembling for collective action. They find that more heterogeneous communities have lower levels of public goods. Similarly, Vigdor (2004) finds that such communities have lower response rates for the US Census, despite the fiscal advantages to a community of responding. Similar organizational problems may plague heterogeneous communities when it comes to negotiating (or opposing) polluting facilities (Videras and Bordoni 2006).

Both these areas are worthy of further exploration, as are no doubt all those discussed in this volume. If the volume succeeds as we hope, it will be in its role as a conversation starter that motivates still more exploration of those topics.

Notes

1. On the location of landfills and hazardous waste facilities, see US GAO (1983); United Church of Christ (1987); Goldman and Fitton (1994); Baden and Coursey (2002); Been (1997); Boer et al. (1997); Pastor, Sadd, and Hipp (2001); Saha and Mohai (2005); Mohai and Saha (2006); Bullard et al. (2007); and Maantay (2007). On the presence of large polluters, see Hersh (1995); Ringquist (1997); Sadd et al. (1999); Fisher, Kelly, and Romm (2006); and Banzhaf, Sidon, and Walsh (Chapter 4). On the emissions of air pollutants, see Kriesel, Centner, and Keeler (1996); Brooks and Sethi (1997); Ringquist (1997); Arora and Cason (1999); and Pastor, Sadd, and Morello-Frosch (2004, 2007). On estimated air pollution concentrations, see Morello-Frosch, Pastor, and Sadd (2001); Ash and Fetter (2004); Fisher, Kelly, and Romm (2006); Pastor, Sadd, and Morello-Frosch (2007); and Depro and Timmins (Chapter 5).

Bullard (1990) is the classic book-length introduction to the entire literature. For more recent reviews and discussion, see Cole and Foster (2001), Bowen (2002), Pastor (2002), Ringquist (2003), Brulle and Pellow (2006), and Noonan (2008). See Ringquist (2005) for a meta-analysis.

2. An exception is the sensitivity of the results to spatial scale, with evidence of the correlation between pollution and demographics stronger at smaller, more disaggregate scales. See Mohai and Saha (2006); Baden, Noonan, and Turaga (2007); and Noonan, Turaga, and Baden (2009).

3. In addition to impeding new permits, sometimes these activities include bargaining for compensation (Jenkins, Maguire, and Morgan 2004).

4. See Lazarus (2000), Binder et al. (2001), and Bullard et al. (2007) on the tangible successes of the environmental justice movement.

5. We particularly thank Joseph Aldy, Vicki Been, Robert Deacon, and Jason Johnston for their valuable and constructive comments.

6. Alchian and Demsetz (1973) point out that ownership is equivalent to the rights to use a resource. Because there may be many uses, property rights are almost infinitely divisible. The owner of "*the* right" to use of a parcel of land, for example, may differ for the right to occupancy, the mineral rights, the water rights, rights-of-way, and so forth. In the same way, even if common law does not give communities a right to be free from pollution, statutory or administrative law may give communities the right to contest the permitting process for citing a facility nearby. It is this right that may give rise to Coasian bargaining, even without plain and unambiguous property rights over every aspect of the resources at stake. Indeed, such actions lie at the heart of the environmental justice movement's strategy today.

7. Loosely, procedural justice in this context refers to the fairness of the processes that determine the ultimate spatial distribution of pollution. Naturally, the EPA is focused on the fairness of federal rule making, but others would emphasize other processes, including business planning, political negotiation, and even the market

itself. Distributive justice refers to the fairness or equity of the ultimate distribution of pollution itself. So long as there is a correlation between pollution and demographics, there is at least a prima facie case for distributive injustice, however it arises. On the interrelationship between procedural and distributive justice issues in the environmental context, see Foster (1998) and Banzhaf (2011).

8. At one time, environmental justice activists sought a remedy in Title VI of the Civil Rights Act, under rules for agencies using federal money. These rules required only proof of discriminatory effect rather than proof of intent. However, the Supreme Court ruled in 2001 in *Alexander v. Sandoval* (532 U.S. 275) that there was no private right of action to enforce such regulations.

9. The tide against explicit discrimination began to turn with the Supreme Court's decision in *Shelley v. Kraemer* (334 U.S. 1 [1948]), striking down restrictive covenants, and with passage of the Fair Housing Act of 1968. While the existence of overt discrimination in housing markets did not immediately disappear, its importance has steadily declined. Nevertheless, discriminatory practices are believed to continue to play a role in the locational opportunities of different racial groups (see Turner et al. 2002; Hanson and Hawley 2011).

References

Alchian, Armen, and Harold Demsetz. 1973. "The Property Right Paradigm." *Journal of Economic History* 33 (1): 16–27.

Alesina, Alberto, Reza Baqir, and William Easterly. 1999. "Public Goods and Ethnic Divisions." *Quarterly Journal of Economics* 114 (4): 1243–84.

Arora, Seema, and Timothy N. Cason. 1999. "Do Community Characteristics Influence Environmental Outcomes? Evidence from the Toxics Release Inventory." *Southern Economic Journal* 65 (4): 691–716.

Ash, Michael, and T. Robert Fetter. 2004. "Who Lives on the Wrong Side of the Environmental Tracks? Evidence from the EPA's Risk-Screening Environmental Indicators Model." *Social Science Quarterly* 85 (2): 441–62.

Baden, Brett M., and Don L. Coursey. 2002. "The Locality of Waste Sites within the City of Chicago: A Demographic, Social, and Economic Analysis." *Resource and Energy Economics* 24 (1–2): 53–93.

Baden, Brett M., Douglas S. Noonan, and Rama Mohana R. Turaga. 2007. "Scales of Justice: Is There a Geographic Bias in Environmental Equity Analysis?" *Journal of Environmental Planning and Management* 50 (2): 163–85.

Banzhaf, H. Spencer. Forthcoming. "Regulatory Impact Analyses of Environmental Justice Effects." *Journal of Land Use and Environmental Law.*

Banzhaf, H. Spencer, and Randall P. Walsh. 2008. "Do People Vote with Their Feet? An Empirical Test of Tiebout's Mechanism." *American Economic Review* 98 (3): 843–63.

———. 2010. "Segregation and Tiebout Sorting: Investigating the Link between Investments in Public Goods and Neighborhood Tipping." NBER Working Paper 16057, National Bureau of Economic Research, Cambridge, MA. http://ideas.repec.org/p/nbr/nberwo/16057.html.

Becker, Gary S. 1957. *The Economics of Discrimination.* Chicago: University of Chicago Press.

———. 1983. "A Theory of Competition among Pressure Groups for Political Influence." *Quarterly Journal of Economics* 98 (3): 371–400.

Becker, Gary S., and Kevin M. Murphy. 2000. *Social Economics: Market Behavior in a Social Environment,* chap. 5. Cambridge, MA: Belknap Press.

Been, Vicki. 1993. "What's Fairness Got to Do with It? Environmental Justice and the Siting of Locally Undesirable Land Uses." *Cornell Law Review* 78:1001–85.

———. 1994. "Locally Undesirable Land Uses in Minority Neighborhoods: Disproportionate Siting or Market Dynamics?" *Yale Law Journal* 103:1383–1422.

Been, Vicki, with Francis Gupta. 1997. "Coming to the Nuisance or Going to the Barrios? A Longitudinal Analysis of Environmental Justice Claims." *Ecology Law Quarterly* 24 (1): 1–56.

Binder, Denis, Colin Crawford, Eileen Gauna, M. Casey Jarman, Alice Kaswan, Bradford C. Mank, Catherine A. O'Neill, Clifford Rechtschaffen, and Robert R. M. Verchick. 2001. "A Survey of Federal Agency Response to President Clinton's Executive Order No. 12898 on Environmental Justice." *Environmental Law Reporter* 31:11133–50.

Blais, Lynn E. 1996. "Environmental Racism Reconsidered." *North Carolina Law Review* 75:75–151.

Boer, J. Tom, Manuel Pastor Jr., James L. Sadd, and Lori D. Snyder. 1997. "Is There Environmental Racism? The Demographics of Hazardous Waste in Los Angeles County." *Social Science Quarterly* 78 (4): 793–810.

Bowen, William M. 2002. "An Analytical Review of Environmental Justice Research: What Do We Really Know?" *Environmental Management* 29 (1): 3–15.

Brooks, Nancy, and Rajiv Sethi. 1997. "The Distribution of Pollution: Community Characteristics and Exposure to Air Toxics." *Journal of Environmental Economics and Management* 32 (2): 233–50.

Brueckner, Jan K., and Stuart S. Rosenthal. 2009. "Gentrification and Neighborhood Housing Cycles: Will America's Future Downtowns Be Rich?" *Review of Economics and Statistics* 91 (4): 725–43.

Brulle, Robert J., and David N. Pellow. 2006. "Environmental Justice: Human Health and Environmental Inequalities." *Annual Review of Public Health* 27:103–24.

Bryant, Bunyan. 1995. "Introduction." In *Environmental Justice: Issues, Policies, and Solutions,* edited by Bunyan Bryant. Washington, DC: Island Press.

Bullard, Robert D. 1990. *Dumping in Dixie: Race, Class, and Environmental Quality.* Boulder, CO: Westview Press.

Bullard, Robert D., Paul Mohai, Robin Saha, and Beverly Wright. 2007. *Toxic Wastes and Race at Twenty: 1987–2007*. Report prepared for the United Church of Christ Justice and Witness Ministries, Cleveland, OH. http://www.ucc.org/assets/pdfs/toxic20 .pdf.

Card, David, Alexandre Mas, and Jesse Rothstein. 2008. "Tipping and the Dynamics of Segregation." *Quarterly Journal of Economics* 123 (1): 177–218.

Coase, Ronald H. 1960. "The Problem of Social Cost." *Journal of Law and Economics* 3 (1): 1–44.

Cole, Luke W., and Sheila R. Foster. 2001. *From the Ground Up: Environmental Racism and the Rise of the Environmental Justice Movement*. New York: New York University Press.

Cutler, David M., Edward L. Glaeser, and Jacob L. Vigdor. 1999. "The Rise and Decline of the American Ghetto." *Journal of Political Economy* 107 (3): 455–506.

Farley, Reynolds, and Maria Krysan. 2002. "The Residential Preferences of Blacks: Do They Explain Persistent Segregation?" *Social Forces* 80 (3): 937–80.

Farley, Reynolds, Howard Schuman, Suzanne Bianchi, Diane Colasanto, and Shirley Hatchett. 1978. "Chocolate City, Vanilla Suburbs: Will the Trend toward Racially Separate Communities Continue?" *Social Science Research* 7 (4): 319–44.

Fisher, Joshua B., Maggi Kelly, and Jeff Romm. 2006. "Scales of Environmental Justice: Combining GIS and Spatial Analysis for Air Toxics in West Oakland, California." *Health and Place* 12 (4): 701–14.

Ford, Richard Thompson. 1994. "The Boundaries of Race: Political Geography in Legal Analysis." *Harvard Law Review* 107:1841–1921.

Foster, Sheila. 1998. "Justice from the Ground Up: Distributive Inequities, Grassroots Resistance, and the Transformative Politics of the Environmental Justice Movement." *California Law Review* 86:775–841.

Goldman, Benjamin A., and Laura Fitton. 1994. *Toxic Wastes and Race Revisited: An Update of the 1987 Report on the Racial and Socioeconomic Characteristics of Communities with Hazardous Waste Sites*. Washington, DC: Center for Policy Alternatives, National Association for the Advancement of Colored People, United Church of Christ.

Hamilton, James T. 1993. "Politics and Social Costs: Estimating the Impact of Collective Action on Hazardous Waste Facilities." *RAND Journal of Economics* 24 (1): 101–25.

———. 1995. "Testing for Environmental Racism: Prejudice, Profits, Political Power?" *Journal of Policy Analysis and Management* 14 (1): 107–32.

Hamilton, James T., and W. Kip Viscusi. 1999. *Calculating Risks? The Spatial and Political Dimensions of Hazardous Waste Policy*. Cambridge, MA: MIT Press.

Hanson, Andrew, and Zackary Hawley. 2011. "Do Landlords Discriminate in the Rental Housing Market? Evidence from an Internet Field Experiment in U.S. Cities." *Journal of Urban Economics* 70 (2): 99–114.

Hersh, Robert. 1995. "Race and Industrial Hazards: An Historical Geography of the Pittsburgh Region, 1900–1990." Discussion Paper 95-18, Resources for the Future, Washington, DC.

Jenkins, Robin R., Kelly B. Maguire, and Cynthia L. Morgan. 2004. "Host Community Compensation and Municipal Solid Waste Landfills." *Land Economics* 80 (4): 513–28.

Kriesel, Warren, Terence J. Centner, and Andrew G. Keeler. 1996. "Neighborhood Exposure to Toxic Releases: Are There Racial Inequities?" *Growth and Change* 27 (4): 479–99.

Lazarus, Richard J. 2000. "'Environmental Racism! That's What It Is.'" *University of Illinois Law Review* 2000:255–74.

Maantay, Juliana. 2007. "Asthma and Air Pollution in the Bronx: Methodological and Data Considerations in Using GIS for Environmental Justice and Health Research." *Health and Place* 13 (1): 32–56.

McCubbins, Matthew D., and Thomas Schwartz. 1984. "Congressional Oversight Overlooked: Police Patrols versus Fire Alarms." *American Journal of Political Science* 28 (1): 165–79.

McGuire, Martin. 1974. "Group Segregation and Optimal Jurisdictions." *Journal of Political Economy* 82 (1): 112–32.

Mohai, Paul, and Robin Saha. 2006. "Reassessing Racial and Socioeconomic Disparities in Environmental Justice Research." *Demography* 43 (2): 383–99.

Morello-Frosch, Rachel, Manuel Pastor, and James Sadd. 2001. "Environmental Justice and Southern California's 'Riskscape': The Distribution of Air Toxics Exposures and Health Risks among Diverse Communities." *Urban Affairs Review* 36 (4): 551–78.

National Environmental Justice Advisory Council (NEJAC). 2006. *Unintended Impacts of Redevelopment and Revitalization Efforts in Five Environmental Justice Communities.* Final Report. http://www.epa.gov/compliance/ej/resources/publications/nejac/redev-revital-recomm-9-27-06.pdf.

Noonan, Douglas S. 2008. "Evidence of Environmental Justice: A Critical Perspective on the Practice of EJ Research and Lessons for Policy Design." *Social Science Quarterly* 89 (5): 1153–74.

Noonan, Douglas S., Rama Mohana R. Turaga, and Brett M. Baden. 2009. "Superfund, Hedonics, and the Scale of Environmental Justice." *Environmental Management* 44 (5): 909–20.

Pastor, Manuel. 2002. "Environmental Justice: Reflections from the United States." Conference Paper 1, Political Economy Research Institute, University of Massachusetts, Amherst.

Pastor, Manuel, Jim Sadd, and John Hipp. 2001. "Which Came First? Toxic Facilities, Minority Move-In, and Environmental Justice." *Journal of Urban Affairs* 23 (1): 1–21.

Pastor, Manuel, James Sadd, and Rachel Morello-Frosch. 2004. "Waiting to Inhale: The Demographics of Toxic Air Release Facilities in 21st-Century California." *Social Science Quarterly* 85 (2): 420–40.

———. 2007. "Still Toxic after All These Years: Air Quality and Environmental Justice in the San Francisco Bay Area." Center for Justice, Tolerance, and Community, University of California, Santa Cruz. http://cjtc.ucsc.edu/docs/bay_final.pdf.

Pulido, Laura. 2000. "Rethinking Environmental Racism: White Privilege and Urban Development in Southern California." *Annals of the Association of American Geographers* 90 (1): 12–40.

Ringquist, Evan J. 1997. "Equity and the Distribution of Environmental Risk: The Case of TRI Facilities." *Social Science Quarterly* 78 (4): 811–29.

———. 2003. "Environmental Justice: Normative Concerns, Empirical Evidence, and Government Action." In *Environmental Policy: New Directions for the Twenty-First Century*, edited by Norman J. Vig and Michael E. Kraft. Washington, DC: CQ Press.

———. 2005. "Assessing Evidence of Environmental Inequities: A Meta-Analysis." *Journal of Policy Analysis and Management* 24 (2): 223–47.

Rosenthal, Stuart S. 2008. "Old Homes, Externalities, and Poor Neighborhoods: A Model of Urban Decline and Renewal." *Journal of Urban Economics* 63 (3): 816–40.

Sadd, James L., Manuel Pastor Jr., J. Thomas Boer, and Lori D. Snyder. 1999. "'Every Breath You Take . . .': The Demographics of Toxic Air Releases in Southern California." *Economic Development Quarterly* 13 (2): 107–23.

Saha, Robin, and Paul Mohai. 2005. "Historical Context and Hazardous Waste Facility Siting: Understanding Temporal Patterns in Michigan." *Social Problems* 52 (4): 618–48.

Schelling, Thomas C. 1971. "Dynamic Models of Segregation." *Journal of Mathematical Sociology* 1 (2): 143–86.

———. 1972. "A Process of Residential Segregation: Neighborhood Tipping." In *Racial Discrimination in Economic Life*, edited by A. Pascal. Lexington, MA: Lexington Books.

Sieg, Holger, V. Kerry Smith, H. Spencer Banzhaf, and Randy Walsh. 2004. "Estimating the General Equilibrium Benefits of Large Changes in Spatially Delineated Public Goods." *International Economic Review* 45 (4): 1047–77.

Tiebout, Charles. 1956. "A Pure Theory of Local Expenditures." *Journal of Political Economy* 64 (5): 416–24.

Turner, Margery Austin, Fred Freiberg, Erin Godfrey, Carla Herbig, Diane K. Levy, and Robin R. Smith. 2002. *All Other Things Being Equal: A Paired Testing Study of Mortgage Lending Institutions*. Urban Institute report prepared for the Office of Fair Housing and Equal Opportunity, US Department of Housing and Urban Development, Washington, DC. http://www.urban.org/UploadedPDF/1000504_All_Other_Things_Being_Equal.pdf.

United Church of Christ. 1987. *Toxic Wastes and Race in the United States: A National Report on the Racial and Socio-Economic Characteristics of Communities with Hazardous Waste Sites.* New York: Public Data Access.

US Environmental Protection Agency (EPA). 2010. http://www.epa.gov/environmental justice.

US General Accounting Office (GAO). 1983. *Siting of Hazardous Waste Landfills and Their Correlation with Racial and Economic Status of Surrounding Communities.* Washington, DC: GAO.

Videras, Julio, and Christopher Bordoni. 2006. "Ethnic Heterogeneity and the Enforcement of Environmental Regulation." *Review of Social Economy* 64 (4): 539–62.

Vigdor, Jacob. 2004. "Community Composition and Collective Action: Analyzing Initial Mail Response to the 2000 Census." *Review of Economics and Statistics* 86 (1): 303–12.

Walsh, Randall P. 2007. "Endogenous Open Space Amenities in a Locational Equilibrium." *Journal of Urban Economics* 61 (2): 319–44.

Wolverton, Ann. 2009. "Effects of Socio-Economic and Input-Related Factors on Polluting Plants' Location Decisions." *Berkeley Electronic Journal of Economic Analysis and Policy, Advances* 9 (1). http://www.bepress.com/bejeap/vol9/iss1/art14.

Household Behavior and Land Markets
Theoretical Considerations

AS NOTED in Chapter 1 of this volume, Tiebout (1956) hypothesized that people "sort" into communities based on their demand for local public goods, including the environment. This section explores this notion and its implications for environmental justice.

In Chapter 2, Eleanor McCormick and I explore an important implication of Tiebout's hypothesis, namely, that well-intended cleanup efforts might harm poor residents through the process of "environmental gentrification." We begin by fleshing out this oft-used but rarely defined term, exploring the various demographic effects gentrification entails. We then turn to a review of the evidence for these effects. We find compelling support for the importance of Tiebout's mechanism and for at least some gentrification effects. Price increases appear to be a more likely outcome than turnover in the racial composition of a community.

Jacob Vigdor continues this discussion in Chapter 3, noting a number of important caveats for the prediction that cleanup will trigger price increases. Perhaps the most important of these is that many environmental justice communities have low occupancy rates for their housing stock. These vacancies represent slackness in housing supply conditions. Even if cleanup increases the demand for housing in the community, the slack may be more than able to absorb this new demand without any effect on prices. Illustrating the importance of such exceptions, Vigdor then examines communities near Superfund sites and finds little evidence for increases in housing prices after they became eligible for federal cleanup dollars by being listed on the Superfund National Priority List.

In Chapter 4, Joshua Sidon, Randall Walsh, and I emphasize the importance of interpreting these housing market dynamics in the context of demographic groups who have preferences not only over local environmental conditions and housing prices but also over the demographic composition of the community itself. We show that, in this context, such forces for segregation reinforce the socioeconomic pressures driving environmental justice correlations. That is, not only can richer whites outbid poorer minorities for cleaner, healthier communities, driving up the cost of accessing these communities, but these communities are even more expensive simply because they are whiter, further driving away minorities. At the same time, however, these forces also mitigate gentrification results: the racial composition of a community is a stabilizing force, making it harder to displace local populations.

Reference

Tiebout, Charles. 1956. "A Pure Theory of Local Expenditures." *Journal of Political Economy* 64 (5): 416–24.

2 Moving beyond Cleanup

Identifying the Crucibles of Environmental Gentrification

H. Spencer Banzhaf and Eleanor McCormick

Introduction

As noted in Chapter 1 of this volume, the socioeconomic mechanisms driving the observed correlations among race, income, and exposure to pollution have crucial implications for the effect of any policies designed to unravel that correlation. They also have substantial implications for the effects of cleaning up pollution. For example, one potential mechanism giving rise to the observed correlations operates through housing markets. Pollution may arise in a location for any of a number of reasons, but when it does, it will make local property less attractive. The consequently diminished demand for housing (or other property) in the area lowers housing prices. Richer households depart in search of more desirable locales, while the poor, unable to afford those other alternatives, move in.

The logic of this mechanism suggests that, by the same token, when pollution is cleaned up, property values will rise and wealthier households may move back in. If the poor residents living in the (once) dirty community owned their own home, they would benefit from the appreciation in their housing assets. But, according to the US Census, 83 percent of people living in poverty and receiving public assistance in the United States are renters. These renters would simply have to pay higher rents to their landlords, who reap the windfall profits. Moreover, existing residents may not value the removal of the disamenity as much as other households, creating a mismatch between their priorities and the new character of the neighborhood. Thus, even if they do not move, existing residents, especially renters, may be harmed by the gentrification effects of cleanup. If many former residents do move, to be replaced by wealthier households, the character of the neighborhood would change further, feeding the gentrification. Such "environmental gentrification" is a key concern of local stakeholders, as emphasized in a recent report from the National Environmental Justice Advisory Council (NEJAC; 2006) on the unintended consequences of redevelopment and revitalization efforts.

Several recent studies have looked at one or more aspects of such cascading gentrification effects.[1] Different authors have come to different conclusions about gentrification, but in part these differences stem from differences in terminology. To date, the economics literature has been quite loose in its use of the term "gentrification." In this chapter, we first develop an operational meaning of the term, drawing on the sociology and anthropology literature as well as on economics. We then go on to consider the evidence for environmental gentrification to date and its implications for public policy.

What Is Gentrification?

Ruth Glass, a sociologist, is credited with coining the term "gentrification." Describing the metropolitan center of London in the 1960s, Glass (1964) portrayed gentrification as a process of *invasion* whereby

> one by one, many of the working class quarters of London have been invaded by the middle classes—upper and lower. Shabby, modest mews and cottages—two rooms up and two down—have been taken over, when their leases have expired, and have become elegant, expensive residences. Larger Victorian houses, downgraded in an earlier or recent period . . . have been upgraded once again . . . . Once this process of 'gentrification' starts in a district it goes on rapidly until all or most of the original working class occupiers are displaced, and the whole social character of the district is changed. (pp. xviii–xix)

Thus, class and class change are at the center of Glass's notion and remain so in contemporary definitions and studies of gentrification. Nevertheless, contemporary definitions and popular understandings have evolved and expanded over the years.

Hallmarks of Gentrification

Today, the concept of gentrification has spread into many disciplines and into popular discourse. Writers across disciplines, and even within them, would not agree on everything that is meant by the term "gentrification." Nevertheless, most would agree on four hallmarks:

1. Rising property values and rental costs, so that even houses that are not upgraded become more expensive.
2. New construction or renovation upgrading the housing stock and perhaps converting it from rental to owner-occupied units.
3. Turnover in the local population bringing in residents with a higher socioeconomic status.[2] Some have suggested that changes in the racial or ethnic composition of the neighborhood may accompany this changing economic status (e.g., Levy, Comey, and Padilla 2006), but McKinnish, Walsh, and White (2010) have found that often this is not the case.
4. Changes in the mix of public goods provided by the community, and even in the mix of private goods offered for sale by local retailers.

Economists have generally stressed the market forces that link many of these characteristics together. As a neighborhood becomes more desirable for any number of reasons, more households, including wealthier ones, want to live there. This increased demand for space increases real estate prices to a level that the wealthier households can still afford but that previous residents might not. The wealthier households, in turn, can also afford to improve their living environments in both size and appearance, and so they renovate their property. This renovation then further increases the expenditure required to obtain a housing unit, reinforcing the trend.

Sociologists emphasize these market forces as well but also describe an aesthetic process. Sharon Zukin (1987), in an excellent introduction to the topic, notes that while gentrification can involve new development, often it involves the renovation or rehabilitation of historic buildings. As with the Victorian mansions in Glass's London (and with the Dupont Circle neighborhood of Washington, DC, where we once lived and worked), this renovation reflects the preferences of specific demographic groups for the architecture in the gentrifying neighborhood. Furthermore, historic preservation ordinances may solidify the process.

Where various depictions of gentrification differ the most is in their understanding and description of the indirect effects that new demographic groups, with their new aesthetics, have on the characteristics of the neighborhood. At the simplest level, the demographic changes themselves may represent a salient change in the neighborhood's character. If racial or socioeconomic groups have differing preferences for the racial or socioeconomic makeup of the neighborhood (perhaps preferring to live with people like themselves), initial demographic changes would fuel further changes in the demographic composition.[3]

Sociologists tend to stress the character of the community that different groups create, adding more flesh to the economists' skeletal model. Some highlight gentrification as the arrival of yuppies. Others stress the arrival of a more bohemian culture. For instance, Zukin (1987) describes gentrification as a radical break with suburbia, "a movement away from child-centered households toward the social diversity and aesthetic promiscuity of city life" (p. 131). She argues that gentrification leads to the visibility and naturalization of a "variety of household structures" (Zukin 1998).

These newcomers to the community may have preferences for different private goods. Thus, another aesthetic aspect of gentrification is the change in the character of local retail and other services. O'Sullivan (2005) develops an economic model in which low- and high-income residents consume distinctive private goods. As more high-income residents move in, local provision of their preferred goods increases (e.g., more coffee shops, florists, bookstores), making the neighborhood more attractive to those households and again reinforcing the demographic shift.[4] O'Sullivan calls this the "Starbucks effect."

Other indirect effects of demographic changes in the community may include changes in the crime rate or quality of local public schools. Crime may first increase following gentrification, as increased inequality creates more conflict and new targets for property crime. The former effect in particular appears strong in the data (Blau and Blau 1982; Morgan 2000). Consistent with these findings, some have suggested that the first wave of gentrifiers has a high tolerance for crime (Skogan 1986; Zukin 1987).[5] In the longer run, as the gentrification process continues, crime would be expected to decrease. Likewise, local school quality might improve, via the peer-group effect in which the higher educational attainment of wealthier families spills over to other children as well or via the rising tax base.[6]

A case study of Portland, Oregon, from 1990 to 2000 highlights many of these changes, including changes in racial composition, income distribution, and housing prices. O'Sullivan (2005) finds that, compared to the Portland area overall, the central city became whiter and grew in the share of households with incomes at least double the poverty rate. Meanwhile, median housing prices increased by a factor of 3.4 in the inner city compared to 2.6 in the rest of the city. In addition, crime decreased by 49 percent in the inner city but only by

5 percent in the rest of the city. A case study of Boston, Massachusetts, from 1970 to 1998 not only found influxes of college-educated households in gentrifying areas but also found citywide increases in land values (Vigdor 2002). It concluded that the effects had more to do with metro-wide changes in income distribution than with local amenities.

So far, we have described what happens in areas we would describe as "gentrifying." The opposite side of the coin is the fate of other areas that do *not* gentrify. Gentrification's contribution to displacement and homelessness has long been a contentious area of study (Zukin 1987). Economists have emphasized the so-called spatial mismatch hypothesis, in which a mismatch of skills of previous blue-collar residents and the requirements of new white-collar jobs leads to unemployment or migration (Kain 1968; Frey 1979; Brueckner and Zenou 2003). In her description of 1960s London, Glass (1964) saw "pockets of blight" (p. xx) growing more dense and areas where "change and stagnation exist side by side" (p. xxv). On this reading, as low-cost neighborhoods gentrify, poorer residents have fewer options, and so they pack into remaining poor neighborhoods more densely.

Theories of Neighborhood Change

The various hallmarks of gentrification discussed previously receive greater or less weight, or are described in different terms, according to different theories of neighborhood change. In addition to neoclassical economics, five social theories of neighborhood change serve as paradigms for descriptions of gentrification (Zukin 1987; Liu 1997). The five theories are the invasion-succession model, the neighborhood life-cycle model, the push-pull model, the institutional theory of neighborhood change, and a Marxist-materialist perspective. Most of these theories have components that resonate with neoclassical economics as well; accordingly, we discuss economic theories alongside the sociological.

Associated with the Chicago school of human ecology, the classical invasion-succession model is based on an ecological process in which a new plant invades a habitat and replaces previous plants as the dominant species, only to be itself replaced by a later invasion. This process, according to the theory, is mirrored in human society, with succeeding demographic waves pouring into a neighborhood (Duncan and Duncan 1957). This may well be what Glass (1964) had in mind when describing gentrification as an "invasion." In Liu's (1997) analysis of the theory, the invasion-succession model implies that relationships between races will be characterized by competition, conflict, and accommodation.

The neighborhood life-cycle model, originally formulated by Hoover and Vernon (1959; cited in Liu 1997), also views neighborhood change as a natural process. Here, the analogy is to generational succession rather than to ecological succession. As a housing stock ages, it becomes less desirable, leading to successive in-migration of lower socioeconomic groups who are willing to occupy it at reduced costs. Eventually, when it deteriorates to a critical point, the housing stock is recycled and renewed. Economists will recognize in this perspective a "filtering" model or a model of the optimal timing of investment (e.g., Somerville and Holmes 2001; Rosenthal 2008; Brueckner and Rosenthal 2009). As a young housing stock first begins to age, renovating it requires high fixed costs and only modest returns. Eventually, as it continues to age, it reaches a point at which investment is economical. This process has been confirmed in empirical work by Helms (2003), who finds age a significant factor in the prediction of housing renovation, and Brueckner and Rosenthal (2009), who find it a significant predictor in where the rich and poor live.

This life-cycle perspective is important for understanding the potential consequences of cleaning up polluted neighborhoods. If local land prices and the socioeconomic status of local residents are correlated with pollution primarily through mutual correlation with the age of a neighborhood, removal of the cleanups would not reverse the basic phenomenon, and gentrification would be less likely to occur. Future work exploring the connection between pollution and the age and life cycle of the nearby housing stock would be useful.

A third sociological theory, the so-called push-pull model, focuses on two related forces. The pushing force includes neighborhood disamenities that make a neighborhood less desirable for residents, for example, air pollution or locally undesirable land uses (LULUs) such as Superfund sites. The pulling force includes amenities, those things that might draw a person to reside in a given neighborhood, for example, parks or employment opportunities. The push force motivates households to relocate, and they then choose a new neighborhood based on its pulling factors (e.g., Frey 1979). Applied to land uses, this theory interprets the cleanup of pollution as pulling in those who are attracted to the new set of amenities and pushing out those who cannot afford to stay (see Liu 1997). The sociologists' push-pull model is quite close to neoclassical economic models of neighborhood choice, in which households choose where to live based on the balancing of prices and desirable and undesirable features. One difference, however, is that economists would tell a story of simultaneous push-and-pull forces. Households may decide to relocate based on changing pull factors elsewhere, even without new push factors in their current neighborhood. This increases the prospects for environmental gentrification, since reducing or cleaning up pollution would be a "pull" factor for many residents.

Fourth, the institutional theory indicates that organizations, including universities, banks, and insurance companies, play a large role in the status of a neighborhood as they make their location, economic, and political decisions. Banks, for example, can consign a neighborhood to decline through the practice of redlining, in which they refuse to finance mortgages or home equity loans in a neighborhood, a practice emphasized by NEJAC (2006) (see, e.g., Ross and Tootell [2004] for evidence of redlining). According to the institutional theory, amenities or push-pull factors play only a minor role. Thus, LULUs would not necessarily be obstacles to neighborhood stability and do not necessarily lead to neighborhood decline.

A fifth and final perspective comes from Marxism, where gentrification is a manifestation of the propensity for capital to reproduce itself. Zukin (1987) writes that, according to this perspective,

> in our time, capital expansion has no new territory left to explore, so it redevelops, or internally dedifferentiates, urban space. Just as the frontier thesis in US history legitimized an economic push through "uncivilized" lands, so the urban frontier thesis legitimizes the corporate reclamation of the inner city from racial ghettos and marginal business uses. (p. 141)

From the materialist viewpoint, such expansion might also partly explain conversion of rental units to owner-occupied units. Zukin explains:

> As a form of homeownership, gentrified dwellings are both a means of accumulation and a means of social reproduction for part of the highly educated middle class. Moreover, as a reference to specific building types in the center of the city, gentrification connotes both a mode of high status cultural consumption and the colonization of an expanding terrain by economic institutions [and employment] associated with the service sector. (1987, p. 144)

Thus, the expansion of capital into the neighborhood may represent the accumulation of wealth, or it may represent the social expansion of capitalists. In any case, capitalists are simply doing what capitalists do.

Although there are many perspectives and ways of describing gentrification, most authors appear to agree on the main signs and indicators. Thus, an operational and widely accepted definition of gentrification might read as follows. Gentrification is a phenomenon with many reinforcing characteristics, incorporating three hallmarks of community change: rising property values and rental costs; renewal or creation of housing stock corresponding to the appreciation of housing values; and changes in demographic composition, especially economic status but perhaps affecting race, education, and household size as well. A fourth set of issues, differing more widely from case to case and writer to writer, is the formation of new amenities, including the aesthetic feel of a neighborhood, its crime rate, and the quality of its schools.

A Conceptual Framework for Gentrification

Since Adam Smith and David Ricardo, economists have understood that more desirable land—for example, more fertile farmland—commands higher values than more marginal land. This commonsense theory, captured in the real estate agent's motto "location, location, location," was expanded by Charles Tiebout (1956) and Wallace Oates (1969) in a much more general model of local amenities, local political economy, demographics, and real estate prices. Tiebout's notion was that households can vote with their feet to live in communities that have their preferred bundle of amenities, tax rates, and housing prices. While everybody likes better schools, parks, a clean environment, and so forth, not everybody is equally willing to pay the higher housing costs (including taxes) required to live near them. Citizens who have a higher willingness to pay for them—because they have more money or because they place a relatively high priority on them—will move into communities with high housing costs and high levels of local public services. Poorer citizens or citizens who place a lower priority on the environment will move into dirtier communities with lower costs. Again, their lower value, in monetary terms, may be a result of either their restricted means or their preferences. In this way, people "sort" themselves into neighborhoods with others with a similar willingness to pay for public goods.

Tiebout's insights have given birth to a large and fruitful literature (see Fischel [2001, 2006] for overviews). The most important connections for our purposes are illustrated in Figure 2.1. The figure shows a pyramid depicting what we might call "the four sides of environmental demography." Each vertex in the pyramid represents one aspect of a model of interconnecting social relations. The top represents environmental quality, for example, the presence or

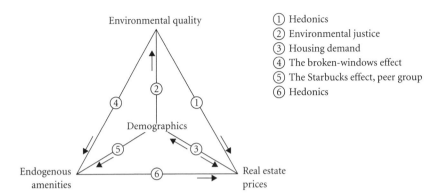

Figure 2.1 Four sides of environmental gentrification

absence of a local polluting facility or a LULU. The back represents the demographic makeup of the local citizenry. The left represents other local amenities (schools, safety, and local retail—as imagined in the "Starbucks effect"). These are labeled "endogenous" to reflect the fact that they are determined in part by the actions of local residents. Finally, the right represents local real estate markets, in which people buy and sell property in communities differentiated by these characteristics.

The environmental justice literature has persuasively documented a correlation between pollution and demographics. This correlation is represented by the vertical line connecting their respective vertices in the pyramid. However, efforts to document causal relationships based on this correlation have been frustrated by the fact that they are interconnected in a larger social system (Foster 1998; Pulido 2000; Noonan, Krupka, and Baden 2007). For example, an equally compelling literature documents that land and housing prices are more expensive in less polluted areas. This literature can be represented by the line connecting the environment and real estate vertices in the figure. Now we immediately see that one could explain the connection between the environment and demographics indirectly via the real estate connection: since the desirability of clean neighborhoods bids up the price, poorer populations (including minorities) will be less likely to obtain housing in those neighborhoods. Thus, after cleanup, the neighborhood might become more expensive as well as wealthier, whiter, and more educated.

We illuminate this connection in more detail using a class of Tiebout models introduced by Epple, Filimon, and Romer (1984), in which households "sort" into communities differentiated by prices and public goods (like environmental quality), based on their incomes and tastes. Versions of the model have been estimated econometrically by Epple and Sieg (1999) and Epple, Romer, and Sieg (2001) and applied to environmental improvements by Sieg et al. (2004), Smith et al. (2004), Walsh (2007), and Wu and Cho (2003). Banzhaf and Walsh (2008) and Vigdor (2006) use this model to gain insights into environmental gentrification. The results presented here are derived in more detail in Chapter 4; here, we give only a brief (and less technical) summary.

In this model, households differ by their income and by their tastes for public goods/bads, including contamination and visual disamenities like brownfields. Consequently, they also differ by their willingness to pay, in terms of higher housing prices, for bundles of public goods. However, they do not differ in how they value one *particular* public good (e.g., parks and green spaces) relative to another (e.g., public schools). Because of the latter simplifying assumption, households agree on their rankings of "most desirable" communities. Because of the higher demand for housing there, housing prices are highest in the most desirable communities; likewise, they are lowest in the least desirable. And because households do differ in their willingness to trade off other goods (medical care, clothing, etc.) for public goods, these price differentials lead households to select different communities. Holding tastes constant, richer households will be in the more desirable communities and poorer households in the less desirable communities.

Figure 2.2 illustrates the situation. The figure shows two demographic types (differing by, e.g., race or educational attainment) with different income distributions. The two curves in the figure are their respective density functions, with type 2 being wealthier, on average, than type 1. Type 2 households may be white, for example, and type 1 minority, or type 2 may be college-educated and type 1 high school dropouts.

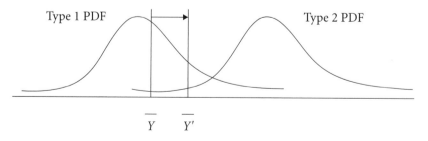

Figure 2.2 Density of income for two household types and shift in community income boundary after improvement in G_1

Holding tastes constant, the income threshold $\overline{Y}$ separates the two demographic types into two different communities: all those with incomes above $\overline{Y}$ are in the more desirable of two communities, while all those with incomes below $\overline{Y}$ are in the less desirable. In the case depicted, the more desirable of the two communities also has more type 2 households. This follows logically whenever type 2's income distribution first-order stochastically dominates type 1's (see Chapter 4)—that is, whenever a greater share of type 2's population than type 1's has income higher than any arbitrary level y.

This model can illuminate what happens to a community, and to other communities, when its public goods improve, as when LULUs are cleaned up and returned to productive uses. Consider an improvement in community 1. After the improvement, households that were somewhat indifferent before will now clearly prefer community 1. As depicted in Figure 2.2, $\overline{Y}$ will shift to the right (shown as $\overline{Y}'$). All the people who preferred community 1 will continue to prefer it, but now additional people (represented by the area between $\overline{Y}$ and $\overline{Y}'$) will as well. In other words, the demand for housing in community 1 will increase, and the demand for housing in community 2 will fall. This will have the effect of increasing the population of community 1 and decreasing the population of community 2.[7] Other things equal, it will also have the effect of increasing housing prices in community 1 and lowering them in community 2. We thus have two clear hypotheses: demand for housing and housing prices will both increase following cleanup and reuse of LULUs. These are some of the classic hallmarks of gentrification.

What about the demographic composition of the communities? Note that the people in the area between $\overline{Y}$ and $\overline{Y}'$, those who previously preferred community 2 but now prefer community 1, are richer, on average, than the original residents of community 1. When they move in following the cleanup of the LULU, they will thus increase the average income of community 1. Note, however, that these people were poorer, on average, than those who remain in community 2. Accordingly, the average income of community 2 will increase as well! Although we can hypothesize an increase in income following cleanup and reuse of LULUs, another hallmark of gentrification, this hypothesis is harder to test in the data, because the process involves movement of supposedly "control" communities in the same direction. However, as discussed by Banzhaf and Walsh (2008), it should be possible to detect this effect in certain cases.

Finally, we cannot say anything about the change in the composition of community 1 with respect to other demographic variables. Common sense seemingly suggests that, as income increases, demographic groups associated with higher incomes should increase as well. However, that need not be the case. If the ratio of type 1 households to type 2 households among those moving into community 1 is greater than the ratio among those previously living in community 1 (to the left of the original $\bar{Y}$), then community 1's share of type 1 households could increase, even while the community becomes richer. Thus, this additional hallmark of gentrification—where it is associated with certain demographic groups, whether it be whites, more educated individuals, or some other group—is the least likely to result from cleanup and reuse of LULUs and the least likely to be found in empirical studies. This is consistent with the findings of McKinnish, Walsh, and White (2010), who find that gentrifying neighborhoods often remain attractive to minority incumbents.

Finally, the left side of Figure 2.1 further complicates the picture. After all, the connection between demographics and other amenities includes those cases in which the new populations change the aesthetic character of the housing stock, are associated with lower crime rates, bring a new peer group to the public schools, or attract new retail (the "Starbucks effect"). More speculatively, changes in environmental amenities might have some direct connection to factors such as crime if there is a "broken windows" effect, wherein the decay represented by a brownfield, for example, engenders social disconnectedness and disregard (e.g., Kelling and Coles 1996). Finally, people may sort on demographic composition as well, as with the phenomenon of "white flight" (Banzhaf and Walsh 2010; see also Chapter 4).

Evidence for the Tiebout Effect

Evidence has accumulated that Tiebout's model is a good description of reality. This evidence can be grouped into two categories. The first category is a check of the model's premise that households are mobile and "sort" into neighborhoods based on their demand for public goods. In fact, Americans are quite mobile. According to the US Census, the average American household moves once every five years, a very high rate. This mobility creates a constant churning that allows the demographic composition of communities to evolve rapidly along with changing amenities. Moreover, as Fischel (1981) has pointed out, residents have many communities from which to choose, with most US metro areas having dozens (or even hundreds) of local jurisdictions. In addition, the distribution of job locations does not appear to restrict households' choices about where to live (Hamilton 1982). All this implies that Tieboutian sorting does not even require that changes in amenities induce individual households to move. If people are moving on a regular basis for other reasons, so long as they look at amenities and housing prices when they do move, households with higher willingness to pay for amenities will "sort" into neighborhoods with those amenities.

This indeed seems to be the case, and evidence of such sorting represents the second category. If Tiebout's mechanism in which households vote with their feet is functioning, areas with better public goods should have higher demand and therefore higher real estate prices. There is plenty of evidence to support this contention. Since the seminal work by Oates (1969), numerous studies have found a correlation between housing prices and local amenities or disamenities, including environmental pollution. For example, housing prices are lower nearer LULUs like Superfund sites and landfills.[8] Of course, as noted in Chapter 1, this correlation may also arise if dirty industries are attracted to areas with cheaper land prices. For this reason, evidence of a correlation between real estate prices and air pollution is particularly supportive of the Tiebout model, because air pollution is often determined by distant emissions, making the correlation less likely to be the result of reverse causation. That is, while residents might respond to pollution that blows in from a great distance, firms are less likely to respond to distant populations when making their pollution decisions. Smith and Huang (1995) found systematic evidence of such a correlation between housing prices and air pollution concentrations in their synthesis of earlier studies. More recently, Bayer, Keohane, and Timmins (2009) have taken an approach that specifically relies on only that portion of local air pollution that does come from distant sources. Similarly, Chay and Greenstone (2005) have looked only at the variation in local air pollution that comes from changes in federal nonattainment status. Both approaches explicitly "net out" any reverse effect of local markets and local demographics on pollution levels, yet continue to find a strong correlation between housing prices and pollution levels.

Demographic patterns similarly are consistent with the Tiebout model. For example, Graves and Waldman (1991) have found that elderly retirees move to counties where public goods are capitalized more into wages than into land prices. Eberts and Gronberg (1981) have found that there is more heterogeneity in income levels within school districts in metro areas with fewer school districts from which to choose. Similarly, Gramlich and Rubinfeld (1982) have shown that in metro areas with a wider "menu" of choices for public service levels, households are more satisfied with the level of such services in their community than are households in rural areas with fewer choices, where many households viewed local service levels as either "too high" or "too low." Both of these studies suggest that, when given the opportunity, households do sort into areas with amenity levels that match their willingness to pay for them. More recently, Epple and Sieg (1999) and Sieg et al. (2004) have found that the ranking of communities by average incomes correlates well with the ranking by price and that, as predicted by their Tiebout model, the income ranking is independent of which income quartile is chosen.

Environmental Gentrification

If such social mechanisms are in operation, they can have profound implications for the distributional effects of environmental cleanup, with seemingly commonsense remedies to environmental injustice actually harming the groups they are intended to help. Of course, if a neighborhood is cleaned up, all residents who live there will enjoy the clean environment. However, because the neighborhood is now more desirable, real estate prices will increase. This appreciation is an added boon to homeowners and to landlords. However, rents will increase, too, offsetting the welfare gain to renters. In fact, Sieg et al. (2004) and Walsh (2007) show that cleaning up a high-pollution neighborhood can actually *harm* existing renters in some circumstances. Sieg et al. call this process "environmental gentrification."

Sieg et al. (2004) study the welfare effects of air pollution improvements in Los Angeles, California, where poorer and more polluted areas have experienced the biggest gains from improving air quality over the past 15 years. The counterintuitive effects arise from the fact that residents who live in such neighborhoods have the lowest willingness/ability to pay for environmental amenities. Given their incomes and tastes, they place a higher priority on affordable housing than on the environment in comparison to other households. When the environment is improved, the change is one that essentially works against these priorities. Other households that had been avoiding the pollution may desire to move back in, driving up housing prices. Competing to live in the neighborhood, those households will bid up prices to their own, higher willingness to pay. The original residents will have to either move out or pay these new premiums. Although they do enjoy the direct benefit of the environmental improvement, these higher rental payments more than offset that gain for them, making them worse off. The biggest gainers are the landlords and even some of the new gentrifying residents.[9]

By and large, the evidence supports the idea that new pollution (or newly discovered pollution) depresses the demand for local housing and that, by the same token, cleaning up pollution increases demand. Kahn (2000) finds that population growth has soared in the Los Angeles counties that have experienced the largest reductions in air pollution. Banzhaf and Walsh (2008) show similar effects at a much more local level. They find that neighborhoods with large polluting facilities within one-quarter mile lose a large share of their population, compared to other neighborhoods within the same zip code or school district but farther away from the facility. The difference is as much as 9 to 12 percentage points. Neighborhoods where such facilities have closed down or substantially reduced their pollution levels, on the other hand, saw *increases* in their population of 4 to 6 percentage points over the same period. By restricting comparisons to the same zip code or school district, this study holds labor market and other regional economic factors constant, while focusing on the differences in proximity to the disamenity.

These population effects essentially imply changes in demand for housing in an area, which, in turn, naturally affects housing prices. Again, there is strong evidence that cleaning up pollution triggers the higher prices associated with gentrification. The largest literature in this area is applied to Superfund and other hazardous waste sites. In one of the first such studies, Kohlhase (1991) finds that land prices in Houston, Texas, were no lower nearer Superfund sites until after the sites were listed on the National Priorities List (NPL) (1986, as compared to 1980 and 1976). One site was cleaned up by 1986, and it does not show the same relationship, suggesting cleanup can raise housing prices.[10]

RSR Corporation's lead smelter in Dallas, Texas, provides another excellent example. After many years of operation, health risks at the plant were officially identified in 1981, and the plant closed in 1984. During cleanup, lead was abated from the soil at homes within a half mile of the facility. A court ruled in 1986 that cleanup was complete, but new concerns arose in 1991 and the site was finally placed on the Superfund NPL in 1993. McCluskey and Rausser (2003) show that the plant depressed local real estate prices somewhat in the early period but that the effect was much larger following official notification of the health risks. Prices then rebounded after the cleanup, only to fall once more following the renewed concerns after 1991 (see also Dale et al. 1999).

This pattern, though common, is not without exception. Messer et al. (2006) have cast doubt on the hypothesis that housing prices inevitably rebound after cleanup. In their study of three Superfund sites, where cleanup at the sites was delayed for 10 to 20 years, property prices near the sites do not seem to have rebounded following cleanup. (See also Ihlanfeldt and Taylor [2004] for a similar finding for brownfields.) More recently, Greenstone and Gallagher (2008) have suggested that such studies may be biased if cleanup is triggered by changes in local demographics and real estate markets. They employ a creative and innovative technique in which they compare sites that were eligible for federal cleanup under Superfund and other hazardous waste sites that just missed qualifying for such cleanup. Qualification was based on a hazard ranking system that was presumably free of political manipulation. Since the objective harm is similar for the two sets of sites, comparisons between them should isolate the effect of cleanup. Using this approach, Greenstone and Gallagher do not find any effect of cleanup on housing prices. Vigdor (see Chapter 3), reanalyzing these data using several refinements, reaches a similar conclusion.

There are good reasons why such exceptions might arise. As Vigdor points out in Chapter 3, some communities near hazards may have many vacant housing units. If so, even if cleanup increases the demand for housing in the area, it may have little price effect because the excess supply can take up the slack. Noonan (see Chapter 7) similarly points out that when cleanup is accompanied by redevelopment of an area, and where that redevelopment involves new housing construction, the supply effect could offset the demand effect.

But as Messer et al. (2006) suggest, in the case of Superfund sites the most likely explanation for these exceptions is that the sites became permanently stigmatized. In effect, the sites never were really cleaned up in the eyes of local residents. In Messer and colleagues' study, cleanup at the sites was delayed many years, even decades, so the potential for stigma is understandable. Supporting this interpretation, recent studies of air quality find real estate prices do appreciate following improvements (e.g., Chay and Greenstone 2005). Unlike Superfund sites, air pollution would not be expected to leave a permanent stigma.

A related concern arises in the case of Greenstone and Gallagher's (2008) study. As Gamper-Rabindran, Mastromonaco, and Timmins (2011) point out, Greenstone and Gallagher combine the effects of final listing on the Superfund's National Priorities List with deletion from the list following cleanup. Their motivation for doing so was that listing implies federal funds for cleanup, so for residents who were already aware of the contamination, listing on Superfund would seem to be good news. However, residents might equally view listing on the Superfund site as bad news about the severity of the toxicity or the legal hurdles facing redevelopment of the site. Accordingly, Gamper-Rabindran, Mastromonaco, and Timmins revisit Greenstone and Gallagher's analysis and find substantial price effects from actual cleanup, in contrast to listing.

We conclude that although there are exceptions, the evidence seems clear that in most cases improvements in local environmental conditions do trigger increases in property prices. What about the other hallmarks of gentrification? Do communities become richer and whiter? As emphasized above, the Tiebout model is surprisingly agnostic about these effects. While it predicts that the poor and minorities will live in more polluted areas, the response to *changes* is far from clear, especially for racial and similar group identities.

Essentially, there may be some hysteresis in community characteristics (McCluskey and Rausser 2003; Cameron and McConnaha 2006). That is, imagine a world with only two communities, one rich and one poor. Which is which may be utterly arbitrary, until some event like the discovery of hazardous waste triggers a process in which the dirty community is bound to be poorer. The residents of their respective communities will over the years build up social systems that fit their respective needs and wants. Removing the hazardous waste removes the initial reason the groups sorted into those communities in which they are found, but given the mobility costs and other neighborhood amenities that have formed, the neighborhood's character may not change as rapidly as simple static models would predict. Banzhaf and Walsh (2010) provide an example in which households choose communities based on their demographic composition as well as their public goods. They show that in this case cleanup can trigger price increases and increases in income but not necessarily changes in other demographic traits such as racial composition. To the contrary, segregation may *increase* following cleanup, because minorities no longer need to pay the price of living in white communities to obtain the public amenities.

Additionally, demographic relationships that are fundamentally *cross-sectional* (e.g., at a point in time, pollution and prices are correlated in space) can be difficult to infer empirically from *changes*. The reason is that the effect in the area of interest needs to be statistically compared to a suitable control group. In the context of local demographics, the best controls would be nearby or similar neighborhoods. However, such neighborhoods are also affected by the change in pollution. For example, when the richest residents of a poor neighborhood flee to a richer neighborhood to escape a new polluting facility, *both* neighborhoods can become poorer on average (see Chapter 4). The reason is that the poor neighborhood loses its richest citizens, bringing down its average income, while the rich neighborhood gains more residents at the poor end of its distribution, bringing down its average income, too—even though the total average income in the population remains unchanged. The comparison is even more complicated when trying to measure changes in racial groups and other groups, because the change in composition will depend on the relative concentrations of the groups at the margin. This poses a dilemma for empirical researchers: control communities are unaffected by the statistical "treatment" of changes in pollution in proportion to their irrelevance to the affected neighborhood.

Despite these potential difficulties, at least 12 studies have looked at the evolution of demographics following the siting of local polluting facilities (or the discovery of pollution) or following cleanup: Baden and Coursey (2002); Banzhaf and Walsh (2008); Been (1994, 1997); Cameron, Crawford, and McConnaha (Chapter 6); Cameron and McConnaha (2006); Depro, Timmins, and O'Neil (2011); Gamper-Rabindran and Timmins (2011); Greenstone and Gallagher (2008); Lambert and Boerner (1997); Pastor, Sadd, and Hipp (2001); and Wolverton (Chapter 8). The evidence is quite mixed. Been (1997) and Pastor, Sadd, and Hipp (2001) find no evidence of increased minority populations following the siting of undesirable land uses. Baden and Coursey (2002), Lambert and Boerner (1997), and Wolverton (Chapter 8), on the other hand, find no such correlation at the time of siting but do in later periods, suggesting the correlation arose, ex post, from migration. Cameron, Crawford, and McConnaha (Chapter 6); Cameron and McConnaha (2006); and Greenstone and Gallagher (2008) find little demographic effect following cleanup of the Superfund sites. Then again, Banzhaf and Walsh (2008) find that median incomes fell after new polluting facilities were sited in, and rose when they exited, local neighborhoods. Gamper-Rabindran and Timmins (2011) find a similar effect, as well as an increase in the share of minorities.

More recently, Depro, Timmins, and O'Neil (2011) have pointed out that observed changes in group populations do not reveal patterns in individuals' behavior. They construct an example illustrating that, even when minorities differentially come to a nuisance, it does not logically follow that the *percentage* of residents who are minorities will increase more in the polluted community than in a control group. The authors offer a simple solution for empirical work: rather than focus on community aggregates, track the migratory adjustments of individual households. Crowder and Downey (2010) take a similar approach. Together, these two studies provide what well may be the most convincing evidence to date that minorities are more likely than whites to "come to the nuisance" (and less likely to flee).

Finally, in addition to the effect of housing price appreciation and demographics, gentrification may bring the left side of the pyramid in Figure 2.1, where other public goods are produced locally, into play as well. For example, the new residents may vote for higher taxes and higher levels of public services and push for a particular mix of services that matches their own priorities. These priorities may differ from those of the original residents because of the different needs of members of different social strata or simply because of the different tastes of different socioeconomic groups. In this way, the initial effects cascade into secondary effects that further harm the original residents.[11] However, this is merely speculative: there is little evidence to support this notion at this time, at least with respect to environmental policy.

A fair summary of the predictions of the Tiebout model as well as the empirical literature appears to be that cleanup leads to increases in housing costs and probably increases in income but not necessarily other changes in demographic composition. This lesson appears consistent with the broader approach taken by McKinnish, Walsh, and White (2010), who find that gentrifying neighborhoods often are associated with rising minority incomes. Nevertheless, it is the increase in housing costs that has the most salient policy implications, as it is those effects that harm poor renters living in gentrifying communities.

Such concerns about "environmental gentrification" are not only the musings of academics delighting in counterintuitive findings. To the contrary, they have been highlighted by grassroots environmental justice activists. For example, the NEJAC (2006) report mentioned previously suggests:

As the waves of new "gentry" move to large scale renovation projects in or near central business or warehouse districts, they come into direct contact with the current residents of these formerly forgotten places. Many of these older urban areas suffered from the industrialized waste practices of the past, and were not in high demand for residential development. Low-income people, recent immigrants, and people of color who were unable to find or afford shelter elsewhere have established communities in these areas. The commodity of land being sold in the real estate market is more than a physical structure or piece of acreage. It is also a neighborhood, a political and cultural entity necessary for the sustainability of a community in that place. Gentrification has placed populations in urban areas in direct competition for inner city space with relatively powerful and privileged groups. Environmental cleanup of these formerly industrialized, now residential, communities can be a powerfully displacing force. (p. 2)

These unintended consequences of environmental cleanup, articulated so well in the NEJAC report, are precisely the types of effects predicted by Tiebout's model.

Conclusion

There are three principal hallmarks of gentrification in virtually every perspective on the subject: rising property values and rental costs, new construction or renovation upgrading the housing stock, and turnover in the local population bringing in residents with a higher socioeconomic status. Various perspectives emphasize other features as well, but most involve some sense of the creation of a new amenity, based on architecture, retail, lifestyle, or peer groups. These new endogenous amenities may further drive gentrification.

Tiebout's process is a market-based phenomenon that can give rise to the observed correlations between pollution and poor and minority populations. This process implies that the exposure of different groups to different levels of pollution arises in part from their individual choices. The word "choice" here must be interpreted carefully. It is not meant to imply that poor minority households are in the same position as rich white households when it comes to the choices they face. It does suggest, however, that these groups are competent to work out how best to improve their own welfare, given the limitations and opportunities that are available to them. By choosing to live in more polluted but lower-cost areas, the poor are revealing that inexpensive housing is a higher priority than environmental amenities.

Because a market is involved in distributing environmental quality to different groups, people pay a price, possibly a hidden one, to obtain a cleaner environment.[12] Cleaning up the environment will impose that price precisely on those groups who have revealed that they would rather not pay it. If the price is higher housing costs, then poor renters—those most disadvantaged—will pay the price. Individual homeowners, too, will pay it but will be compensated by their appreciating housing values. Landlords will benefit the most, receiving a windfall of higher rents.

For existing cleanup efforts such as Superfund and the Brownfields Program, these market models suggest guidelines that can help minimize these unintended consequences. Three recommendations stand out. First, redevelopment (or "reuse") projects that fit the existing character of the community are less likely to trigger gentrification. That is, new housing, retail, or public amenities should be of a kind that is appealing to existing residents, rather than to outsiders who might move in and bid up rents. Consistent with this point, the NEJAC (2006) report on unintended consequences stresses the importance of community involvement in planning reuse projects.

Second, given the role of racial and other demographic preferences in maintaining equilibrium, targeting more homogeneous communities may be less likely to trigger gentrification as well. These communities are probably farther from a "tipping point" at which they would switch over to a new demographic composition.

Third, the work of Sieg et al. (2004) and Smith et al. (2004) suggests that when large policies target several communities within a metropolitan area, gentrification effects are likely to be smaller. While improving a single community is likely to increase its attractiveness relative to all other communities, creating incentives for other households to move in and driving up its housing prices, improving many communities would neutralize this effect, lifting all boats equally.

But there is a larger point at stake. When experiencing poor environmental quality is a consequence, rather than a cause, of poverty, then cleaning up the environment to help the poor is like treating the symptom rather than the disease. Some symptoms, like a moderate fever, represent the body's best efforts to heal itself. In such cases, treating the symptom may actually be counterproductive.

This does not mean there is no role for a physician. But the best physician facilitates the body's natural healing processes. Like the body, the market is a remarkably efficient machine. It provides goods, including local environmental amenities, to those who demand them most—and who have the resources to pay for them. It follows that the best way to help disadvantaged groups is to empower them, strengthening their position within the market system. Redistributing income to the poor, for example, would provide them with more resources to pay for those things they most want, including, if they so choose, a cleaner environment. Encouraging homeownership would put more people in a position to truly benefit from neighborhood improvements such as environmental cleanups.[13] Providing legal aid, facilitating conflict resolution, and otherwise helping poor residents in environmental disputes can help the Coasian process to function better and enable the poor to participate in it fully. These may be the more effective routes for helping the poor—and prove to have "win-win" outcomes for society.

Notes

Support for this research was provided by Industrial Economics, Inc. and the US EPA. Additional support for Spencer Banzhaf came from the Property and Environment Research Center (PERC), especially through a Julian Simon fellowship supported by the Searle Freedom Trust. We thank Terry Anderson, Robin Jenkins, Elizabeth Kopits, Roger Meiners, Brian Morrison, David Simpson, Kris Wernstedt, and Jeffrey Zabel for comments and suggestions. We also thank participants at seminars at EPA/NCEE, PERC, and a PERC Lone Mountain Forum.

1. Prominent among them in the economics literature are Sieg et al. (2004), who coined the term "environmental gentrification"; Vigdor (2002; see also Chapter 3); and McKinnish, Walsh, and White (2010).

2. This may be accompanied by abnormal rates of turnover in a rapidly changing neighborhood, but not necessarily. Nationally, almost half of all households move within a five-year period. Such a baseline rate of mobility may be sufficient to bring about a change in character.

3. On this, see the economic literature on "endogenous" racial amenities and sorting, for example, Schelling (1969, 1972); Becker and Murphy (2000); Sethi and Somanathan (2004); Bayer, Fang, and McMillan (2005); Bayer, Ferreira, and McMillan (2007); Bayer and McMillan (2005); Banzhaf, Sidon, and Walsh (Chapter 4); and Banzhaf and Walsh (2010). For discussion in the law literature, see Ford (1994). Finally, see the survey work by Farley et al. (1978) and Farley and Krysan (2002).

4. Although these are private goods for all practical purposes, technically small economies of scale in production induce some publicness, with the goods only provided if local demand is high enough.

5. This finding is confirmed by information on residents' reactions to and opinions on their newly resettled homes and neighborhoods as solicited in both the Mount Pleasant and the Capitol Hill neighborhoods in Dennis Gale's survey of Washington, DC, in the 1970s. Even with a majority of respondents reporting personal victimization and unease pertaining to the level of criminal activity, most saw crime as a necessary price to pay to enjoy the benefits of inner-city living (Laska and Spain 1980; Gale 1984).

6. But, as Vigdor (2002) notes, if gentrifying households do not have children, they would have little impact on schools.

7. This increase in population density could follow the development of undeveloped land, rezoning developments for more dense uses, and/or changes in vacancy rates. To the extent these mechanisms are restricted, changes in population density likewise would be restricted and price effects would be greater.

8. See E2 Inc. (2005), Farber (1998), Ihlanfeldt and Taylor (2004), Kiel (1995), Kiel and McClain (1995), Kiel and Williams (2007), and Smith and Desvousges (1986) for examples and Boyle and Kiel (2001) for an overview.

9. To our knowledge, Alchian ([1979] 2006) was the first to make precisely this point, also as it happens in the context of Los Angeles air quality improvements.

10. In a similar study of hazardous waste sites in Boston, Michaels and Smith (1990) find a positive effect of distance on prices, but again that it is only significant after discovery and publication. In a study designed to further explore these information effects, Gayer, Hamilton, and Viscusi (2000) find that the depressing effect on prices of seven Superfund sites in Grand Rapids, Michigan, declined after the EPA released information on objective health risks, illustrating that the markets react to changes in perceptions (see also Gayer, Hamilton, and Viscusi 2002). This suggests that they might react to objective changes from cleanup as well.

11. On this, see the wider literature on gentrification, such as Zukin (1987). Banzhaf and McCormick (2006) review these general equilibrium effects in more detail.

12. A similar point might be made about the Coasian process discussed in Chapter 1. There, the price takes the form of refusing compensation for the pollution, rather than foregoing lower housing prices.

13. Of course, it goes without saying that the strength of homeownership for local communities must be balanced against the cost of encouraging people to own homes when they cannot afford them—as the recent housing crisis has reminded us. As an alternative, Levy, Comey, and Padilla (2006) suggest various affordable housing strategies to help low-income residents when gentrification threatens. These strategies include using zoning and other tools to encourage production of affordable units, retention of existing affordable housing units, and asset building for current residents and neighborhood families. These strategies were found to be effective in six case studies (see also Kennedy and Leonard 2001).

References

Alchian, Armen. (1979) 2006. "The Beneficiaries of Cleaner Air." In *Property Rights and Economic Behavior*. Vol. 2 of *The Collected Works of Armen A. Alchian*, edited by Daniel K. Benjamin. Indianapolis, IN: Liberty Fund.

Baden, Brett M., and Don L. Coursey. 2002. "The Locality of Waste Sites within the City of Chicago: A Demographic, Social, and Economic Analysis." *Resource and Energy Economics* 24 (1–2): 53–93.

Banzhaf, H. Spencer, and Eleanor McCormick. 2006. "Moving beyond Cleanup: Identifying the Crucibles of Environmental Gentrification." Working Paper 07-02, National Center for Environmental Economics, US Environmental Protection Agency, Washington, DC. http://yosemite.epa.gov/EE/epa/eed.nsf/WPNumberNew/2007-02?OpenDocument.

Banzhaf, H. Spencer, and Randall P. Walsh. 2008. "Do People Vote with Their Feet? An Empirical Test of Tiebout's Mechanism." *American Economic Review* 98 (3): 843–63.

———. 2010. "Segregation and Tiebout Sorting: Investigating the Link between Investments in Public Goods and Neighborhood Tipping." NBER Working Paper 16057, National Bureau of Economic Research, Cambridge, MA. http://ideas.repec.org/p/nbr/nberwo/16057.html.

Bayer, Patrick, Hanming Fang, and Robert McMillan. 2005. "Separate When Equal? Racial Inequality and Residential Segregation." NBER Working Paper 11507, National Bureau of Economic Research, Cambridge, MA. http://www.nber.org/papers/w11507.

Bayer, Patrick, Fernando Ferreira, and Robert McMillan. 2007. "A Unified Framework for Measuring Preferences for Schools and Neighborhoods." *Journal of Political Economy* 115 (4): 588–638.

Bayer, Patrick, Nathaniel Keohane, and Christopher Timmins. 2009. "Migration and Hedonic Valuation: The Case of Air Quality." *Journal of Environmental Economics and Management* 58 (1): 1–14.

Bayer, Patrick, and Robert McMillan. 2005. "Racial Sorting and Neighborhood Quality." Mimeo, Yale University, New Haven, CT.

Becker, Gary S., and Kevin M. Murphy. 2000. *Social Economics: Market Behavior in a Social Environment*, chap. 5. Cambridge, MA: Belknap Press.

Been, Vicki. 1994. "Locally Undesirable Land Uses in Minority Neighborhoods: Disproportionate Siting or Market Dynamics?" *Yale Law Journal* 103:1383–1422.

Been, Vicki, with Francis Gupta. 1997. "Coming to the Nuisance or Going to the Barrios? A Longitudinal Analysis of Environmental Justice Claims." *Ecology Law Quarterly* 24 (1): 1–56.

Blau, Judith R., and Peter M. Blau. 1982. "The Cost of Inequality: Metropolitan Structure and Violent Crime." *American Sociological Review* 47 (1): 114–29.

Boyle, Melissa A., and Katherine A. Kiel. 2001. "A Survey of House Price Hedonic Studies of the Impact of Environmental Externalities." *Journal of Real Estate Literature* 9 (2): 117–44.

Brueckner, Jan K., and Stuart S. Rosenthal. 2009. "Gentrification and Neighborhood Housing Cycles: Will America's Future Downtowns Be Rich?" *Review of Economics and Statistics* 91 (4): 725–43.

Brueckner, Jan K., and Yves Zenou. 2003. "Space and Unemployment: The Labor-Market Effects of Spatial Mismatch." *Journal of Labor Economics* 21 (1): 242–66.

Cameron, Trudy Ann, and Ian T. McConnaha. 2006. "Evidence of Environmental Migration." *Land Economics* 82 (2): 273–90.

Chay, Kenneth Y., and Michael Greenstone. 2005. "Does Air Quality Matter? Evidence from the Housing Market." *Journal of Political Economy* 113 (2): 376–424.

Crowder, Kyle, and Liam Downey. 2010. "Inter-Neighborhood Migration, Race, and Environmental Hazards: Modeling Micro-Level Processes of Environmental Inequality." *American Journal of Sociology* 115 (4): 1110–49.

Dale, Larry, James C. Murdoch, Mark A. Thayer, and Paul A. Waddell. 1999. "Do Property Values Rebound from Environmental Stigmas? Evidence from Dallas." *Land Economics* 75 (2): 311–26.

Depro, Brooks, Christopher Timmins, and Maggie O'Neil. 2011. "Meeting Urban Housing Needs: Do People Really Come to the Nuisance?" Mimeo, RTI International, Research Triangle Park, NC.

Duncan, Otis D., and Beverly Duncan. 1957. *The Negro Population of Chicago.* Chicago: University of Chicago Press.

E2 Inc. 2005. *Superfund Benefits Analysis.* Draft report prepared for the US Environmental Protection Agency. http://www.epa.gov/superfund/news/benefits.pdf.

Eberts, Randall W., and Timothy J. Gronberg. 1981. "Jurisdictional Homogeneity and the Tiebout Hypothesis." *Journal of Urban Economics* 10 (2): 227–39.

Epple, Dennis, Radu Filimon, and Thomas Romer. 1984. "Equilibrium among Local Jurisdictions: Toward an Integrated Approach of Voting and Residential Choice." *Journal of Public Economics* 24 (3): 281–308.

Epple, Dennis, Thomas Romer, and Holger Sieg. 2001. "Interjurisdictional Sorting and Majority Rule: An Empirical Analysis." *Econometrica* 69 (6): 1437–66.

Epple, Dennis, and Holger Sieg. 1999. "Estimating Equilibrium Models of Local Jurisdictions." *Journal of Political Economy* 107 (4): 645–81.

Farber, Stephen. 1998. "Undesirable Facilities and Property Values: A Summary of Empirical Studies." *Ecological Economics* 24 (1): 1–14.

Farley, Reynolds, and Maria Krysan. 2002. "The Residential Preferences of Blacks: Do They Explain Persistent Segregation?" *Social Forces* 80 (3): 937–80.

Farley, Reynolds, Howard Schuman, Suzanne Bianchi, Diane Colasanto, and Shirley Hatchett. 1978. "Chocolate City, Vanilla Suburbs: Will the Trend toward Racially Separate Communities Continue?" *Social Science Research* 7 (4): 319–44.

Fischel, William A. 1981. "Is Local Government Structure in Large Urbanized Areas Monopolistic or Competitive?" *National Tax Journal* 34:95–104.

———. 2001. *The Homevoter Hypothesis: How Home Values Influence Local Government Taxation, School Finance, and Land-Use Policies.* Cambridge, MA: Harvard University Press.

———. 2006. *The Tiebout Model at Fifty: Essays in Public Economics in Honor of Wallace Oates.* Cambridge, MA: Lincoln Institute of Land Policy.

Ford, Richard Thompson. 1994. "The Boundaries of Race: Political Geography in Legal Analysis." *Harvard Law Review* 107:1841–1921.

Foster, Sheila. 1998. "Justice from the Ground Up: Distributive Inequities, Grassroots Resistance, and the Transformative Politics of the Environmental Justice Movement." *California Law Review* 86:775–841.

Frey, W. H. 1979. "Central City White Flight: Racial and Nonracial Causes." *American Sociological Review* 44 (3): 425–88.

Gale, Dennis E. 1984. *Neighborhood Revitalization and the Postindustrial City: A Multinational Perspective.* Toronto: Lexington Books.

Gamper-Rabindran, Shanti, Ralph Mastromonaco, and Christopher Timmins. 2011. "Valuing the Benefits of Superfund Site Remediation: Three Approaches to Measuring Localized Externalities." NBER Working Paper 16655, National Bureau of Economic Research, Cambridge, MA. http://www.nber.org/papers/w16655.

Gamper-Rabindran, Shanti, and Christopher Timmins. 2011. "Hazardous Waste Cleanup, Neighborhood Gentrification, and Environmental Justice: Evidence from Restricted Access Census Block Data." *American Economic Review* 101 (3): 620–24.

Gayer, Ted, James T. Hamilton, and W. Kip Viscusi. 2000. "Private Values of Risk Tradeoffs at Superfund Sites: Housing Market Evidence on Learning about Risk." *Review of Economics and Statistics* 82 (3): 439–51.

———. 2002. "The Market Value of Reducing Cancer Risk." *Southern Economic Journal* 69 (2): 266–89.

Glass, Ruth. 1964. "Introduction: Aspects of Change." In *London: Aspects of Change*, edited by Ruth Glass et al. London: MacGibbon & Kee.

Gramlich, Edward M., and Daniel L. Rubinfeld. 1982. "Micro Estimates of Public Spending Demand Functions and Tests of the Tiebout and Median-Voter Hypotheses." *Journal of Political Economy* 90 (3): 536–60.

Graves, Philip E., and Donald M. Waldman. 1991. "Multimarket Amenity Compensation and the Behavior of the Elderly." *American Economic Review* 81 (5): 1374–81.

Greenstone, Michael, and Justin Gallagher. 2008. "Does Hazardous Waste Matter? Evidence from the Housing Market and the Superfund Program." *Quarterly Journal of Economics* 123 (3): 951–1003.

Hamilton, Bruce W. 1982. "Wasteful Commuting." *Journal of Political Economy* 90 (5): 1035–53.

Helms, Andrew C. 2003. "Understanding Gentrification: An Empirical Analysis of the Determinants of Urban Housing Renovation." *Journal of Urban Economics* 54 (3): 474–98.

Ihlanfeldt, Keith R., and Laura O. Taylor. 2004. "Externality Effects of Small-Scale Hazardous Waste Sites: Evidence from Urban Commercial Property Markets." *Journal of Environmental Economics and Management* 47 (1): 117–39.

Kahn, Matthew E. 2000. "Smog Reduction's Impact on California County Growth." *Journal of Regional Science* 40 (3): 565–82.

Kain, John F. 1968. "Housing Segregation, Negro Employment, and Metropolitan Decentralization." *Quarterly Journal of Economics* 82 (2): 32–59.

Kelling, George L., and Catherine M. Coles. 1996. *Fixing Broken Windows.* New York: Touchstone.

Kennedy, Maureen, and Paul Leonard. 2001. "Dealing with Neighborhood Change: A Primer on Gentrification and Policy Choices." Discussion paper prepared for the Brookings Institution Center on Urban and Metropolitan Policy.

Kiel, Katherine A. 1995. "Measuring the Impact of the Discovery and Cleaning of Identified Hazardous Waste Sites on House Values." *Land Economics* 71 (4): 428–35.

Kiel, Katherine A., and Katherine T. McClain. 1995. "The Effect of an Incinerator Siting on Housing Appreciation Rates." *Journal of Urban Economics* 37 (3): 311–23.

Kiel, Katherine A., and Michael Williams. 2007. "The Impact of Superfund Sites on Local Property Values: Are All Sites the Same?" *Journal of Urban Economics* 61 (1): 170–92.

Kohlhase, Janet E. 1991. "The Impact of Toxic Waste Sites on Housing Values." *Journal of Urban Economics* 30 (1): 1–26.

Lambert, Thomas, and Christopher Boerner. 1997. "Environmental Inequity: Economic Causes, Economic Solutions." *Yale Journal on Regulation* 14 (1): 195–234.

Laska, Shirley Bradway, and Daphne Spain, eds. 1980. *Back to the City: Issues in Neighborhood Renovation.* New York: Pergamon Press.

Levy, Diane K., Jennifer Comey, and Sandra Padilla. 2006. *In the Face of Gentrification: Case Studies of Local Efforts to Mitigate Displacement.* Washington, DC: Urban Institute. http://www.urban.org/UploadedPDF/411294_gentrification.pdf.

Liu, Feng. 1997. "Dynamics and Causation of Environmental Equity, Locally Unwanted Land Uses, and Neighborhood Changes." *Environmental Management* 21 (5): 643–56.

McCluskey, Jill J., and Gordon C. Rausser. 2003. "Stigmatized Asset Value: Is It Temporary or Long-Term?" *Review of Economics and Statistics* 85 (2): 276–85.

McKinnish, Terra, Randall Walsh, and T. Kirk White. 2010. "Who Gentrifies Low-Income Neighborhoods?" *Journal of Urban Economics* 67 (2): 180–93.

Messer, Kent D., William D. Schulze, Katherine F. Hackett, Trudy Ann Cameron, and Gary H. McClelland. 2006. "Can Stigma Explain Large Property Value Losses? The Psychology and Economics of Superfund." *Environmental and Resource Economics* 33 (3): 299–324.

Michaels, R. Gregory, and V. Kerry Smith. 1990. "Market Segmentation and Valuing Amenities with Hedonic Models: The Case of Hazardous Waste Sites." *Journal of Urban Economics* 28 (2): 223–42.

Morgan, Kelly. 2000. "Inequality and Crime." *Review of Economics and Statistics* 82 (4): 530–39.

National Environmental Justice Advisory Council (NEJAC). 2006. *Unintended Impacts of Redevelopment and Revitalization Efforts in Five Environmental Justice Communities.* Final Report. http://www.epa.gov/compliance/ej/resources/publications/nejac/redev-revital-recomm-9-27-06.pdf.

Noonan, Douglas S., Douglas J. Krupka, and Brett M. Baden. 2007. "Neighborhood Dynamics and Price Effects of Superfund Site Clean-Up." *Journal of Regional Science* 47 (4): 665–92.

Oates, Wallace E. 1969. "The Effects of Property Taxes and Local Public Spending on Property Values: An Empirical Study of Tax Capitalization and the Tiebout Hypothesis." *Journal of Political Economy* 77 (6): 957–71.

O'Sullivan, Arthur. 2005. "Gentrification and Crime." *Journal of Urban Economics* 57 (1): 73–85.

Pastor, Manuel, Jim Sadd, and John Hipp. 2001. "Which Came First? Toxic Facilities, Minority Move-In, and Environmental Justice." *Journal of Urban Affairs* 23 (1): 1–21.

Pulido, Laura. 2000. "Rethinking Environmental Racism: White Privilege and Urban Development in Southern California." *Annals of the Association of American Geographers* 90 (1): 12–40.

Rosenthal, Stuart S. 2008. "Old Homes, Externalities, and Poor Neighborhoods: A Model of Urban Decline and Renewal." *Journal of Urban Economics* 63 (3): 816–40.

Ross, Stephen L., and Geoffrey M. B. Tootell. 2004. "Redlining, the Community Reinvestment Act, and Private Mortgage Insurance." *Journal of Urban Economics* 55 (2): 278–97.

Schelling, Thomas C. 1969. "Models of Segregation." *American Economic Review* 59 (2): 488–92.

———. 1972. "A Process of Residential Segregation: Neighborhood Tipping." In *Racial Discrimination in Economic Life,* edited by A. Pascal. Lexington, MA: Lexington Books.

Sethi, Rajiv, and Rohini Somanathan. 2004. "Inequality and Segregation." *Journal of Political Economy* 112 (6): 1296–1321.

Sieg, Holger, V. Kerry Smith, H. Spencer Banzhaf, and Randy Walsh. 2004. "Estimating the General Equilibrium Benefits of Large Changes in Spatially Delineated Public Goods." *International Economic Review* 45 (4): 1047–77.

Skogan, Wesley. 1986. "Fear of Crime and Neighborhood Change." *Crime and Justice* 8:203–229.

Smith, V. Kerry, and William H. Desvousges. 1986. "The Value of Avoiding a LULU: Hazardous Waste Disposal Sites." *Review of Economics and Statistics* 68 (2): 293–99.

Smith, V. Kerry, and Ju-Chin Huang. 1995. "Can Markets Value Air Quality? A Meta Analysis of Hedonic Property Value Models." *Journal of Political Economy* 103 (1): 209–27.

Smith, V. Kerry, Holger Sieg, H. Spencer Banzhaf, and Randy Walsh. 2004. "General Equilibrium Benefits for Environmental Improvements: Projected Ozone Reductions under EPA's Prospective Analysis for the Los Angeles Air Basin." *Journal of Environmental Economics and Management* 47 (3): 559–84.

Somerville, C. Tsuriel, and Cynthia Holmes. 2001. "Dynamics of the Affordable Housing Stock: Microdata Analysis of Filtering." *Journal of Housing Research* 12 (1): 115–40.

Tiebout, Charles. 1956. "A Pure Theory of Local Expenditures." *Journal of Political Economy* 64 (5): 416–24.

Vigdor, Jacob L. 2002. "Does Gentrification Harm the Poor?" *Brookings Papers on Urban Affairs* 3:133–82.

———. 2006. "Does Urban Decay Harm the Poor?" Mimeo, Duke University, Durham, NC.

Walsh, Randall P. 2007. "Endogenous Open Space Amenities in a Locational Equilibrium." *Journal of Urban Economics* 61 (2): 319–44.

Wu, JunJie, and Seong-Hoon Cho. 2003. "Estimating Households' Preferences for Environmental Amenities Using Equilibrium Models of Local Jurisdictions." *Scottish Journal of Political Economy* 50 (2): 189–206.

Zukin, Sharon. 1987. "Gentrification: Culture and Capital in the Urban Core." *Annual Review of Sociology* 13:129–47.

———. 1998. "Urban Lifestyles: Diversity and Standardisation in Spaces of Consumption." *Urban Studies* 35 (5–6): 825–39.

3 Does Environmental Remediation Benefit the Poor?

Jacob L. Vigdor

Introduction

Private industry and government have collectively spent billions of dollars to remediate the consequences of past polluting activity and to reduce the amount of pollution emitted in the future. These costs have been incurred in the belief that they deliver substantial benefits to society. In addition to arguments that the benefits of remediation exceed the costs to society, it is often argued that carefully targeted cleanups can have a progressive impact, disproportionately improving the quality of life of poor households, while progressive taxation ensures that the costs disproportionately fall on the more affluent.

Is it correct, however, to assert that environmental cleanups—even those targeted at economically distressed cities and neighborhoods—yield benefits to the poor? There are several potential intervening mechanisms that might prevent environmental remediation from translating into a clear improvement in quality of life. Indeed, they present the real possibility of decreased living standards for some households. Local environmental improvements may lead to increases in property values, which translate into a clear gain for homeowners but not for renters. At one extreme, environmental cleanups might lead to wholesale displacement of poor residents akin to that purported to occur in gentrifying neighborhoods.

Property markets are not the only potential intervening mechanism. If environmental improvements raise production costs for local employers, they may respond by offering lower wages or exiting the labor market altogether. The implication for health insurance, provided either by the government or through private markets, is that the benefits of lower health care costs accrue not to the individuals requiring less health care but to the parties required to pay for it.[1]

A final concern regarding the progressivity of remediation-related benefits is that poor residents may place little value on environmental quality. For example, if poor households place no value on environmental quality, then it is impossible to design a progressive environmental remediation program. If remediation leads to property value increases, then poor renters are actually harmed by remediation. A more paternalistic analysis might arrive at a different conclusion, but such an analysis must make assumptions regarding the magnitude of benefits rather than estimate them using traditional empirical methods such as hedonic analysis. Moreover, the social benefits of separating people from environmental hazards may be achieved more cost effectively by moving residents away from hazards rather than cleaning them up. Such a scenario is most likely to occur in declining housing markets.

This chapter considers these potential limitations to the overall benefits and progressivity of environmental remediation. It begins by presenting a basic economic model of housing price responses to environmental improvements, or capitalization. Alterations to the basic model then introduce the possibility that consumers are imperfectly informed about the environmental hazards in their neighborhoods, that environmental changes are capitalized into wages rather than housing prices, and other modifications. The general theoretical prediction is clear throughout: market reactions to improvements in environmental quality should occur, but they might not be of sufficient magnitude to offset the potential quality-of-life improvements to local residents.

The question of whether price changes, displacement, and other mechanisms offset all the potential benefits of remediation is inherently empirical. This chapter thus follows up the theoretical discussion with a review of existing evidence on whether environmental improvements raise housing prices, lower wages, or lead to displacement. The best available evidence suggests that, as predicted by the simple model, areas with known environmental hazards have lower property values, and the discovery of new hazards drives prices down. There is less consensus, however, that remediation leads to increases in prices. Evidence suggests that responses to remediation are different in tight housing markets relative to slack ones and that reductions in air pollution may induce a larger response than the cleanup of hazardous waste sites. Overall, the evidence indicates that those who live near a hazardous waste site and place a value on its removal stand to reap benefits from remediation, but only a small proportion of households near hazardous waste sites actually place a large value on environmental quality.

Economic Framework

Economists have established a method of evaluating environmental benefits, rooted in the presumption that people who value environmental improvements will be willing to pay more for housing in the vicinity of a hazardous waste site after it has been remediated. The value of an environmental cleanup can thus be approximated by the increase in the value of housing located close to a site.

The basic economic logic underlying this prediction reflects a long legacy of models of capitalization and residential sorting, dating at least to Epple and Romer (1991). Thorough expositions of varying technical rigor can be found in Been (1997), Sieg et al. (2004), and Smith et al. (2004); see also Chapters 2 and 4. What follows here is a very basic, nontechnical discussion.

Households face an array of neighborhood location choices, each with its own bundle of amenities and local public goods. Specific housing units are allocated to those individuals with the highest willingness to pay for the associated bundle, plus any characteristics that are specific to the unit. Neighborhoods with severe environmental problems are not likely to be favored by many households. To the extent that they are inhabited at all, residents will tend to be either unconcerned about proximity to concentration or poor enough that they have been priced out of more attractive neighborhood alternatives. As there is little competition for housing in contaminated neighborhoods, the price of a housing unit is expected to remain low.

When environmental remediation occurs, the direct effect is to improve the lives of those who live in proximity to the hazard. At the same time, however, households that once shunned the neighborhood because of contamination will now reconsider it.[2] In some cases, formerly contaminated neighborhoods may be highly valued because they are proximate to other valued resources, such as central business districts or scenic waterfronts. To remain housed, the original residents must either pay higher rent in the remediated neighborhood, pay the market rate in some other neighborhood, or crowd into a smaller unit while paying a comparable amount. The arrival of new, and in many cases more affluent, households in newly remediated neighborhoods is often described as "environmental gentrification." As in other cases of gentrification, the original residents who own their homes are spared these immediate negative impacts and receive a windfall gain from the increase in the value of their property.

For renters, the direct positive effect of an environmental cleanup may thus be partially or wholly offset by an indirect decrease in well-being associated with reduced housing consumption; reduced consumption of other goods; or a move to a neighborhood that, by revealed preference, the household considered inferior to the "pre-remediation" neighborhood. The potential for indirect negative effects on utility to swamp the direct positive effects of environmental remediation results from an equilibrium pattern that might seem paradoxical to the layperson but is quite logical to an economist. The set of households that choose to live close to environmental hazards are those that place very little value on environmental quality in general. Presumably, this group consists disproportionately of poor households whose willingness to pay is low in part because their ability to pay is low.

Complications

The simple model presented above necessarily abstracts from many important aspects of the real world. In reality, many neighborhoods contain undeveloped land, meaning that the number of parcels available for interested households can vary. Neighborhoods that become more attractive will expand, and those that become less attractive will contract. These expansions and contractions will act to mitigate any price response to environmental remediation. In the extreme case, rather than become relatively more expensive, the neighborhoods experiencing cleanups may become larger or more populous relative to others. The potential for expansion thus takes some of the price pressure off of households that place little value on a remediation that takes place near their home. It also suggests that quantities, rather than just prices, should be taken into consideration when evaluating the benefits of remediation in the housing market.

In some cases, environmental remediation may not generate either a price response or a quantity response. Suppose that a remote mine is the source of contamination and the extent of the environmental hazard is revealed upon the mine's closure. The mine's closure removes the rationale for human habitation in the area; remediation can have no impact on the housing market because, for all intents and purposes, that market has ceased to exist. Housing units may remain in the vicinity, but they will remain vacant in the absence of some new compelling economic rationale for individuals to locate in the area.

Similar arguments can be made not just for remote communities engaged in natural resource extraction but also for many large but declining industrial cities. For example, remediating a contaminated site in an abandoned section of Detroit, Michigan, would be of little to no value because the city's population decline has resulted in a housing glut.[3]

The housing market response to environmental remediation can be minimal, even in cities not marked by widespread abandonment. In the initial scenario described above, price increases and gentrification were rationalized by presuming that a group of nonresident consumers placed both a strong negative value on environmental hazards and a strong positive value on some other neighborhood amenity—such as waterfront views or proximity to a central business district. Once the hazard is removed, it is this group who bids up housing values in the neighborhood.

This presumption could fail in one of two ways. First, the contaminated neighborhood may, in fact, be devoid of other amenities, in which case the cleanup may be completely irrelevant from the nonresident consumer's perspective. Second, nonresident consumers might place a value on environmental quality that is not very different from that of residents. In such a scenario, prices might increase somewhat, but the increase would only be commensurate with residents' valuation of the neighborhood improvement, and displacement would not occur.

Overall, then, the property value method of evaluating the benefits of environmental remediation introduces a form of catch-22. Either cleanups have little or no impact on the housing market, in which case there are no benefits, or there is an impact on the housing market, in which case society as a whole benefits, but the original renters most likely suffer, because they are unwilling to pay the rent premium associated with the improvement in environmental quality. In either case, environmental remediation does not benefit the poor, unless they happen to own their homes and experience a windfall gain associated with gentrification.

Do Property Markets Really Capture the Entire Welfare Gain?

The value that an individual consumer attaches to environmental remediation may be different from the value society places on exposing that consumer to fewer hazards. There are two main arguments for why this might be the case. Consumers may be misinformed about the extent and nature of the risks associated with exposure to environmental hazards. On the one hand, consumers may lack information about the presence of hazards or of the link between the hazards and specific consequences. The notion that the mere cleanup of an environmental hazard provides consumers with knowledge that the hazard existed in the first place underlies the so-called stigma hypothesis for why cleanups may not improve property values (Messer et al. 2006). Individuals may also be myopic regarding the valuation of consequences occurring far in the future. On the other hand, a considerable amount of research demonstrates that individuals often overestimate the probability of rare events by orders of magnitude, implying that they assume too strong a correlation between proximity to environmental hazards and the risk of specific illnesses or disorders (Kahneman and Tversky 1979). It is also true that a great deal of uncertainty surrounds the estimation of causal relationships between exposure to environmental hazards and health risks. Depending on the type of misinformation affecting consumer decisions, the private value attached to remediation may be either higher or lower than an objective estimate of the benefits (see, e.g., Gayer, Hamilton, and Viscusi 2000).

The second reason to think consumers may view remediation differently from society as a whole is that they may be insured against the costs associated with proximity to environmental hazards. The costs of treating most medical conditions, for example, are borne not by any single individual but by their health insurer. From the individual's perspective, as long as premiums are not adjusted to reflect the risk of proximity to hazards, avoidance of these medical costs does not result in a direct improvement in living standards. From society's perspective, however, the cost savings are important. Similar insurance mechanisms prevent consumers from considering the full cost of outcomes such as disability. The indifference of consumers to hazards that create costs for society but not directly to themselves is a classic example of moral hazard.

An alternative method of computing the benefits of environmental remediation uses scientific models associating exposure to environmental hazards with medical conditions. The change in exposure can then be transformed into a change in risk of disease. This change in risk can then be used in two ways. A cost-effectiveness analysis compares the cost of a cleanup to the proportionate decrease in risk. The output of such an analysis is measured in dollars per case avoided. A full cost-benefit analysis translates the disease risk into a dollar amount, quantifying the average costs associated with treating the disease and the decrease in duration and quality of life associated with that disease. The dollar value of benefits associated with cleanup can then be compared to the dollar value of costs. This alternative method of evaluation is known variously as the "benefits transfer," "integrated assessment," or "damage-cost approach" (Desvousges, Johnson, and Banzhaf 1998; Navrud and Ready 2007).

The primary drawback of the health-oriented approach is the number of assumptions required to arrive at a dollar value. To see this, consider the following equation, which summarizes the steps necessary to translate a change in environmental hazards to monetary benefits:

$$B = N \sum_i \Delta T \frac{\Delta H_i}{\Delta T} \frac{C_i}{H_i},$$

where B is a measure of the dollar value of health risk reduction associated with an environmental cleanup; ΔT is the change in environmental hazards brought about by the remediation; the ratio $\Delta H_i/\Delta T$, taken from the scientific literature, is the reduction in probability of contracting disease i associated with a unit reduction in environmental hazards; N is the population to which the risk reduction applies; and the ratio C_i/H_i measures the dollar value of averting one case of disease i. There are potential controversies at each stage of this process. How definitive is the link between an environmental hazard and disease i? Exactly how large is the population at risk? How should we evaluate the benefits of avoiding disease, particularly the intangible benefits such as reductions in pain and suffering?

Still another method of computing benefits is the so-called stated-preference approach (Alberini and Kahn 2006). Based on surveys, this approach suffers from divergences between what people say they will do and what they actually do. In sum, there is no perfect method of evaluating the benefits of environmental remediation, and, as a result, there is also no perfect method of determining whether those benefits are progressive. The arguments presented above, however, do not alter the conclusion that poor residents of environmentally contaminated areas may perceive little gain from remediation, except possibly if they are homeowners and cleanup leads to gentrification.

Evaluating Existing Evidence

Do housing prices in neighborhoods undergoing environmental remediation rise relative to other areas in the same housing market? Do these price changes result in the displacement of the original residents? Do wage levels decline? These questions are critically important, as they potentially indicate the existence and magnitude of benefits to society associated with environmental remediation. They are also inherently difficult questions to answer, for they require researchers to infer what would have happened to relative prices and wages in the absence of a remediation.

The ideal method of identifying the effect of remediation would be to take a set of known hazardous waste sites and randomly assign them to be cleaned up or left alone. A researcher could then observe differences in trajectories between the sites that were cleaned up and the sites that were not cleaned up and attribute any differences between them to the cleanup. Nothing approximating this scientific experiment has ever been conducted. First, the announcement of a cleanup often occurs simultaneously with the release of information regarding the degree of contamination at a site. Second, the decision to clean up a hazardous waste site is generally made in an environment of scarce resources, in which the sites posing greater risks receive higher priority. A simple effort to track the trajectory of property values around a site from before until after the cleanup thus runs the risk of confounding the effect of the cleanup with the effect of revealing information about the hazard in the first place, and with other trends common to neighborhoods hosting hazardous waste sites. In recent decades, the most significant confounding trend in most of the United States is the decline of manufacturing industry employment, as many hazardous waste sites are associated with industrial activity.

Efforts to infer the impact of remediation on the composition of neighborhoods, housing prices, or earnings of residents face the fundamental challenge of identifying a counterfactual scenario: What would have happened in a local area in the absence of the cleanup? These efforts also face common methodological concerns relating to external validity: the experience of one or a handful of sites may not be representative of hazardous waste sites in general. The following review both summarizes the main findings of the studies and critically analyzes the assumptions made regarding counterfactual scenarios and the representativeness of the sites examined.

Studies of Housing Prices and Quantities

Several studies have evaluated the impact of proximity to environmental hazards, or remediation of those hazards, on property values. To identify this impact, these studies generally take advantage of discrete events, such as the arrival of a new polluting firm in a neighborhood or the revelation of information about a hazard, and infer the impact of the event by comparing subsequent price trends in the immediate area with quasi–control group neighborhoods elsewhere.

Michaels and Smith (1990), for example, analyze the impact of the revelation of information about 11 hazardous waste sites near Boston, Massachusetts. Their estimates rely on the presumption that the impact on property values decays over space, implying that the effects can be measured by contrasting price trends in proximate areas with those in slightly more distant areas. Michaels and Smith report a significant impact on property values, particularly higher-end properties. Their finding makes sense economically. Environmental quality is most likely a normal good, which means higher-income households should exhibit a stronger response to new information about hazards.

Similar methods have been used by Kohlhase (1991) in her study of the impact of Superfund site proclamations near Houston, Texas; by Kiel (1995) and Kiel and Zabel (2001) in studies of sites in Woburn, Massachusetts; and by McCluskey and Rausser (2003) in their study of neighborhoods near a lead smelter in Dallas, Texas. Ihlanfeldt and Taylor (2004) find evidence that proximity to hazardous waste sites affects the market for commercial property in Atlanta, Georgia. Each study finds evidence that the revelation of information about a hazardous waste site leads to declines in property values. But each can be criticized on the grounds that their limited geographic scope potentially limits the generalizability of the results. It is also less clear from these studies whether the remediation of Superfund sites reverses property value declines. For example, Messer et al. (2006) argue that delays in cleanup can lead to "stigma" effects whereby property value declines persist even after cleanup has taken place.

Greenstone and Gallagher (2008) use an alternative method of inferring the impact of Superfund site selection and consequent cleanup. They note that initial placement on the Superfund National Priorities List (NPL) in the early 1980s was determined by first scoring each of several hundred nominated sites on a scale known as the Hazardous Ranking System (HRS). A fixed number of sites were then admitted to the NPL on the basis of their HRS scores. Greenstone and Gallagher's empirical strategy rests on a comparison of sites just above the HRS cutoff for immediate inclusion on the NPL with those just below the cutoff. Figure 3.1, reprinted from the original article, shows the estimated probability that a site is placed on the NPL as a function of its HRS score. It shows that sites on either side of the arbitrary HRS cutoff of 28.5 faced dramatically different probabilities of being placed on the NPL and hence of undergoing remediation.[4]

Greenstone and Gallagher's main results focus on property values, population, and counts of housing units in census tracts surrounding each of these

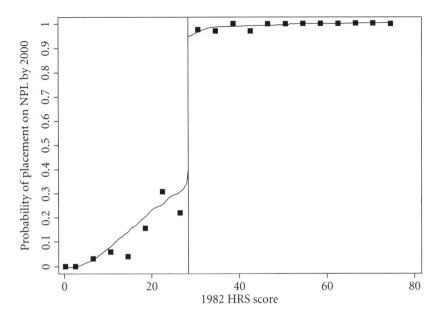

Figure 3.1 Probability a site is listed on the NPL, by HRS score. Reprinted from Greenstone and Gallagher (2008). Permission to reprint granted by Oxford University Press.

sites in 2000, the point at which remediation activities were at least under way for most sites on the initial NPL. They raise one concern with this strategy, which is that sites just above the cutoff for inclusion on the original NPL had significantly lower property values in 1980. This difference in pretreatment characteristics does not persist, however, when controlling for other pretreatment characteristics, which also appear in the authors' preferred 2000 specifications. The results indicate that NPL placement had no significant effect on property values or housing rents, while showing, if anything, that NPL placement had a negative impact on population and the size of the housing stock.

Although Greenstone and Gallagher interpret their results as indicating that remediation had no effect on property values and further argue that the benefits of remediation are therefore slight, it is important to recall that previous studies have shown property declines in areas surrounding a hazardous waste site at the time it was placed on the NPL. Greenstone and Gallagher argue that similar negative impacts should have also applied to the "control" sites with HRS scores below the cutoff for inclusion on the NPL. This argument would certainly carry weight in models assuming that consumers correctly perceive all relevant information in making location decisions. If, on the other hand, consumers place undue weight on NPL placement relative to the underlying characteristics, those sites initially placed on the NPL may have witnessed larger initial declines in property values.

Are consumers unduly influenced by differences in discrete categorizations when underlying continuous phenomena show little meaningful variation? There is at least some evidence that they do. Figlio and Lucas (2004) show significant property value reactions to minor differences in school average test scores in Florida, when those small average differences are also associated with discrete differences in letter grades assigned by the state government.

A word of caution is in order. Greenstone and Gallagher's regression discontinuity methodology identifies what is known as a "local average treatment effect": the impact of remediation on sites that were very close to the cutoff for inclusion on the NPL. Essentially, it compares sites just below the threshold of an HRS score of 28.5, which did not receive Superfund funding, and those just above the threshold, which did. The strength of this approach is that the two groups are similar in terms of the HRS score as well as other factors. The limitation is that it provides little or no information on the impact of remediation on sites that were far above the cutoff or the potential impact on sites well below the cutoff. It is conceivable, for example, that remediation had a more positive impact on sites ranked well above the threshold for placement on the NPL.[5]

Below, I present additional analysis using Greenstone and Gallagher's original data set. Part of this supplemental analysis considers whether any improving trend in property values can be observed in sites above the NPL threshold between 1990, the point at which no cleanup activities were under way for many sites on the NPL, and 2000. A second component considers whether there are important differences between Superfund sites very close to the NPL cutoff thresholds and those at higher priority.

Studies of Demographic Change

Much of the literature on environmental hazards and neighborhood demographics has focused on the question of whether polluting firms locate in poor neighborhoods or whether neighborhoods with polluting firms attract poor residents. More recently, investigators have extended this literature to consider whether improvements in environmental conditions in particular neighborhoods lead those areas to undergo demographic changes.

Been (1997) demonstrates that hazardous waste, treatment, storage, and disposal facilities tend to be sited in census tracts with relatively low poverty rates. Any cross-sectional correlation between poverty and environmental hazards thus appears to be driven by residential sorting rather than explicit decisions to locate hazardous waste sites in poor areas (see Chapter 8). While such a sorting model is entirely consistent with the model above, Been does not actually provide affirmative evidence of sorting, nor do they specifically consider whether the removal of an environmental hazard causes reverse sorting.

Cameron and McConnaha (2006) examine demographic trends in neighborhoods surrounding four NPL sites and report some evidence of declines in neighborhood socioeconomic status once a site is placed on the NPL and of improvements once the site is cleaned up. The strongest results pertain to a Superfund site in the relatively densely populated suburbs of New York City on Long Island, consistent with the view that price escalation and gentrification following cleanup are most likely to occur in relatively tight housing markets.

Greenstone and Gallagher (2008) use the methodology described above to determine whether demographic changes occurred in neighborhoods adjacent to sites that barely qualified for inclusion on the initial NPL relative to those that did not. They find no consistent evidence of differences as of 2000. These findings can once again be questioned for potentially confounding the effect of initial placement on the NPL with subsequent cleanup, in the case where placement on the NPL has independent effects over and above those that would be predicted on the basis of HRS scores alone. There are also concerns that the local average treatment effect derived from the regression discontinuity misses important effects for sites well away from the margin. The analysis in the subsequent section provides some opportunity to assess this claim.

Banzhaf and Walsh (2008) investigate the impact of proximity to firms emitting air pollutants in urban areas of California during the 1990s. Using information from the Toxics Release Inventory (TRI), they take advantage of the fact that polluters enter and exit locations with some frequency. They find that areas gaining polluters become less populated and poorer, on average, while areas losing polluters tend to see opposite trends. The stronger evidence of sorting in that article may reflect the authors' use of uniformly defined circles of common radius as a neighborhood construct, rather than census tracts. It should be noted, however, that the relatively coarse timing of demographic observations from the 1990 and 2000 Census enumerations makes it difficult to infer exactly whether demographic trends precede or follow the entry or exit of polluting firms.

In all, studies of the impact of remediation on property values and demographics agree with the economic insight that the impact of hazardous waste cleanups may be different in housing markets with varying degrees of slack. The strongest evidence of a sorting response, for example, has been found in the relatively high cost housing areas of urban California and suburban parts of northeastern cities. In these areas, environmental remediation may lead more affluent households to consider selecting a residence in a neighborhood they would have shunned before remediation. In areas with slack housing markets, such as the declining cities of the industrial Midwest, the impact of remediation may be less significant. In such cities, remediation may be insufficient for affluent households to consider residing in a neighborhood, given the abundance of inexpensive alternatives.

Studies of Earnings

To date, few studies have explicitly examined the potential link between environmental remediation and earnings. Greenstone and Gallagher (2008) use their regression discontinuity methodology to examine indicators of income and wealth but find few consistent results. Given the absence of true longitudinal data in the US Census, it is not clear whether evidence of changes in income should be construed as changes in the composition of a neighborhood or as changes in the fortunes of the original residents. The following analysis provides some additional insight into the relationship between environmental remediation and the labor market.

New Evidence

The empirical analysis in this section is based on data on the location of nearly 700 hazardous waste sites initially evaluated by the US Environmental Protection Agency in the early 1980s for possible inclusion on the NPL, a precursor to cleanup under the Comprehensive Environmental Response, Compensation, and Liability Act of 1980 (CERCLA), commonly known as Superfund. This is the same data set used by Greenstone and Gallagher (2005, 2008) in their analysis of the impact of placement on the NPL on property values. As noted above, this study focused on the relationship between NPL placement and median 2000 owner-occupied housing values and reported impacts that were generally not statistically significant, with positive but modest point estimates. The same analysis found no significant impact on housing supply, the demographic composition of neighborhoods, or basic measures of income.

This section presents graphical evidence corroborating many of Greenstone and Gallagher's results and provides additional evidence on the relationship between environmental remediation and earned income, to assess the likelihood that improvements in standards of living have led households to accept lower wages rather than pay higher rents. It also presents additional evidence from 1990, to assess whether restricting the analysis to patterns in 1980 and 2000 overlooks important intervening trends. This simple analysis exploits the fact that hazardous waste sites receiving HRS scores above 28.5 were placed on the initial NPL, and those with scores below were not. As Figure 3.1 indicates, sites with scores above this threshold were virtually always placed on the NPL. Sites with lower scores were sometimes placed on the NPL, but there is a clear discontinuity at 28.5. The following regression discontinuity analyses estimate so-called intent-to-treat effects, which infer the impact of the *initial* placement decision, rather than the final decision, on later trends.

As noted above, the regression discontinuity methodology identifies a "local average treatment effect" for hazardous sites very close to the 28.5 threshold. Are these sites representative of all remediated sites? One way to gauge this is from the geographic patterns across sites. Among the 343 hazardous waste sites with HRS scores above 32.5, well above the NPL threshold, about one-third are in New York, New Jersey, or Florida—states with generally robust housing markets. Just over one-quarter come from the Rust Belt states of Pennsylvania, Ohio, Indiana, Michigan, and Illinois—states in which industrial and population decline has limited the vitality of housing markets.

The 108 "marginal" sites close to the 28.5 cutoff are distributed very differently from those well above the threshold: 41 percent are in the Rust Belt states of Pennsylvania, Ohio, Indiana, and Michigan, while only 14 percent are in New York, New Jersey, and Florida. The share of "barely treated" sites just above the 28.5 threshold tilts even more heavily toward the Rust Belt: 47 percent are located in the five-state belt between Pennsylvania and Illinois.

Is it conceivable that local average treatment effects, even if reliably estimated using the regression discontinuity methodology, understate the impact of remediation of severely contaminated sites in high-density, tight housing markets such as those in the Northeast, Florida, and California? Absolutely. It is impossible, of course, to know for certain what the treatment effects are in these types of sites since there is no viable control group for them. It is not necessarily inconsistent, however, to point simultaneously to significant effects in smaller event studies and insignificant regression discontinuity effects.

With this caveat in mind, the remainder of this section provides some basic exploration of Greenstone and Gallagher's methods and results. The outcome variables considered in this analysis pertain to census tracts with area-weighted centroids within 2 miles of a hazardous waste site with a 1982 HRS score. Tracts are excluded from the sample, however, if any portion lies within 3 miles of a second hazardous waste site. This addresses a concern not discussed in Greenstone and Gallagher (2008), namely, that many hazardous waste sites were clustered geographically, implying that some tracts were proximate to both "treated" and "control" sites. This restriction therefore reduces the likelihood that tracts on one side of the discontinuity are tainted by proximity to a site on the other side. A substantial proportion of tracts are eliminated with this restriction; more than 1,000 tracts have some portion within 3 miles of multiple hazardous waste sites, and one tract has a portion of its land area within 3 miles of nine distinct sites. While the restriction has little impact on estimates, it does increase confidence that the absence of significant impacts reflects the true absence of an effect and not simply contamination of the treatment.

Figure 3.2 shows the relationship between the 1982 HRS score and the logarithm of median gross rent at the tract level at three points in time: 1980, 1990, and 2000. The unit of observation is the census tract; tracts have been aggregated to the nearest integer value of the HRS score of the corresponding hazardous waste site. The curve fitted to the data is a cubic, with a discontinuity permitted at the NPL cutoff of 28.5.

Focusing first on the point of discontinuity, in this sample there is no evidence of any discontinuity in rents at the NPL cutoff as of 1980, assuaging concerns raised originally by Greenstone and Gallagher themselves. In later years, there is no evidence that sites barely eligible for the NPL witnessed any excess rent appreciation relative to those sites barely ineligible, on the other side of the discontinuity. If anything, the neighborhoods on the untreated side of the discontinuity exhibited faster growth, although the 2000 discontinuity is not significantly different from 0. These results support Greenstone and Gallagher's conclusion that Superfund cleanups have no impact on property values or rents.

If we look farther from the discontinuity, however, there are interesting things happening. In the neighborhoods surrounding the worst hazardous waste sites, on the right side of Figure 3.2, we see a pronounced "dip" in the

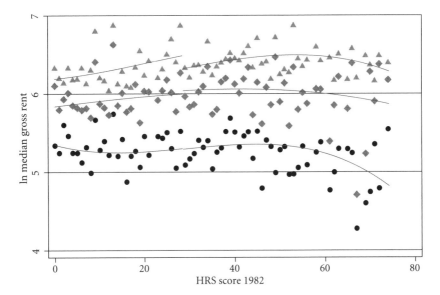

Figure 3.2 Relationship between HRS score and median gross rent, 1980 (circles), 1990 (diamonds), and 2000 (triangles). Note: Unit of observation is the set of census tracts with centroids within 2 miles of a hazardous waste site with an HRS score within a one-point range, excluding those tracts with any portion lying within 3 miles of one or more additional sites. Sites with HRS scores above 28.5 were automatically placed on the NPL in 1980.

fitted cubic model for 1980, indicating that median rents were low in these areas compared to places with somewhat less severe cleanup problems. By 1990, this initial dip has disappeared, and it does not reappear in 2000. It is not appropriate to make a causal claim on the basis of this evidence, as there may have been many unrelated trends in the neighborhoods in question between 1980 and 2000. Nonetheless, the evidence is fundamentally consistent with the idea that remediation had a significant impact on property values in the worst-case sites, while having little to no impact on marginal sites. The local average treatment effect estimated with the regression discontinuity offers no opportunity to support or deny this claim.

Whereas Figure 3.2 looks at price effects in the housing market, Figure 3.3 focuses on quantity. From an expositional perspective, Figure 3.2 had the advantage of exploiting inflation, which ensured that the data points and fitted cubics did not overlap much from one decade to the next. This is not the case when examining housing units, but in spite of this problem, a definite trend

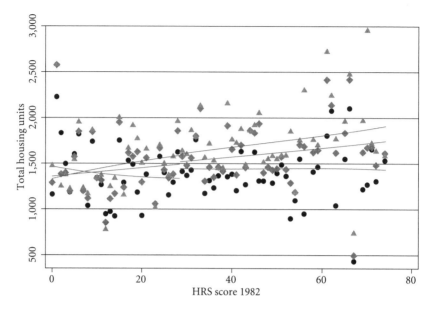

Figure 3.3 Relationship between HRS score and total housing units, 1980 (circles), 1990 (diamonds), and 2000 (triangles). Note: Unit of observation is the set of census tracts with centroids within 2 miles of a hazardous waste site with an HRS score within a one-point range, excluding those tracts with any portion lying within 3 miles of one or more additional sites. Sites with HRS scores above 28.5 were automatically placed on the NPL in 1980.

can be discerned. Once again, focusing on the point of discontinuity leads us to conclusions that mirror those of Greenstone and Gallagher. There is no evidence of a significant difference in the total number of housing units in the tracts surrounding waste sites that just barely made and missed inclusion on the initial NPL at any point in time.

Consistent with the basic pattern in Figure 3.2, there is a different story to be told on the right side of the graph. Whereas the fitted cubics indicate almost no net change in the number of housing units surrounding sites with very low HRS scores (between, say, 0 and 15), there is a more substantial estimated mean difference in areas surrounding sites with more severe contamination. Whereas these areas held an average of around 1,400 housing units per tract in 1980, by 2000, the average was closer to the 1,700 to 1,800 range, an increase of more than 20 percent. The same caveat that applied in Figure 3.2 applies here: we can't really be confident that what we are observing reflects the impact of remediation. It is consistent, however, with the idea that remediation had very little impact on marginal sites and had a more significant positive impact on the demand for housing surrounding the worst-off sites, which translated into increases in both price and quantity.

For the sake of argument, let's accept for now the conjecture that remediation of the sites with the highest 1982 HRS scores increased demand in the housing market. Can we be certain that the demand reflects a higher willingness to pay among the original residents of the neighborhood? Or does it rather reflect the arrival of a more environmentally conscious class of consumer, who bestowed windfall profits on those original residents who owned homes but otherwise caused those residents to choose between paying for a neighborhood amenity they did not value or moving somewhere else? We can't really answer this question directly using the data presently available, but we can at least look for a separate symptom of gentrification and displacement: significant changes in the income levels of area residents.

There is a second reason for examining income, noted above. In scenarios where consumers value remediation but firms do not, we might expect the economic response to take the form of lower wages as well as higher rents. Firms will only be willing to pay higher rent in remediated areas if they are compensated in the form of a lower wage bill. Consumers may willingly assent to this trade-off if they attach sufficiently high values to the environmental improvements.

Figure 3.4 shows data on the average earnings of workers in areas surrounding hazardous waste sites in 1980, 1990, and 2000. Looking at the point of discontinuity, there is evidence that workers near sites just barely eligible for the original NPL consistently earn less than their counterparts below the threshold, although this pattern is never statistically significant. Similar to the results of Greenstone and Gallagher, the conclusion here is that environmental remediation appears to have had little in the way of labor market effects at marginal sites.

In this particular case, there is little evidence of any radical changes in the labor market in neighborhoods close to the most severely contaminated sites. The fitted polynomials for 1980 and 1990 are close to vertical translations of one another, indicating that nominal wages rose proportionately in all places over that decade. The cubic fit for 2000 indicates a slightly more noticeable degree of trailing off on the right side of the graph, indicating that, if anything, the average earnings of workers near the sites of highest priority on the NPL failed to keep up with their counterparts residing closer to low-priority sites.

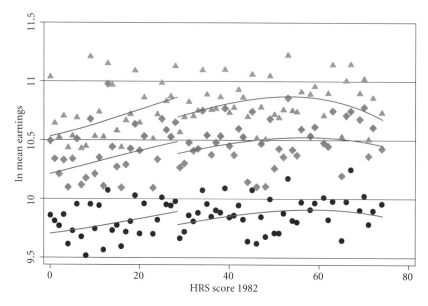

Figure 3.4 Relationship between HRS score and log of mean earnings, 1980 (circles), 1990 (diamonds), and 2000 (triangles). Note: Unit of observation is the set of census tracts with centroids within 2 miles of a hazardous waste site with an HRS score within a one-point range, excluding those tracts with any portion lying within 3 miles of one or more additional sites. Sites with HRS scores above 28.5 were automatically placed on the NPL in 1980.

This is more consistent with a story of firms requiring workers to accept lower wages in areas undergoing land value appreciation than with a story of gentrification; there is nothing to say, however, that both phenomena could not occur simultaneously. As with Figures 3.2 and 3.3, we also must be very clear in stating that causal inference is not directly supported with this methodology.

Conclusion

In the context of a classical economic model, it is difficult to argue that environmental remediation benefits the poor in light of evidence that such households place little value on environmental quality in the first place. The best available evidence suggests that placement of a pollution-emitting firm, or revelation of information about a local hazard, causes property values to decline in the immediate surroundings. As households that place a value on environmental quality abandon these areas, they are replaced by households that place less value on this amenity. While environmental remediation may be associated with increased property values in some circumstances, it is likely that the process relies, at least to some extent, on the return of households that place a value on environmental quality.

A series of empirical questions lies at the heart of the debate about the effects of remediation and their distribution, and these questions are very difficult to answer. One emerging pattern in the literature is that the response to environmental remediation is heterogeneous in an economically sensible way. In slack housing markets, where contamination-free neighborhoods are not a scarce commodity, the impact of remediation is negligible. By a similar token, cleaning up hazardous waste sites in completely uninhabited areas is likely to generate few benefits. In at least some cases, the more economically defensible response to contamination is to move people away from hazards, rather than remove the hazards themselves.

In the nation's tightest housing markets, where the supply of neighborhoods has failed to keep up with the demand, environmental remediation stands a better chance of generating tangible benefits. Individual case studies point to strong effects of cleaning up sites at the core or periphery of growing cities; a reexamination of the data on sites listed on the original NPL suggests that high-priority sites, which were disproportionately located in parts of the country with tight housing markets, had more robust responses than the lower-priority sites that were barely included on the NPL.

The impacts on property values, to the extent that they exist, threaten to negate some or all of the benefits that accrue to renter households, particularly when neighborhoods become crowded with more affluent households that place a higher value on environmental amenities. The basic evidence introduced here, however, shows little sign of gentrification occurring in remediated high-priority neighborhoods. The notion that the impacts of neighborhood amenity improvements are modest relative to residents' willingness to pay is consistent with Vigdor (2010), who analyzes the impact of various forms of neighborhood quality change on equilibrium prices using the longitudinal American Housing Survey. That study does not explicitly consider environmental amenities, however, and a more direct analysis of housing prices and willingness to pay with longitudinal data would seem to be a promising avenue for future research.

Notes

I am grateful to Michael Greenstone for sharing the HRS data and to Spencer Banzhaf for guidance on writing this chapter. All errors are my own.

1. Lower health care costs could, in theory, result in lowered insurance premiums. In practice, market regulations may prohibit insurers from pricing environmental risks into premiums.

2. In theoretical models of this type, it is typical to assume that there are no moving costs, in which case a change in neighborhood quality will instantaneously cause some individuals to switch neighborhoods. It is more realistic, however, to think that households face specific fixed costs associated with moving, from the costs of searching for a new home, to the up-front costs of arranging financing for that home, to the costs of physically moving. Each of these costs will tend to dampen the response to a change in neighborhood quality. In fact, if moving costs are high enough, they will prevent any movement at all, in which case it would be inappropriate to evaluate the benefits of environmental remediation using property values. In most metropolitan areas, however, there is a nearly continuous flow of newly arrived households for whom the costs of moving are sunk. These households can adjust their neighborhood choice instantaneously in response to new information.

3. A more general statement of this point follows the logic of Roback (1982), who argues that both firms and workers compete for land in any city and that both land prices and wages adjust to ensure an economic equilibrium. Amenities will tend to drive up land values the most if they are attractive to both workers and firms. There is some evidence that firms place a positive value on environmental quality; see Ihlanfeldt and Taylor (2004). In some cases, however, environmental remediation may follow a new regulation that prohibits a firm from using a certain production technology. In that case, the firm's demand for land may decrease, even as households attempt to bid up land prices as environmental quality improves. In such a scenario, the less ambiguous implication of remediation is a reduction in market wages.

4. It is true that some sites with scores below the cutoff were eventually remediated. For purposes of inference, this "noncompliance" is not particularly troubling; the only requirement for inferring local average treatment effects using a regression discontinuity framework such as Greenstone and Gallagher's is that the probability of treatment differs on either side of the arbitrary cutoff point.

5. See Imbens and Lemieux (2008) for an introduction to regression discontinuity methods.

References

Alberini, Anna, and James R. Kahn, eds. 2006. *Handbook on Contingent Valuation*. Cheltenham, UK: Edward Elgar.

Banzhaf, H. Spencer, and Randall P. Walsh. 2008. "Do People Vote with Their Feet? An Empirical Test of Tiebout's Mechanism." *American Economic Review* 98 (3): 843–63.

Been, Vicki, with Francis Gupta. 1997. "Coming to the Nuisance or Going to the Barrios? A Longitudinal Analysis of Environmental Justice Claims." *Ecology Law Quarterly* 24 (1): 1–56.

Cameron, Trudy Ann, and Ian T. McConnaha. 2006. "Evidence of Environmental Migration." *Land Economics* 82 (2): 273–90.

Desvousges, William H., F. Reed Johnson, and H. Spencer Banzhaf. 1998. *Environmental Policy Analysis with Limited Information: Principles and Applications of the Transfer Method.* Cheltenham, UK: Edward Elgar.

Epple, Dennis, and Thomas Romer. 1991. "Mobility and Redistribution." *Journal of Political Economy* 99 (4): 828–58.

Figlio, David, and Maurice Lucas. 2004. "What's in a Grade? School Report Cards and the Housing Market." *American Economic Review* 94 (3): 591–604.

Gayer, Ted, James T. Hamilton, and W. Kip Viscusi. 2000. "Private Values of Risk Tradeoffs at Superfund Sites: Housing Market Evidence on Learning about Risk." *Review of Economics and Statistics* 82 (3): 439–51.

Greenstone, Michael, and Justin Gallagher. 2005. "Does Hazardous Waste Matter? Evidence from the Housing Market and the Superfund Program." NBER Working Paper 11790, National Bureau of Economic Research, Cambridge, MA. http://ideas .repec.org/p/nbr/nberwo/11790.html.

———. 2008. "Does Hazardous Waste Matter? Evidence from the Housing Market and the Superfund Program." *Quarterly Journal of Economics* 123 (3): 951–1003.

Ihlanfeldt, Keith R., and Laura O. Taylor. 2004. "Externality Effects of Small-Scale Hazardous Waste Sites: Evidence from Urban Commercial Property Markets." *Journal of Environmental Economics and Management* 47 (1): 117–39.

Imbens, Guido W., and Thomas Lemieux. 2008. "Regression Discontinuity Designs: A Guide to Practice." *Journal of Econometrics* 142 (2): 615–35.

Kahneman, Daniel, and Amos Tversky. 1979. "Prospect Theory: An Analysis of Decision under Risk." *Econometrica* 47 (2): 263–91.

Kiel, Katherine A. 1995. "Measuring the Impact of the Discovery and Cleaning of Identified Hazardous Waste Sites on House Values." *Land Economics* 71 (4): 428–35.

Kiel, Katherine, and Jeffrey Zabel. 2001. "Estimating the Economic Benefits of Cleaning Up Superfund Sites: The Case of Woburn, Massachusetts." *Journal of Real Estate Finance and Economics* 22 (2–3): 163–84.

Kohlhase, Janet E. 1991. "The Impact of Toxic Waste Sites on Housing Values." *Journal of Urban Economics* 30 (1): 1–26.

McCluskey, Jill J., and Gordon C. Rausser. 2003. "Hazardous Waste Sites and Housing Appreciation Rates." *Journal of Environmental Economics and Management* 45 (2): 166–76.

Messer, Kent D., William D. Schulze, Katherine F. Hackett, Trudy Ann Cameron, and Gary H. McClelland. 2006. "Can Stigma Explain Large Property Value Losses? The Psychology and Economics of Superfund." *Environmental and Resource Economics* 33 (3): 299–324.

Michaels, R. Gregory, and V. Kerry Smith. 1990. "Market Segmentation and Valuing Amenities with Hedonic Models: The Case of Hazardous Waste Sites." *Journal of Urban Economics* 28 (2): 223–42.

Navrud, Ståle, and Richard Ready, eds. 2007. *Environmental Values Transfer: Issues and Methods.* Dordrecht, Netherlands: Kluwer.

Roback, Jennifer. 1982. "Wages, Rents, and the Quality of Life." *Journal of Political Economy* 90 (6): 1257–78.

Sieg, Holger, V. Kerry Smith, H. Spencer Banzhaf, and Randy Walsh. 2004. "Estimating the General Equilibrium Benefits of Large Changes in Spatially Delineated Public Goods." *International Economic Review* 45 (4): 1047–77.

Smith, V. Kerry, Holger Sieg, H. Spencer Banzhaf, and Randy Walsh. 2004. "General Equilibrium Benefits for Environmental Improvements: Projected Ozone Reductions under EPA's Prospective Analysis for the Los Angeles Air Basin." *Journal of Environmental Economics and Management* 47 (3): 559–84.

Vigdor, Jacob L. 2010. "Is Urban Decay Bad? Is Urban Revitalization Bad Too?" *Journal of Urban Economics* 68 (3): 277–89.

4 Environmental Gentrification and Discrimination

H. Spencer Banzhaf, Joshua Sidon, and Randall P. Walsh

Introduction

As emphasized in Chapter 1 of this volume, evaluating claims of discrimination and injustice as well as the potential success of various legal and policy remedies to environmental inequities requires an understanding of the social causes lying behind the correlation between pollution and demographics (for further discussion, see Been 1993; Foster 1998; see also Chapter 2). There are at least three potentially nonexclusive interpretations of this correlation. The simplest interpretation is that firms react to demographics in determining their pollution patterns. Under this interpretation, firms may be discriminating out of racist motives or, more subtly, may be seeking out areas with weaker political power. Consistent with this view, Hamilton (1993), Brooks and Sethi (1997), and Arora and Cason (1999) have found evidence for a correlation between pollution and proxies for political power such as turnout in elections. A second, similar interpretation is that firms are attracted to factors spatially correlated with demographics: low land prices, access to transportation corridors, and proximity to other similar firms (see Chapter 8).

A third interpretation, known as "coming to the nuisance," essentially reverses the causality. Once an area becomes polluted, irrespective of the cause of the pollution, it becomes a less desirable place to live. Wealthier households leave, land and housing values fall, and the poor may even move in, attracted by lower housing costs. In this way, the correlation may arise ex post (Been 1993, 1994, 1997; see also Chapter 8). This interpretation is essentially an application of Tiebout's (1956) model of local public finance, in which households sort geographically according to their willingness to pay, in land prices and taxes, for amenities (see Chapter 2).

Understanding which of these explanations is correct is important for several reasons. First, if the Tiebout sorting explanation is correct, it would color the interpretation of injustice, moving it from firm behavior to more fundamental grounds such as inequity in the distribution of income. Second, it would cast doubt on the efficacy of policies designed to reverse the correlation through the targeting of firm behavior. As pointed out by Been (1993), as long as some areas are more polluted than others, migration might always reestablish the correlation.

Finally, it could have important and counterintuitive implications for household welfare. For example, Sieg et al. (2004) and Walsh (2007) find that targeting dirty, poor neighborhoods for improvements with the intention of helping the local residents can have perverse results. The reason is that residents who sort into dirtier communities place a relatively high priority on low-cost housing compared to the environment. Thus, cleaning up the environment may increase those costs by more than their willingness to pay, as other households bid property values up by their own higher willingness to pay. Moreover, as they generally rent their housing, poor residents stand to lose from these increased housing costs. Sieg et al. (2004) refer to this effect as "environmental gentrification." Such perverse distributional effects are not only a concern of the academic literature: they have emerged as a top concern of grassroots movements as well, as expressed in a recent report from the National Environmental Justice Advisory Council (NEJAC; 2006).

To date, evidence on whether the correlation between pollution and poor and minority populations arises more from firm behavior or from household behavior is mixed, and we will not claim to settle the issue here.[1] Rather, our contribution is to evaluate the potential for gentrification, in a world in which Tiebout sorting by households is assumed to be the predominant factor. Banzhaf and Walsh (2008) have recently shown that, in a Tiebout framework, demand and price effects can be expected from exogenous environmental improvements. However, since Glass (1964) first coined the term, "gentrification" has meant a set of effects, including the influx of wealthier white households, increased land values, and renovation and remodeling of the housing stock (see Chapter 2). Although gentrification—vaguely defined—seems an intuitive outcome of such exogenous improvements, beyond price effects they have not been established in the theoretical or empirical literature to date.

We begin with a simple model in which households sort over neighborhoods differing by exogenously determined public goods (e.g., air quality or the presence of hazardous waste facilities) and extend it to include preferences over endogenously determined demographic composition. We first show that Tiebout sorting over amenities and housing prices is sufficient to generate correlations between pollution and poor and minority populations. Next, we show that there is a surprising asymmetry in the demographic effects of introducing pollution into a community and then cleaning it up. Beginning from such a pattern of exposure, cleaning up the environment is likely to cause the neighborhood to become richer but not necessarily whiter. Moreover, when sorting occurs on endogenous demographic attributes as well, there are reasons the *opposite* may occur with the communities becoming even more racially segregated. Essentially, before the cleanup, rich minorities were forced to live in the largely white community to acquire public goods, paying a social cost of living among another group and the pecuniary cost of the higher housing prices of white communities (Ford 1994). As a poor, minority neighborhood becomes less polluted, rich minorities move back in, because they no longer have to pay the added costs of a mostly white community to acquire the public good. Thus, speaking loosely, the demographics may exhibit hysteresis.

In addition to these theoretical results, we provide an empirical analysis of environmentally induced migration that attempts to overcome the limitations of some previous studies. We evaluate the correlation between local demographics and large air polluters registered in the Toxics Release Inventory (TRI), a common application in the environmental justice literature. We also evaluate the impact of entry and exit of TRI facilities, as well as changes in toxicity-weighted emission levels, on changes in local community demographics, controlling for baseline conditions. As our unit of analysis, we use a set of "communities" defined by equally spaced half-mile-diameter circles and attach TRI emissions to these communities based on their location relative to the facility. Our results illustrate the predictions of the model: communities near polluting facilities are poorer on average, have more minorities, and have lower average educational attainment. However, cleaning up the communities does not necessarily reduce their preexisting demographic differences with other communities.

These theoretical and empirical findings are important for two reasons. First, they speak to the policy concerns about gentrification such as those expressed in the NEJAC report, clarifying the sense in which gentrification may occur. Second, our results also clarify recent findings of the demographic effects following cleanup of Superfund sites (Cameron and McConnaha 2006; Greenstone and Gallagher 2008). Finding no clear demographic responses, these authors raise the possibility that Superfund cleanup is perceived to be ineffective or that cross-sectional evidence of the depressing effects of such sites was invalid in the first place. Our model suggests that inferences about initial sorting patterns based on results from demographic differences in differences following cleanups is fraught with danger.[2]

A Simple Model of Sorting over Neighborhoods with Exogenous Amenities

To see the implications of a simple Tiebout model for gentrification and other demographic dynamics, we begin with a model of vertically differentiated communities, similar to the one first introduced by Epple, Filimon, and Romer (1984). Sieg et al. (2004), Smith et al. (2004), Walsh (2007), and Wu and Cho (2003) have employed this model empirically to estimate the distributional welfare effects of environmental policies. Banzhaf and Walsh (2008) recently employed it to test the Tiebout hypothesis more generally. Here, we extend that work to demographic effects.

Consider households that are differentiated by their income y, which is drawn from a continuous distribution over the interval $[y_l, y_h]$. Households, indexed by i, also belong to one of two "types," which differ by their income distributions. Type w incomes are given by the density function $f^w(y)$ and cumulative distribution $F^w(y)$, type m incomes by $f^m(y)$ and $F^m(y)$. Type w is a richer group than type m, in the sense that its income distribution first-order stochastically dominates type m; that is, $F^w(y) < F^m(y)$ for all values of y. These types may be thought of as racial groups (think w for white and m for minorities), but any typology with different income distributions is consistent with the model: family structure (traditional families being richer, on average, than single-parent families), educational attainment (college graduates being richer than high school dropouts), and so on.

Households choose to live in one of two communities j. Household preferences are represented by the conditional indirect utility function $V(y_i, P_j, G_j)$, where P_j is the price of a unit of housing in community j.[3] G_j represents a single public good (or an index of public goods)—call it "environmental quality." The fact that there is a single public good implies that all households agree on the more desirable community. It follows that in equilibrium this higher-ranked community will also have higher prices. We will refer to the less desirable community as community 1 and the more desirable community as community 2. Conditional on the community chosen, households then choose their optimal amount of housing. The associated housing demand function is assumed independent of the level of G and is given by $D(P, y)$.[4] Each community is characterized by a continuous housing supply function $S_j(P)$ and an exogenously determined level of environmental quality G_j.[5]

Finally, assume that household preferences satisfy the "single crossing" property. Single crossing in this context means simply that a household's willingness to pay for G, in terms of increased P, is increasing in income. Single crossing guarantees that there is a unique value of y, which we denote by $\bar{Y}$, at which households are indifferent between the two communities. It also leads to perfect income stratification of households across communities: households with incomes below $\bar{Y}$ will prefer community 1, and richer households will prefer community 2 (Epple, Filimon, and Romer 1984).[6]

Unique equilibrium prices P_j and boundary incomes $\bar{Y}$ are implicitly defined by the following equilibrium conditions:

$$V(\bar{Y},P_1,G_2)=V(\bar{Y},P_2,G_2),$$
$$M \int_{y\in C_j} D(P_j,y)f(y)dy = S^j(P_j) \quad \forall j \in \{1,2\}, \tag{4.1}$$

where M is the total mass of households and C_j is the set of incomes locating in community j. These equations formalize the boundary indifference condition and the requirement that the housing markets clear in both communities. Figure 4.1 provides a graphic representation of equilibrium. It shows the densities of type 1 and type 2 individuals over income and the value of $\bar{Y}$ at which households are indifferent between the two communities. All households of either type with incomes to the left of $\bar{Y}$ sort into community 1, all to the right into community 2.

The following propositions follow immediately from the model:

Proposition 1. Mean incomes are lower in community 1.

Proposition 2. The ratio of type m to type w citizens will be greater in community 1 than in community 2.

Proposition 1 is simply a restatement of the definition of $\bar{Y}$ together with income stratification. Proposition 2 follows from the fact that the distribution of income for type w first-order dominates type m. At any value of $\bar{Y}$, a greater

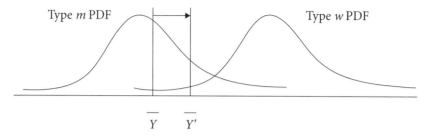

Figure 4.1 Density of income for two household types and community income boundary and shift in community income boundary after improvement in G_1

proportion of the type m population will be in community 1 than type w's population. The proposition then follows by arithmetic.[7]

Now consider the effect of changes in public goods on the equilibrium of the model, under the assumption of costless mobility for households. We consider the effects of improvements in the low-public-good community, represented by an increase in G_1. (Declines will have the opposite effect, as will improvements in G_2.) Banzhaf and Walsh (2008) show that for an increase in G_1, the comparative statics can be illustrated by Figure 4.1, with $\bar{Y}$ shifting to the right to $\bar{Y}'$. Previously indifferent households will now strictly prefer community 1. For large nonmarginal improvements in G_1—large enough that the communities switch rankings and community 1 becomes the more desirable community—the model predicts that households will switch communities, with community 1 now having the richer citizens above the new $\bar{Y}$. From these basic insights, they prove the following results for this model:

> *Proposition 3* (Banzhaf and Walsh 2008). Marginal and nonmarginal improvements in G_1 will lead to an increase in the price of housing in community 1 and a decrease in the price of housing in community 2.
>
> *Proposition 4* (Banzhaf and Walsh 2008). Marginal improvements in G_1 will lead to an increased population in community 1 and a decreased population in community 2 "almost everywhere." Nonmarginal improvements usually will have the same effect.
>
> *Proposition 5* (Banzhaf and Walsh 2008). Marginal improvements in G_1 will lead to an increase in the mean income in community 1 *and* in community 2. Thus, the change in mean income in community 1 *relative* to that in community 2 is indeterminate for marginal changes in G. However, *nonmarginal* changes in G_1 that make community 1 more

desirable than community 2 will lead to an unambiguous increase in community 1's mean income relative to that of community 2.

Propositions 3 and 4 are essentially the effects of supply and demand. When G_1 improves, more people would like to live there (in Figure 4.1, the interval from the initial $\bar{Y}$ to the new higher $\bar{Y}'$). This increased demand raises the price of housing in the community, which generally leads to smaller average housing units in equilibrium. The qualifications in Proposition 4 ("almost everywhere," "usually") relate to a single point in the domain of G, where $G_1 = G_2$. At that point, the sudden switch in the rankings of the communities leads to a discontinuous increase in mean income in community 1. That discontinuous income effect dominates the price effect, so that the average size of housing units actually increases; supply conditions then imply that populations must shrink.

The first part of Proposition 5 follows from the fact that, after a marginal improvement in G_1, the poorest people in community 2 move to community 1 (those people between the vertical lines in Figure 4.1), where they are now the richest. Community 1's mean income increases, because it gained richer citizens than it had before. This can be thought of as an absolute income effect. Unfortunately, community 2's mean income increases as well, because it lost its poorest citizens. This makes a relative income effect difficult to infer from empirical work, unless the data include "control" observations that are not close substitutes. However, as noted above, if G_1 improves enough that the rankings of the communities change, the model predicts that households will switch places, and community 1 will become the richer of the two. The second part of Proposition 5 then follows by the same logic of Proposition 1. In this case, income effects can be detected empirically.

We now consider the effect of a cleanup in community 1 on the relative proportions of type m and type w households. In the following section, we extend the model further still to the case where these proportions enter household preferences.

> *Proposition 6.* Marginal changes in G_1 will have an ambiguous effect on the ratio of type m citizens to type w citizens in community 1. Hence, they will also have an ambiguous effect on this ratio in community 1 relative to community 2. Nonmarginal changes in G_1 that make community 1 more desirable than community 2 will lead to an unambiguous decrease in the proportion of type m citizens in community 1 relative to that in community 2.

To see this, let N_1^m denote the initial type m population in community 1 and let N_1^w denote the initial type w population in community 1. A marginal change in G_1 makes those with incomes $\overline{Y}$ strictly prefer community 1. After this transition, the ratio of type m to type w citizens in community 1 can be written as a weighted average of that proportion among the original citizens $\dfrac{N_1^m}{N_1^w}$ and among the new citizens $\dfrac{f^m(\overline{Y})}{f^w(\overline{Y})}$. Although $F^m(\overline{Y}) > F^w(\overline{Y})$, this need not be true of the density function. That is, around the boundary income $\overline{Y}$, the proportion of type m citizens may be greater than at lower incomes. Accordingly, for marginal changes, there is neither an absolute nor a relative effect predicted for the composition of communities by type.

The second part of the proposition, for large nonmarginal changes that reverse the rankings of communities, follows from Proposition 2. Proposition 2 states that, initially, a greater proportion of community 1's citizens will be of type m relative to that of community 2. By the same logic, if community 1 becomes the more desirable community, a *smaller* proportion of community 1's citizens will now be of type m relative to that of community 2. The second part of Proposition 6 follows immediately. In this case, cleanup can affect the proportion of racial groups and similar groups, as with income effects.

Extension to Preferences for Endogenous Demographic Composition

The above model is driven solely by demands for housing and public goods, with race and other such characteristics merely being correlated with incomes. However, race itself has been a historically important factor in the formation of neighborhoods. There is strong evidence that non-Hispanic whites have preferred to live with one another (or away from minorities), while ethnic groups also form their own cohesive neighborhoods. Evidence for such sorting comes directly from surveys (Farley et al. 1978, 1994; Farley and Krysan 2002; Bobo and Zubrinsky 1996; Emerson, Chai, and Yancey 2001). It also comes indirectly via economic models of housing markets, both theoretical and empirical. Such studies include Schelling (1969, 1971, 1972); King and Mieszkowski (1973); Clark (1991); Cutler, Glaeser, and Vigdor (1999); Becker and Murphy (2000); Bayer, Fang, and McMillan (2005); Bayer and McMillan (2005); Bayer, Ferreira, and McMillan (2007); and Card, Mas, and Rothstein (2008). Taken together, these studies provide substantial evidence that racial preferences contribute to observed differences in the locational choice across race.

In this chapter, we refer to racial or group preferences, which give rise to segregation through processes such as "white flight," which Cutler, Glaeser, and Vigdor (1999) refer to as "decentralized racism."[8] In a nutshell, the basic consequence of incorporating group preferences into the model is to support a much greater variety of sorting than in the basic Tiebout model of the previous section. Moreover, improvements in environmental quality are liable to lead to counterintuitive results, such as an increase in racial segregation and an increased proportion of minorities in the improved neighborhood. Our response to these complexities is to greatly simplify the model in other respects. In particular, we will allow only two levels of income ("rich" and "poor") and abstract from scale effects and housing demand effects by fixing the supply of housing in each community and exogenously fixing housing units to a uniform size.[9] We also restrict the preference space by assuming a Cobb-Douglas functional form for utility. While in some contexts such a simplified model might be viewed as a limitation, in our context it actually serves to strengthen the take-away message: that a wide range of sorting responses to changes in public goods are conceivable. Since our simple model would always be nested in more complex models as a special case, adding complexity cannot reduce the set of feasible sorting responses.

Additional Model Assumptions

Individuals have one of two income levels, low (L) and high (H). Together with the two groups (indexed by r), this results in four possible types $i \in \{w_H, w_L, m_H, m_L\}$.[10] Although we will often speak in terms of racial groups, the earlier comment about the interpretation of types still holds, with the model applicable to any demographic groups who are correlated with income. The population is exogenously known and is equal to $N = \sum_i \sum_{j=1}^{2} n_j^i$, where n_j^i represents the number of individuals of type i living in community j. In addition, define N_1 and N_2 as the total population residing in community 1 and community 2, respectively, and define N^w and N^m as the total number of type w and type m households in the economy, respectively. Each of the two regions consists of an equal amount of homogeneous land and housing, with quantities fixed at l. The two communities differ by their endogenously determined racial composition $SHARE_{rj}$ (the share of citizens in community j who are type r), as well as G_j.

Individuals choose community 1 or 2 to maximize their utility. The indirect utility function, conditional on the choice of community, is given by

$$V_{ij} = v(y_i, P_j, R_{rj}, G_j),$$

where R_{rj}, a transformation of racial composition $SHARE_{rj}$, is r's perception of the demographic desirability of community j. For tractability, we assume a Cobb-Douglas functional form for utility:

$$V_{ij} = \left(y_i - P_j\right)^\alpha R_{rj}^\eta G_j^\gamma. \tag{4.2}$$

We also assume that R_{rj} is determined by a quadratic loss function around a "demographic bliss point" D_r:

$$R_{rj} = 1 - (D_r - SHARE_{rj})^2. \tag{4.3}$$

That is, each type would ideally like to live in a community D_r percent of which is composed of citizens of its own race.

With two community attributes and with discretized income distributions, the equilibrium conditions of the model can no longer be written in terms of $\bar{Y}$. Nevertheless, equilibrium can still be characterized by indifference and preference relationships. Thus, we require:

$$V_{ij} \geq V_{ik} \text{ if } n_{ij} > 0 \text{ and } n_{ik} = 0 \tag{4.4}$$

and

$$V_{ij} = V_{ik} \text{ if } n_{ij}, n_{ik} > 0. \tag{4.5}$$

That is, if type i resides in both communities, that type must be indifferent between the two; if type i resides in only one community, it must prefer it. We also continue to require that no households are homeless:

$$\sum_{j=1,2} n_{wj} = N_w \text{ and } \sum_{j=1,2} n_{bj} = N_b \tag{4.6}$$

and that the housing market clears:

$$\sum_{i=w_H, w_L, b_H, b_L} n_{i1} = l_1 \text{ and } \sum_{i=w_H, w_L, b_H, b_L} n_{i2} = l_2. \tag{4.7}$$

Since lot size is fixed at 1, the proportion of each type will dictate the possible distributions across regions. For example, with more whites than minorities and equal-sized communities, whites would have to reside in both regions. More generally, in equilibrium, at least one of the four types will have to be in both communities. For those types, Equation (4.5) will hold.

This insight is key to deriving results for the model. Given our parameterization of $V(\ )$, it implies for a type i living in both communities that

$$\left(y_i - P_1\right)^\alpha R_{i1}^\eta G_1^\gamma = \left(y_i - P_2\right)^\alpha R_{i2}^\eta G_2^\gamma, \tag{4.8}$$

which can be rewritten as

$$P_1 = y_i - \left(y_i - P_2\right)R_i G, \tag{4.9}$$

where $R_i = \left(\dfrac{R_{i2}}{R_{i1}}\right)^{\eta/\alpha}$ and $G = \left(\dfrac{G_2}{G_1}\right)^{\gamma/\alpha} > 1$. Equation (4.9) determines an equilibrium price for community 2, given P_2, R, and G, that will support an equilibrium with type i straddled across both communities.

By the same logic, for some type i that is segregated into community 1 in equilibrium,

$$P_1 \le y_i - \left(y_i - P_2\right)R_i G. \tag{4.10}$$

That is, P_1 is low enough to make them prefer community 1, given P_2, R, and G. For any type segregated into community 2, the inequality is reversed.

Analytical Results with Two Types

To build intuition, we begin by simplifying the model still further, gradually building up to the more general version given above. In particular, suppose there are only two types, $i \in \{w_H, m_L\}$, or rich whites and poor minorities. If we assume there are more whites than minorities, and if the housing stock is equal in the two communities, whites will have to live in both communities. In this case, there are only three feasible equilibria: complete integration (*INT*; with both races in both communities), partial segregation with all minorities in community 1 (*SEG1*), and partial segregation with all minorities in community 2 (*SEG2*).

As a starting point, and to provide a bridge to the earlier section, set $\eta = 0$, so there are no racial preferences. We know that Equation (4.8) must hold for whites. Without racial preferences, this condition simplifies to

$$P_1 = y_w - (y_w - P_2)G. \tag{4.11}$$

By assumption, however, whites are richer than minorities. It follows that, for minorities,

$$P_1 < y_m - (y_m - P_2)G. \tag{4.12}$$

The price in community 1 is below that which would make minorities indifferent.[11] Thus, only sorting with all minorities in community 1 (*SEG1*) is supportable as an equilibrium. Community 1 is therefore poorer and has a higher concentration of minorities than community 2. This result is completely consistent with Propositions 1 and 2 in the previous section.

Now consider the effect of incorporating racial preferences into the model. Equation (4.8) must still hold for whites:

$$P_1 = y_w - (y_w - P_2)R_w G.$$

The indifference price, while still determined by whites, now depends on both environmental quality and the perceived racial amenity. G is exogenously determined, and $SHARE_j$ (and hence R) is trivially determined by Equations (4.6) and (4.7) and by the relative populations of each type.

Which of the three feasible community compositions are supportable equilibria will depend on whether

$$P_1 >/< y_m - (y_m - P_2)R_m G, \tag{4.13}$$

that is, on whether

$$y_w - (y_w - P_2)R_w G >/< y_m - (y_m - P_2)R_m G.$$

Without racial preferences, we found that this relationship was characterized by $<$. However, introducing racial preferences complicates the relationship because the two types now have a unique perception of the desirability of the two communities. In the general case, without restricting the weights η and γ and without specifying the demographic bliss point, all of the three feasible community compositions are supportable as equilibria.

Consider, for example, the case where both racial groups always prefer living in communities with more of their own race ($D_r = 1$ in Equation [4.3]). In this case, the previous equilibrium, with all minorities in community 1, is still supported. The reason is that, because it is an all-white community, whites have an additional reason to prefer community 2, lowering the indifference price P_1. And the lower price in community 1, combined with the attractiveness of more fellow minorities, further strengthens the attraction of minorities to community 1.

But other equilibria are also possible. Consider next the equilibrium with minorities residing entirely in community 2 (*SEG2*). The white population must continue to reside in both regions, resulting in the same condition as above. The equilibrium condition for minorities is reversed:

$$P_1 \geq y_m - (y_m - P_2)R_mG$$

or

$$y_w - (y_w - P_2)R_wG > y_m - (y_m - P_2)R_mG.$$

With the presence of racial preferences, it is now possible to support this sorting in equilibrium. For example, suppose, with all minorities in community 2, we have $R_w < 1 < R_m$; that is, whites prefer the demographic characteristics of community 1 and minorities those of community 2.[12] As we increase η, the taste parameter on racial composition, R_w becomes smaller and R_m bigger, augmenting the inequality. For sufficiently strong racial tastes, and with minorities in community 2, minorities' willingness to pay for community 2 will rise above that of whites, who in extreme cases will even require lower prices to live there despite the higher public good. More precisely, the equilibrium will be supported whenever

$$R_m > \left[\left(y_w - P_2 \right)R_w - \frac{y_w - y_m}{G} \right] \frac{1}{y_m - P_2}.$$

Minorities' perceived racial amenity in community 2 relative to community 1 must be greater than whites', with adjustments for relative incomes, public good differences, and price differences. Note that whenever this equilibrium is supported, *SEG1* is supported as well. With all minorities in community 1, the strong racial preferences will reinforce the previous results.

Finally, consider the case of complete integration, with both types in each community. Equilibrium requires

$$y_w - (y_w - P_2)R_wG = P_1 = y_m - (y_m - P_2)R_mG.$$

In the absence of racial preferences, it was shown that the wealthy white population will always have a higher willingness to pay for environmental quality. Therefore, again, in order for this equilibrium to exist, the perceived racial quality gap for the minority population must both favor the high environmental quality region and exceed the gap perceived by the white population. In this case, the expression (4.13) must hold with equality. Although it can accordingly exist for suitable parameter values, this equilibrium is always unstable. A marginal change in environmental quality or population composition will cause the model to tip to one of the other two equilibria. Specifically, with any marginal change, the indifference prices for both populations will deviate from indifference prices observed prior to the change. For example, if either community experiences an improvement in G_j, richer whites, with higher marginal willingness to pay for G, will outbid minorities for the available housing in that community. This behavior will continue until a stable segregated equilibrium is reached.

Simulations with Two and Four Types

We illustrate the above results with simulations. To do so, we assume the following parameterization. The supply of housing in each community is normalized to 1, so the total population in this society is normalized to 2. We assume a distribution of 85 percent whites ($N_w = 1.7$) and 15 percent minorities ($N_w = 0.3$). This is the approximate distribution of whites and blacks in the United States in the 2000 Census. We also assume minorities' income is two-thirds that of whites, with $Y_H = 1$ and $Y_L = 0.67$.[13] We set the exogenous public goods to $G_1 = 1$ and $G_2 = 2$. We set a (the taste for the numeraire good) equal to 0.7 and allow the taste parameters for R_j and G_j to vary over the region $\eta + \gamma < 0.3$, $\eta > 0$, $\gamma > 0$.[14]

Finally, we set the racial bliss point $D = 0.9$ for both races. This value is consistent with recent work by Card, Mas, and Rothstein (2008), who econometrically estimate a "tipping point" for whites between 5 and 20 percent minority composition, at which point they flee. We also consider values of 0.8 for both types as well as 0.9 for whites and 0.5 for minorities.[15] The latter model is consistent with survey findings from Farley et al. (1978) and Farley and Krysan (2002).

Figure 4.2 summarizes the results of the simulations. The lower right corner of the figure represents strong racial preferences relative to environmental preferences, the upper left corner the opposite. The figure shows that, intuitively, as the taste for the environment becomes stronger relative to the taste for racial composition, only *SEG1* is supported, so that the minorities are in community 1. This result is consistent with that from the previous section, in which with no racial preferences there is sorting by income, with community 1 having a greater share of minorities. As racial preferences become stronger, other equilibria can now be supported as well, although *SEG1* always remains a possibility. The figure also shows the result of reducing the racial bliss point to 0.8. This effect is essentially the same as reducing the racial taste parameter:

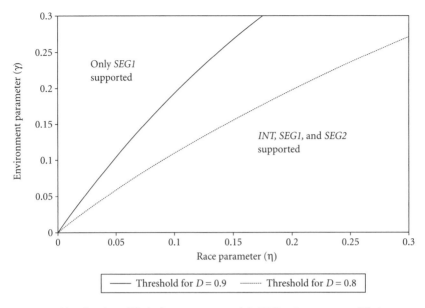

Figure 4.2 Simulated equilibria for two-type model. *SEG1* refers to an equilibrium with all minorities in community 1 (with lower public goods). *SEG2* refers to an equilibrium with all minorities in community 2. *INT* refers to an integrated equilibrium with both racial groups in each community. *D* is the racial bliss point for both types.

relative to the contribution of public goods to the relative utilities of the two communities, the contribution of racial composition is smaller, since for each community the less preferred composition is no longer so far from the bliss point. Consequently, lowering the bliss point reduces the parameter space supporting *SEG2* and *INT*.

We complete our analysis with simulations of the most general version of the model (i.e., with four types). We partition N_w into $n_{wH} = 0.95$ and $n_{wL} = 0.75$, and N_m into $n_{wH} = 0.1$ and $n_{wL} = 0.2$. Note the total white population exceeds the total minority population and the total rich population exceeds the total poor population, so both white and rich individuals will reside in both regions.

The assumed population distribution reduces the set of feasible demographic distributions. For example, it is not possible to have the rich white population living entirely within a region with the entire population of any other type. Table 4.1 lists potential feasible equilibria. It gives a shorthand abbreviation, the locations of each type, and the resulting mean income and

Table 4.1 Candidate equilibria for the four-type case

Case	Types that may be found in the indicated communities			Percentage minority		Mean income		Supportable	Reason unsupportable
	Both	C_2	C_1	C_2	C_1	C_2	C_1		
Stratification by race—minority population in community 1 (RM1)									
RM1.WH	w_H	w_L	m_H, m_L	0	0.3	0.75	0.93	No[a]	$V_{w_L 2} \leq V_{w_L 1}$
RM1.WL	w_L	w_H	m_H, m_L	0	0.3	0.98	0.70	Yes	—
Stratification by race—minority population in community 2 (RM2)									
RM2.WH	w_H	m_H, m_L	w_L	0.3	0	0.93	0.75	Yes	—
RM2.WL	w_L	m_H, m_L	w_H	0.3	0	0.70	0.98	Yes[b]	—
Stratification by income—poor population in community 1 (IP1)									
IP1.WH	w_H	m_H	w_L, m_L	0.1	0.2	1.0	0.69	No[c]	$V_{m_H 2} \leq V_{m_H 1}$
IP1.MH	m_H	w_H	w_L, m_L	0.05	0.25	1.0	0.69	Yes	—
Stratification by income—poor population in community 2 (IP2)									
IP2.WH	w_H	w_L, m_L	m_H	0.2	0.1	0.69	1.0	No	$V_{w_L 2} \leq V_{w_L 1}$ and $V_{m_H 2} \geq V_{m_H 1}$
IP2.MH	m_H	w_L, m_L	w_H	0.25	0.05	0.69	1.0	No	$V_{w_L 2} \leq V_{w_L 1}$ and $V_{m_L 2} \leq V_{m_L 1}$
Other									
O.9	w_H	w_L, m_H	m_L	0.1	0.2	0.75	0.93	No	$V_{w_L 2} \leq V_{w_L 1}$ and $V_{m_H 2} \geq V_{m_H 1}$
O.10	w_H	m_L	w_L, m_H	0.2	0.1	0.93	0.75	No	$V_{m_H 2} \geq V_{m_H 1}$
O.11	m_L	w_H	w_L, m_H	0.05	0.25	0.98	0.70	No	$V_{w_L 2} \geq V_{w_L 1}$
O.12	m_L	w_L, m_H	w_H	0.25	0.05	0.70	0.98	No	$V_{w_H 2} \geq V_{m_H 1}$

[a] Becomes supportable if $D = 0.8$.
[b] Not supportable if $D = 0.8$.
[c] Supportable only if $\eta = 0$; not supportable for all $\eta > 0$.

percentage of minorities in each community.[16] (The first letter in the abbreviation is R or I, for stratification by race or income; the second letter is M or P, which is followed by a number representing whether minorities or the poor, respectively, are segregated away from others and into which community they are segregated; the two letters after the dot represent the type straddling both communities.)

With the assumed parameters, only four of these distributions are supportable equilibria:

- Stratification by race with minorities in community 1 and poor whites in both communities (RM1.WL)
- Stratification by race with minorities in community 2 and rich whites in both communities (RM2.WH)
- Stratification by race with minorities in community 2 and poor whites in both communities (RM2.WL)
- Stratification by income with the poor in community 1 and rich minorities in both communities (IP1.MH)

For the other eight candidates listed in the table, which cannot be supported, the table summarizes a relationship that violates an equilibrium condition. In these eight cases, given the prices determined by the hypothesized indifference relationship (for the type hypothesized to straddle two communities), at least one other type can be made better off by switching communities.

Figure 4.3 depicts where, in the space of η and γ, these equilibria can be supported. Again, the lower right corner represents strong racial preferences relative to environmental preferences, the upper left the opposite. As with the two-type case, when racial preferences dominate, it is possible to support counterintuitive equilibria with the minorities in the high-public-good community (RM2.WL and RM2.WH). In the extreme case, it is even possible that the high-public-good community has lower mean incomes as well (RM2.WL).[17] However, in these cases, the more intuitive equilibria found in the environmental justice literature hold as well. Moreover, as the taste parameter on public goods increases, the counterintuitive equilibria fall away. In the upper two regions of the figure, all equilibria give community 2 (with the better public good) a higher mean income and lower proportion of minorities. At this extreme, as racial considerations pale relative to the public good, sorting is driven by income differences, with rich minorities outbidding poor whites for the public good.

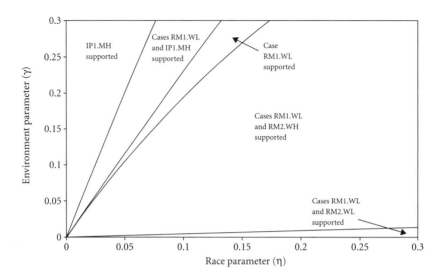

Figure 4.3 Simulated equilibria for four-type model

In summary, the range of equilibria that can be supported by racial preferences is much broader, and Propositions 1 and 2 above no longer hold with
certainty. We revise them as follows:

> *Proposition 1b.* With racial preferences, mean incomes *may* be higher in
> either community. However, any parameter values that support an
> equilibrium with higher mean incomes in C_1 will also support an equi-
> librium with higher mean incomes in C_2, but the reverse is not true.
>
> *Proposition 2b.* With racial preferences, the ratio of type 1 (or minority) to
> type 2 (or white) citizens *may* be lower in either community. However,
> any parameter values that support an equilibrium with a lower ratio of
> type *m* to type *w* in C_1 than in C_2 will also support a lower ratio of type
> 1 to type 2 in C_2, but the reverse is not true.

Thus, with racial preferences, the correlations found in the environmental justice literature do not follow inevitably from a Tiebout model, but they are still
"more likely" in the sense of the second part of Propositions 1b and 2b: the set
of parameters supporting the environmental justice correlations is larger than
and contains the set supporting other demographic distributions.

Dynamics of an Environmental Improvement

Consider now the effect of improving the public good in community 1 (but without making it higher than community 2's). In the previous section, we saw that in a model with continuous income distributions and no racial preferences, community 1 would become richer (though not necessarily more so than community 2) but that there was no definitive effect on racial composition. Not surprisingly, generalizing the model by introducing racial preferences does not reduce the range of possible outcomes. However, it does create a specific dynamic adjustment process in which we expect community 1 to become richer and have a *higher* concentration of minorities.

Figure 4.4 illustrates the effect of an improvement in G_1 (in this case, from 1.0 to 1.5). The improvement shifts up all the boundaries between equilibria in the parameter space. The reason is intuitive: as the communities become more similar in terms of public goods, differences in racial composition are more likely to drive behavior. This change in emphasis is comparable to lowering the taste parameter for public goods γ.

With demographics relatively more important, any initial equilibria with racial stratification will continue to be supportable after the improvement.

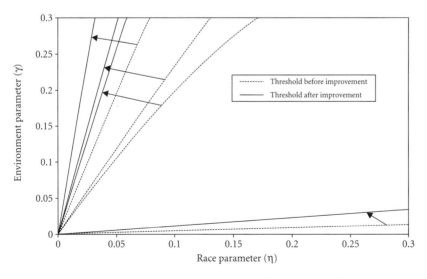

Figure 4.4 Improvement in environmental quality in C_1 (increase in G from 1.0 to 1.5)

Specifically, RM1 and RM2 equilibria will continue to be supported.[18] However, if the economy reflected stratification by income prior to the improvement (IP1.MH), it is possible that this equilibrium would become unsupportable. Furthermore, the most likely result would be a shift to RM1. Specifically, at the indifference price for the rich minority population, the poor white population would be better of living in C_2. Consequently, the poor white population will migrate to C_2 by outbidding the rich minorities for housing there. Equilibrium will be reached when the distribution reflects RM2 and prices reflect indifference for the poor white population. Or, to put it in other terms, with the differences in public goods no longer as important, at the prevailing housing prices that previously made them indifferent, rich minorities will now clearly prefer C_1, where the concentration of other minorities is higher. Thus, Proposition 5 continues to hold. In fact, it is strengthened insofar as any nonmarginal improvement will lead (weakly) to a relative increase in income (even if the relative rankings are no longer reversed). However, Proposition 6 must be amended:

> *Proposition 6b*. With tastes for demographic composition, nonmarginal changes, even large changes that reverse rankings, may lead to an *increase* in the proportion of type m citizens in community 1 relative to that in community 2. In general, the effect is ambiguous.

In summary, our simplest model, with no demographic preferences, suggests that, in a cross section, dirtier communities will be poorer and have a greater proportion of minorities (or other groups who are poorer on average). This is precisely the pattern found in the environmental justice literature. However, our model also shows that the adjustment effects of changes in amenities are not as intuitive as this correlation would suggest. In particular, while we show that a marginal improvement in the amenities of the dirty community will lead to an increase in income, it may not do so relative to its substitutes. Even if the community does become relatively wealthier, it may not become more dominated by richer demographic groups. Moreover, in models that do include group demographic preferences, there is a particular reason the opposite may happen: richer members of the group will sort back into the community to be with their demographic type, no longer needing to avoid the disamenity. Such a scenario strengthens the income effect but has a counterintuitive effect on the composition of types.

These results have implications for what we would empirically expect to find in differences-in-differences type of applications in comparison to cross-sectional applications. In particular, they suggest that general equilibrium responses to cleanup of dirtier sites can be expected to change the reduced-form correlation between pollution and race, actually strengthening the relationship. As Banzhaf and Walsh (2010) show in more detail, this can bias downward the estimates of simple differences-in-differences regressions. Additionally, these results have important policy implications, especially for the sense in which cleanup is likely to trigger gentrification. They suggest that the group dynamics are forces that help keep communities more stable after cleanup, rather than rapidly turning over their demographic composition.

Testing the Model: Past Work and New Empirical Strategy

Recent studies looking at trends in local demographics around Superfund sites, before and after cleanup, have found conflicting evidence of seemingly expected patterns. Cameron, Crawford, and McConnaha (see Chapter 6) and Cameron and McConnaha (2006) have conducted careful and focused evaluations of a small number of case studies, over periods that include the discovery of the sites and in some cases cleanup. Cameron and McConnaha look at four Superfund sites, Cameron et al. at seven. Cameron and McConnaha suggest that the Old Bethpage Landfill on Long Island, New York, which was listed early and was cleaned up in 1993 (though not delisted), is one of the most likely places to observe any gentrification effects. As our model predicts, they do find that average income rises. Significantly, and consistent with the message of this chapter, they do not find patterns with respect to race or family structure.

In national studies, Greenstone and Gallagher (2008), using an innovative regression discontinuity design to account for the endogeneity of which sites are cleaned up, find no statistically significant effect on population density or average income in census tracts with Superfund sites eligible for federal cleanup relative to those ineligible. Considering similar questions but with more local measures of demographics, Gamper-Rabindran and Timmins (2011) do find these relationships.

These studies represent significant advances in the environmental justice literature. Our own empirical illustration extends their work on several fronts. First, we study a much larger set of communities. Second, we focus on air emissions from major polluters as reported in the TRI, rather than on Superfund sites. This allows us to control for the level of baseline emissions and changes in emissions, in addition to the mere presence of a facility. Moreover, an elimination of air emissions may be easier for local communities to perceive (and verify) than a cleanup of polluted land and water.

Third, both studies follow earlier work by Been (1997) and others in using census tracts as the basic geographic unit. However, the use of census tracts as "communities" may be problematic for three reasons. First, census tracts are locally defined to create relatively homogeneous entities. Although some see this as a virtue as it gives more integrity to the concept of community, such gerrymandering may also bias results. For example, if polluting sites have an impact on the demographics of only the most local neighborhoods, and these neighborhoods are conjoined with other neighborhoods with similar characteristics to form census tracts, it would induce correlation between the polluting site and the wider geographic entity (the census tract). Second, although roughly equal in terms of population, census tracts range greatly in size. For example, in California, tracts range in size from less than a tenth of a square mile to more than one thousand square miles. This creates problems in controlling for this large degree of heterogeneity when estimating migration models. Finally, previous research on the correlation between race and environmental quality has shown that results can be quite sensitive to community definitions (Hersh 1995; Mohai and Saha 2006; Baden, Noonan, and Turaga 2007; Gamper-Rabindran and Timmins 2011).

For these reasons, we take a different approach to neighborhood definitions. We follow an approach used by Banzhaf and Walsh (2008), who test our Propositions 4 and 5 (scale and income effects) and extend their work to cross-sectional effects (Propositions 1 and 2) and other demographic effects (Proposition 6). In particular, we define neighborhoods as a set of tangent half-mile-diameter circles evenly distributed across the urbanized portion of California, resulting in 25,166 "communities" (for details, see Banzhaf and Walsh 2008). This approach has the virtue of establishing equally sized communities with randomly drawn boundaries. Each of these communities is then assigned demographic and pollution characteristics as described in the following section.

Data

Our empirical investigation of gentrification effects requires three types of data: demographic data, TRI pollution data, and other spatial amenities.

Census Data

In 1990 and 2000, respectively, we obtained block-level census data on the total populations of each racial group, both as individuals and as households, and socioeconomic variables, including family types, homeownership rates, rental rates, and self-assessed home values. We also collected block group–level data including average incomes, educational attainment, and workforce descriptors. We then apportioned these census data into our circle communities. See Banzhaf and Walsh (2008) for details.

Across circle communities, the average 1990 population is about 772 persons. Most communities are also largely non-Hispanic white, with a mean share of 67 percent across communities. However, this share decreased, on average, by 9 percent from 1990 to 2000. Hispanics are the largest and fastest-growing minority, with an average 19 percent share in 1990. Blacks and Asians represent smaller minorities, with average 1990 shares of 5 percent and 8 percent, respectively. But there is also substantial variation in these data. Among communities with more than 100 residents, there is at least one in which each racial group is completely absent and at least one in which each racial group makes up 90 percent or more of the population. Additionally, in the average community, 8 percent of households are single-parent families, and 10 percent of individuals over the age of 25 did not graduate from high school. Table A.4.1 in the online appendix provides additional details on these data.[19]

TRI Data

As a measure of pollution exposure, we use the Toxics Release Inventory (TRI), a database available from the US Environmental Protection Agency (EPA), to find releases of environmental pollution at firms throughout the United States (the TRI is a commonly used metric in the environmental justice literature).[20] Firms handling more than 10,000 pounds each year of certain hazardous chemicals have been required to report these emissions since 1987.[21] This censoring at the reporting threshold gives rise to a kind of errors-in-variables problem. As in the usual case, this is likely to have a "conservative" effect on our results, biasing them to 0, as some exposed communities are included in the control group. See de Marchi and Hamilton (2006) for further discussion of the data. We use a toxicity-weighted index of all emissions in the TRI, developed by the EPA and available in its Risk-Screening Environmental Indicators (RSEI) model.[22]

We construct quarter-mile buffers around each TRI site and then assign emissions from a given TRI site to the communities that lie within the given buffer, weighted by the proportion of the TRI site's buffer area that falls within the community (for details, see Banzhaf and Walsh 2008). About 10 percent of half-mile communities were exposed in the baseline period (1988–1990), with 4 percent losing exposure by 1998–2000 and 1 percent gaining exposure.

The small number gaining exposure will make testing hypotheses for declines in environmental quality more difficult than improvements. Among exposed communities, most are exposed to 1 to 3 TRI facilities (the interquartile range), with a maximum of 19 facilities for one community. Again, additional details can be found in Table A.4.1 of the online appendix.[23]

Additional Spatial Variables

As additional controls, we include in some models coarse controls for location effects, including distance to the coast, degrees latitude, and crime rates. However, our main approach to controlling for unobserved spatial amenities is to employ school district or zip code dummy variables. School districts have the advantage of mapping directly into an important but difficult-to-measure local public good. We find the share of each community that falls within each of the 226 school districts in our urban areas and assign a continuous variable on [0, 1] to that community for each school district. Seventy-six percent of half-mile communities lie entirely within one school district, 21 percent within two, and the remainder within three or four. The median school district is assigned 94 half-mile circle communities. Zip codes are even more local measures. Here, we simply assign each community to one of the 883 zip codes in our area based on the zip code of the community centroids. The median zip code has 21 circle communities.

Estimation Strategy and Results

Using these data, we test the gentrification hypotheses derived in our theoretical models.

Contemporaneous Patterns in Exposure

We begin by confirming, in our own data, the premise that there is a correlation between pollution and minorities, as found in the environmental justice literature. As shown in Propositions 1 and 2, this correlation would be expected to arise from Tiebout sorting of households in response to amenities and prices. Propositions 1b and 2b, which allow for sorting in response to endogenous demographics as well, weaken the prediction. They suggest that alternative equilibria are possible for some parameter values but that the initial predictions of Propositions 1 and 2 remain possible equilibria for all parameter values.

We begin by considering income correlation (Propositions 1 and 1b). We regress the groups' representation in a given community on the presence of a

TRI site and TRI emissions, as well as locational variables. The basic model for the income case is

$$INC_i = \beta_0 + \beta_{BL} BL_i + \beta_y y_i + \beta_L L_i + e_i, \tag{4.14}$$

where i indexes communities, BL is an indicator for whether the community receives any exposure, y_i is the observed toxicity-weighted TRI exposure of a community (it is 0 whenever BL is 0), and L is a vector of locational variables (latitude and distance to coast or school district fixed effects). We next test for group effects (Propositions 2 and 2b), replacing INC in Equation (4.14) with the percentage of minorities, the percentage of single-parent households, and the percentage of non–high school graduates, three groups with lower average incomes.

The results with school district fixed effects are shown in Table 4.2. The top panel shows an unweighted model, the bottom panel a model in which communities are weighted by baseline population. The results are strongly consistent with the most straightforward predictions of the model. The presence of a TRI site is associated with poorer households, more minorities, more single parents, and more high school dropouts. The inframarginal effect of dirtier plants generally augments the effect but is not statistically significant. The third row shows the combined effect $(\beta_y y_i + \beta_{BL} BL_i)$ at the mean value of y among communities with some exposure. This combined effect is the expected sign and is significant at 1 percent in all cases. A comparison of the two panels shows the estimates are insensitive to weighting. The results also are robust to simple continuous spatial variables for controls rather than school district effects; in fact, in that case the inframarginal effect by itself is always the expected sign and is significant in about half of the four models.

Responses to Changes

Having confirmed this pattern in a single cross section, our next goal is to develop a model that allows us to test for demographic *responses* associated with *changes* in toxic emissions from TRI sites. Propositions 4 and 5 predict that, following an environmental improvement in a community, population density and average income will increase. Banzhaf and Walsh (2008) confirm these hypotheses using these data. We extend their work to Proposition 6, which addresses changes in racial composition and changes in similar categorical types who differ by average income. Proposition 6, derived in a model with no demographic sorting, already shows that the effect is ambiguous. Not

Table 4.2 Baseline composition as function of exposure

	Dependent variable			
Independent variable	Median household income	Share minority (pct pts)	Share non–high school grad (pct pts)	Share single parent (pct pts)
Panel A: Unweighted				
Presence of TRI site	−16,083***	12.4***	1.2***	2.7***
	(<0.01)	(<0.01)	(<0.01)	(<0.01)
Toxicity-weighted TRI emissions	−1.42e−5	5.95e−8*	−7.27e−9	9.30e−9
	(0.44)	(0.09)	(0.67)	(0.44)
Joint effect at mean	−16,126***	12.6***	1.2***	2.7***
	(<0.01)	(<0.01)	(<0.01)	(<0.01)
R^2	0.36	0.41	0.45	0.16
Panel B: Population weighted				
Presence of TRI site	−9,128***	12.1***	1.0***	2.8***
	(<0.01)	(<0.01)	(<0.01)	
Toxicity-weighted TRI emissions	8.68e−6	3.75e−8	3.07e−9	3.22e−8
	(0.72)	(0.36)	(0.88)	(0.12)
Joint effect at mean	−9,102***	12.3***	1.0***	2.9***
	(<0.01)	(<0.01)	(<0.01)	(<0.01)
R^2	0.30	0.49	0.46	0.26

Note: All models contain school district fixed effects. p values, based on robust standard errors, are shown in parentheses.

*Significant at 10%; **significant at 5%; ***significant at 1%.

surprisingly, this (lack of) prediction remains when we generalize the model to allow for tastes over demographic composition. In fact, the model predicts that in some cases the share of minorities and similar groups may increase following cleanup, if richer minorities, no longer needing to avoid the environmental disamenity, move back in to join their group.

Ultimately, this is an empirical question. We regress 1990–2000 changes in the share of white residents, high school dropouts, and single-parent households on a large set of baseline demographics,[24] TRI exposure, and locational variables (latitude and distance to coast, crime rate, school district fixed effects, and/or zip code fixed effects).

TRI exposure is measured as the three-year lagged average, anchored, respectively, on 1990 and 2000, of the toxicity-weighted emissions of the chemicals, allocated to each community as described previously. As exposure variables, we include measures of both shocks and baseline exposure. As shocks, we include discrete indicators for when a community changes status from exposed to not exposed (or vice versa),[25] plus continuous measures of the change in emission levels (which picks up the magnitude of those entering or exiting facilities as well as changes at those continuously emitting). Because, in reality, populations do not adjust instantaneously, we also include an indicator and continuous measure of 1990 exposure to pick up lagged reactions to previous exposure.

The model for the scale effect regression analysis is

$$\Delta PCTMINORITY_i = \delta_0 + \delta_{BL} I_i^{BL} + \delta_{NEW} I_i^{NEW} + \delta_{EXIT} I_i^{EXIT} + \delta_y y_i^{1990}$$
$$+ \delta_{Dy+}(\Delta y_i | \Delta y_i > 0) + \delta_{Dy-}(\Delta y_i | \Delta y_i < 0) \quad (4.15)$$
$$+ \delta_D \Delta_i + \delta_L L_i + u_i,$$

where $DPCTMINORITY$ is the change (or percentage change) in the minority population from 1990 to 2000; I^{BL}, I^{NEW}, and I^{EXIT} are indicator variables for whether the community had any 1990 baseline exposure, went from no exposure to some exposure, or went from some exposure to no exposure; y^{1990} is the level of baseline toxicity-weighted exposure; $\Delta y | \Delta y > 0$ is the change in toxicity-weighted exposure, if positive; and $\Delta y | \Delta y < 0$ is the change in toxicity-weighted exposure, if negative. For regression models of other effects, $\Delta PCTMINORITY$ is simply replaced by the appropriate measure (change in share of whites, high school dropouts, or single-parent families).

We focus on three treatment effects. The "average effect of baseline TRI exposure" estimates the average differential effect on a neighborhood's 1990 to 2000 population change from being exposed to TRI emissions in 1990. The "average effect of new TRI exposure" estimates the average differential effect on a previously unexposed neighborhood of becoming exposed to TRI emissions. And the "average effect of exiting TRI exposure" estimates the average differential effect on a previously exposed neighborhood of losing all its TRI exposure. These treatment effects are calculated as combinations of the estimated coefficients on both indicator and continuous variables. Specifically,

$$\text{Average baseline treatment} = \hat{\delta}_{BL} + \hat{\delta}_y \left(\frac{1}{N_{BL}} \sum_{i \in BL} y_i^{1990} \right), \quad (4.16)$$

$$\text{Average new treatment} = \hat{\delta}_{NEW} + \hat{\delta}_{\Delta y+} \left(\frac{1}{N_{NEW}} \sum_{i \in NEW} \Delta y_i \right),$$

$$\text{Average exit treatment} = \hat{\delta}_{\text{EXIT}} + \hat{\delta}_{\Delta y-}\left(\frac{1}{N_{\text{EXIT}}}\sum_{i\in EXIT}\Delta y_i\right),$$

where, for example, N_{BL} is the number of communities with baseline exposure. Thus, the estimated effect of average baseline TRI exposure, relative to no exposure, is the estimated indicator variable for exposure plus the estimated coefficient on the continuous measure of exposure times the average baseline exposure among those communities with baseline exposure. Similar logic holds for the effect of new and exiting exposure. Note that the first two treatments are relative to communities that never experience exposure, while the exit treatment is relative to the set of communities that had baseline exposure.

We estimate five basic regression models with different levels of control for confounding factors (the D and L variables). Our first model includes no controls. Our second model controls for the baseline demographic variables noted above. As an important spatial amenity, it also includes the Federal Bureau of Investigation (FBI) crime rate imputed from overlapping political jurisdictions and spatial effects measured by latitude and distance to the coast in kilometers. Our third and fourth models contain the same demographic controls but replace the spatial variables with school district fixed effects and zip code fixed effects, respectively. One potential concern with our regressions is that our treatment effects may be endogenous if changes in pollution patterns are a response to unobserved changes in economic conditions that also drive demographic changes. Our local fixed effects help overcome these problems as long as labor and output markets operate on a larger spatial scale than the school district or zip code. Our estimated treatment effects, on the other hand, capture only the differential effect within those areas. If the actual area of impact is larger, our estimates will be biased toward 0.

Our fifth model uses a nonparametric matching estimator rather than least squares. In this model, we match each treated community to its four "most similar" control communities, where "similar" is defined as the Euclidean distance in the space of the variables controlled for in the regressions. We similarly match each control community to its four most similar treatments and combine the differences for a nonparametric estimate of the average treatment effect in the sample. We also adjust for the effect of any differences in the observable characteristics between the matched observations with linear regression. See Heckman, Ichimura, and Todd (1997, 1998) and Abadie and Imbens (2006) for examples and discussion.

Tables 4.3a and 4.3b summarize the estimated treatment effects for unweighted and population-weighted models, respectively. The results underscore the lesson of our theoretical models. Even in contexts where the predictions of Propositions 1, 2, 4, and 5 all hold—that is, even where there is a cross-sectional

Table 4.3a Estimated composition effects[a] from changes in pollution (unweighted)

Model	Average effect of baseline TRI exposure	Average effect of new TRI exposure	Average effect of exiting TRI exposure	R^2
Change minority (pct pts)				
No controls	0.9	1.9**	1.0	0.00
	(0.19)	(0.02)	(0.11)	
Basic controls	1.8***	1.6**	−0.4	0.21
	(<0.01)	(0.03)	(0.50)	
School district fixed effects	1.1*	1.0	−0.1	0.35
	(0.06)	(0.14)	(0.81)	
Zip code fixed effects	1.3**	1.6**	−0.3	0.45
	(0.02)	(0.02)	(0.58)	
Matching estimator	−0.2	−3.6***	−0.2	—
	(0.68)	(<0.01)	(0.69)	
Change high school dropout (pct pts)				
No controls	14.9***	8.8***	−4.2***	0.07
	(<0.01)	(<0.01)	(<0.01)	
Basic controls	1.8***	−0.1	−0.8*	0.74
	(<0.01)	(0.84)	(0.09)	
School district fixed effects	1.5***	0.0	−0.8*	0.77
	(<0.01)	(0.93)	(0.07)	
Zip code fixed effects	1.5***	0.5	−0.9**	0.82
	(<0.01)	(0.460)	(0.02)	
Matching estimator	0.1	0.5	−0.7	—
	(0.91)	(0.78)	(0.37)	
Change single parent (pct pts)				
No controls	−1.2***	−0.6	0.2	0.00
	(<0.01)	(0.16)	(0.51)	
Basic controls	0.2	0.2	−0.2	0.05
	(0.40)	(0.43)	(0.32)	
School district fixed effects	0.2	0.2	−0.2	0.37
	(0.39)	(0.54)	(0.34)	
Zip code fixed effects	0.2	0.3	−0.2	0.43
	(0.35)	(0.34)	(0.31)	
Matching estimator	−0.02	0.33	−0.0	—
	(0.24)	(0.36)	(0.95)	

Note: *p* values, based on robust standard errors, are shown in parentheses. Robust standard errors for matching models are based on Abadie and Imbens (2006).

[a]See Equation (4.16) for definition of the treatment effects.

*Significant at 10%; **significant at 5%; ***significant at 1%.

Table 4.3b Estimated composition effects[a] from changes in pollution (weighted)

Model	Average effect of baseline TRI exposure	Average effect of new TRI exposure	Average effect of exiting TRI exposure	R^2
Change minority (pct pts)				
No controls	−1.3***	0.0	1.1***	0.00
	(<0.01)	(0.94)	(<0.01)	
Basic controls	−0.3	0.2	0.0	0.36
	(0.35)	(0.75)	(0.90)	
School district fixed effects	−0.0	0.0	−0.0	0.52
	(0.82)	(0.34)	(0.41)	
Zip code fixed effects	0.5*	1.0***	−0.3	0.68
	(0.08)	(<0.01)	(0.22)	
Matching estimator	−0.4*	−1.4***	0.1	—
	(0.05)	(<0.01)	(0.56)	
Change high school dropout (pct pts)				
No controls	15.8***	12.2***	−5.7***	0.06
	(<0.01)	(<0.01)	(<0.01)	
Basic controls	0.3	−0.4	−0.2	0.87
	(0.49)	(0.65)	(0.65)	
School district fixed effects	0.1	−0.0	−0.4	0.90
	(0.69)	(0.94)	(0.34)	
Zip code fixed effects	0.1	−0.0	−0.3	0.92
	(0.64)	(0.89)	(0.50)	
Matching estimator	0.5	1.3	0.0	—
	(0.72)	(0.10)	(0.95)	
Change single parent (pct pts)				
No controls	−1.3***	−0.8***	0.5***	0.01
	(<0.01)	(<0.01)	(<0.01)	
Basic controls	0.2	0.3*	−0.0	0.36
	(0.12)	(0.08)	(0.94)	
School district fixed effects	0.3**	0.4**	−0.1	0.44
	(0.02)	(0.04)	(0.22)	
Zip code fixed effects	0.4***	0.3*	−0.2*	0.54
	(<0.01)	(0.07)	(0.10)	
Matching estimator	0.0	0.2	0.0	—
	(0.80)	(0.30)	(0.77)	

Note: p values, based on robust standard errors, are shown in parentheses. Robust standard errors for matching models are based on Abadie and Imbens (2006).

[a]See Equation (4.16) for definition of the treatment effects.

*Significant at 10%; **significant at 5%; ***significant at 1%.

correlation between pollution and demographic groups (race, family structure, education) as shown in Table 4.2—and even where the predicted scale and income responses to a cleanup occur (Banzhaf and Walsh 2008), there need not be responses in the composition of demographic groups.

The tables show some weak evidence for demographic sorting consistent with what one might expect from gentrification, but the effects are generally not robust to changes in specification or to weighting. In the case of minority populations, the matching model in particular stands out for reversing the sign on the estimates. In the case of education, the effect found in the unweighted model appears to disappear when weighting. We should note that it is not just a question of the standard errors. There are over 25,000 observations, and the estimated point estimates tend to be small. While one might always hypothesize that more time than a single decade is necessary to allow any re-sorting, this explanation is unlikely, given that almost 50 percent of Americans move within any five-year period and that income effects have been found in these data (Banzhaf and Walsh 2008). The pattern of results appears to be that income effects can occur without attending effects on group composition, as highlighted by our models. This result is also consistent with the findings of McKinnish, Walsh, and White (2010) that gentrification often occurs through increasing incomes of minorities.

Conclusion

In a world where households sort in response to changes in environmental quality, the bulk of the benefits of a policy that successfully cleans up dirtier neighborhoods where the poor live may actually be captured by rich households. As the neighborhood amenity improves, wealthier households may move in, driving up rents. If the poor do not own their homes, landlords would capture the capital appreciation of the local housing, while the poor pay higher rents. This "environmental gentrification" may actually more than offset the direct gain of the environmental improvement, so that the original residents are actually worse off.

Standard models of gentrification would predict that these changes in real estate prices would be accompanied by other social changes, including dislocation of incumbent residents who may be replaced by transplants who are richer and whiter on average (see Chapter 2). However, our model suggests that insights into the more general equilibrium welfare properties of changes in public goods should be revisited with models that account for demographic sorting. While gentrification in the narrow sense of rising housing costs remains likely, other changes may be less likely. Indeed, we show that cleaning up pollution in minority neighborhoods, far from displacing minorities, may actually increase the share of minorities in that community.

Notes

Support for this research was provided by the National Science Foundation, NSF SES-03-21566. Additional support for Banzhaf was provided by the Property and Environment Research Center (PERC) through the Julian Simon fellowship supported by the Searle Freedom Trust. In addition to these generous supporters, we thank Jason Boardman, Nicholas Flores, Phillip Graves, Terra McKinnish, and seminar participants at PERC and the University of Wyoming for helpful comments and suggestions.

1. For evidence for and against the presence of migratory responses to pollution, see Baden and Coursey (2002); Banzhaf and Walsh (2008); Been (1997); Pastor, Sadd, and Hipp (2001); and Wolverton (Chapter 8).

2. Note that we refer here only to the demographic effects. Greenstone and Gallagher's primary application is to hedonic price effects. Their important finding that there are no price effects following cleanup remains surprising.

3. $V(\ )$ is assumed to be continuous with bounded first derivatives that satisfy $V_y > 0$, $V_G > 0$, and $V_P < 0$.

4. The housing demand function is also continuous with bounded first derivatives $D_y > 0$ and $D_P < 0$. Demand is assumed to be strictly positive and bounded from above.

5. Each community's housing supply function incorporates a bounding price P_j^l such that $\forall P \le P_j^l$, $S_j(P) = 0$, and $\forall P > P_j^l$, $0 < S_j(P) < \infty$ (i.e., supply is 0 at or below the bounding price and finite otherwise).

6. It is straightforward to relax this assumption by introducing heterogeneity in tastes so that there is income heterogeneity within each community, but perfect stratification by tastes for each income (see Sieg et al. 2004). Accordingly, this assumption is not critical for the following implications of the model.

7. Let N^w be the number of type w citizens and let N^m be the number of type m citizens. Let a be the percentage of type m citizens who live in community 1 (i.e., the percentage with incomes below $\bar{Y}$), with $0 < a < 1$. Let β be the percentage of type w citizens in community 1, $0 < \beta < 1$. First-order stochastic dominance, together with income stratification, implies that $a > \beta$. Thus, $\dfrac{\alpha}{\beta} > \dfrac{1-\alpha}{1-\beta}$ and $\dfrac{\alpha N^m}{\beta N^w} > \dfrac{(1-\alpha)N^m}{(1-\beta)N^w}$.

8. Historically, overdiscrimination through collective action has been important in shaping neighborhoods as well (Massey and Denton 1994). Antidiscrimination reforms in the housing market were first introduced with the adoption of the Fair

Housing Act of 1968. However, discriminatory practices are believed to continue to play a role in the locational opportunities of different racial groups (Turner et al. 2002).

9. These assumptions simplify the presentation of the model, but the conclusions in no way depend on them. Results using a more general version of the model with elastic housing supply are available from the authors.

10. The assumption of two income levels simplifies the analysis but is not necessary. See Banzhaf and Walsh (2010) for an extension to continuous income distributions.

11. To see this, rewrite Equation (4.11) as $P_1 = y_w(1 - G) + P_2G$. Since $G > 1$ and $y_m < y_w$, $y_m(1 - G) > y_w(1 - G)$. It follows that $P_1 < y_m(1 - G) + P_2G$.

12. Although intuitive, this condition is sufficient but not necessary.

13. In the 2000 Census, the median white household income was $44,687 compared to $29,423 for blacks. The latter is 65.8 percent of the former—approximately two-thirds.

14. The Consumer Expenditure Survey shows housing accounts for about 30 percent of the average American's budget, and all other goods 70 percent. Locational amenities like R and G are capitalized into local housing costs and bundled with housing costs in such tabulations.

15. As shown below, with these normalized populations and community sizes, only bliss points for whites above 0.85 will trigger a ceteris paribus preference to live in an all-white community over the segregated community with minorities.

16. For tractability, only distributions that have one type split across regions will be explicitly considered. Several distributions in which two types lived across regions were tested and none were supported in equilibrium.

17. As noted in the table, with the racial bliss point set at 0.8, this equilibrium is no longer supportable and is replaced by RM1.WH. The reason for this is that, in this case, whites perceive the racial composition to be more desirable in the community with minorities (70 percent white being closer than 100 percent to the bliss point of 80 percent). Consequently, rich whites outbid poor whites for the privilege of living with more minorities. Since with these normalized populations and community sizes the phenomenon of "white flight" is in this way eliminated for bliss points lower than 0.85, we believe the higher bliss point is of more interest.

18. However, any RM2.WH equilibria just above the lowest boundary in the figure will change to RM2.WL, as rich whites now prefer the all-white community but lower public goods to the mixed community with higher public goods, and therefore outbid poor whites for community 1 housing.

19. The online appendix can be found at http://www.sup.org/environmentaljustice.

20. See, for example, Arora and Cason (1999); Brooks and Sethi (1997); Kriesel, Centner, and Keeler (1996); Morello-Frosch, Pastor, and Sadd (2001); Ringquist (1997); and Sadd et al. (1999).

21. The list of chemicals was greatly expanded in 1994. To maintain a consistent comparison of TRI emissions over time, we have limited the data to the common set of chemicals used since 1988.

22. Information about this model is available at http://www.epa.gov/opptintr/rsei.

23. The online appendix can be found at http://www.sup.org/environmentaljustice.

24. These include population density, percentage black, percentage Hispanic, percentage Asian, percentage other minority, percentage of households with single-parent families, mean rental rate, mean housing value, percentage owning their home, percentage employed, percentage employed in manufacturing (if employed), percentage not graduating from high school, percentage with bachelor's degrees, and the median household income—plus squares of these terms.

25. Note that the discrete variables indicate proximity of a community to any facilities over time, which is related to but not the same as the entry and exit of firms.

References

Abadie, Alberto, and Guido Imbens. 2006. "Large Sample Properties of Matching Estimators for Average Treatment Effects." *Econometrica* 74 (1): 235–67.

Arora, Seema, and Timothy N. Cason. 1999. "Do Community Characteristics Influence Environmental Outcomes? Evidence from the Toxics Release Inventory." *Southern Economic Journal* 65 (4): 691–716.

Baden, Brett M., and Don L. Coursey. 2002. "The Locality of Waste Sites within the City of Chicago: A Demographic, Social, and Economic Analysis." *Resource and Energy Economics* 24 (1–2): 53–93.

Baden, Brett M., Douglas S. Noonan, and Rama Mohana R. Turaga. 2007. "Scales of Justice: Is There a Geographic Bias in Environmental Equity Analysis?" *Journal of Environmental Planning and Management* 50 (2): 163–85.

Banzhaf, H. Spencer, and Randall P. Walsh. 2008. "Do People Vote with Their Feet? An Empirical Test of Tiebout's Mechanism." *American Economic Review* 98 (3): 843–63.

———. 2010. "Segregation and Tiebout Sorting: Investigating the Link between Investments in Public Goods and Neighborhood Tipping." NBER Working Paper 16057, National Bureau of Economic Research, Cambridge, MA. http://ideas.repec.org/p/nbr/nberwo/16057.html.

Bayer, Patrick, Hanming Fang, and Robert McMillan. 2005. "Separate When Equal? Racial Inequality and Residential Segregation." NBER Working Paper 11507, National Bureau of Economic Research, Cambridge, MA. http://www.nber.org/papers/w11507.

Bayer, Patrick, Fernando Ferreira, and Robert McMillan. 2007. "A Unified Framework for Measuring Preferences for Schools and Neighborhoods." *Journal of Political Economy* 115 (4): 588–638.

Bayer, Patrick, and Robert McMillan. 2005. "Racial Sorting and Neighborhood Quality." Mimeo, Yale University, New Haven, CT.

Becker, Gary S., and Kevin M. Murphy. 2000. *Social Economics: Market Behavior in a Social Environment*, chap. 5. Cambridge, MA: Belknap Press.

Been, Vicki. 1993. "What's Fairness Got to Do with It? Environmental Justice and the Siting of Locally Undesirable Land Uses." *Cornell Law Review* 78:1001–85.

———. 1994. "Locally Undesirable Land Uses in Minority Neighborhoods: Disproportionate Siting or Market Dynamics?" *Yale Law Journal* 103:1383–1422.

Been, Vicki, with Francis Gupta. 1997. "Coming to the Nuisance or Going to the Barrios? A Longitudinal Analysis of Environmental Justice Claims." *Ecology Law Quarterly* 24 (1): 1–56.

Bobo, Lawrence, and Camille L. Zubrinsky. 1996. "Attitudes on Residential Integration: Perceived Status Differences, Mere In-Group Preference, or Racial Prejudice?" *Social Forces* 74 (3): 883–909.

Brooks, Nancy, and Rajiv Sethi. 1997. "The Distribution of Pollution: Community Characteristics and Exposure to Air Toxics." *Journal of Environmental Economics and Management* 32 (2): 233–50.

Cameron, Trudy Ann, and Ian T. McConnaha. 2006. "Evidence of Environmental Migration." *Land Economics* 82 (2): 273–90.

Card, David, Alexandre Mas, and Jesse Rothstein. 2008. "Tipping and the Dynamics of Segregation." *Quarterly Journal of Economics* 123 (1): 177–218.

Clark, W. A. V. 1991. "Residential Preferences and Neighborhood Racial Segregation: A Test of the Schelling Segregation Model." *Demography* 28 (1): 1–19.

Cutler, David M., Edward L. Glaeser, and Jacob L. Vigdor. 1999. "The Rise and Decline of the American Ghetto." *Journal of Political Economy* 107 (3): 455–506.

de Marchi, Scott, and James T. Hamilton. 2006. "Assessing the Accuracy of Self-Reported Data: An Evaluation of the Toxics Release Inventory." *Journal of Risk and Uncertainty* 32 (1): 57–76.

Emerson, Michael O., Karen J. Chai, and George Yancey. 2001. "Does Race Matter in Residential Segregation? Exploring the Preferences of White Americans." *American Sociological Review* 66 (6): 922–35.

Epple, Dennis, Radu Filimon, and Thomas Romer. 1984. "Equilibrium among Local Jurisdictions: Toward an Integrated Approach of Voting and Residential Choice." *Journal of Public Economics* 24 (3): 281–308.

Farley, Reynolds, and Maria Krysan. 2002. "The Residential Preferences of Blacks: Do They Explain Persistent Segregation?" *Social Forces* 80 (3): 937–80.

Farley, Reynolds, Howard Schuman, Suzanne Bianchi, Diane Colasanto, and Shirley Hatchett. 1978. "Chocolate City, Vanilla Suburbs: Will the Trend toward Racially Separate Communities Continue?" *Social Science Research* 7 (4): 319–44.

Farley, Reynolds, Charlotte Steeh, Maria Krysan, Tara Jackson, and Keith Reeves. 1994. "Stereotypes and Segregation: Neighborhoods in the Detroit Area." *American Journal of Sociology* 100 (3): 750–80.

Ford, Richard Thompson. 1994. "The Boundaries of Race: Political Geography in Legal Analysis." *Harvard Law Review* 107:1841–1921.

Foster, Sheila. 1998. "Justice from the Ground Up: Distributive Inequities, Grassroots Resistance, and the Transformative Politics of the Environmental Justice Movement." *California Law Review* 86:775–841.

Gamper-Rabindran, Shanti, and Christopher Timmins. 2011. "Hazardous Waste Cleanup, Neighborhood Gentrification, and Environmental Justice: Evidence from Restricted Access Census Block Data." *American Economic Review* 101 (3): 620–24.

Glass, Ruth. 1964. "Introduction: Aspects of Change." In *London: Aspects of Change*, edited by Ruth Glass et al. London: MacGibbon & Kee.

Greenstone, Michael, and Justin Gallagher. 2008. "Does Hazardous Waste Matter? Evidence from the Housing Market and the Superfund Program." *Quarterly Journal of Economics* 123 (3): 951–1003.

Hamilton, James T. 1993. "Politics and Social Costs: Estimating the Impact of Collective Action on Hazardous Waste Facilities." *RAND Journal of Economics* 24 (1): 101–25.

Heckman, James J., Hidehiko Ichimura, and Petra Todd. 1997. "Matching as an Econometric Evaluation Estimator: Evidence from Evaluating a Job Training Program." *Review of Economic Studies* 64 (4): 605–54.

———. 1998. "Matching as an Econometric Evaluation Estimator." *Review of Economic Studies* 65 (2): 261–94.

Hersh, Robert. 1995. "Race and Industrial Hazards: An Historical Geography of the Pittsburgh Region, 1900–1990." Discussion Paper 95-18, Resources for the Future, Washington, DC.

King, A. Thomas, and Peter Mieszkowski. 1973. "Racial Discrimination, Segregation, and the Price of Housing." *Journal of Political Economy* 81 (3): 590–606.

Kriesel, Warren, Terence J. Centner, and Andrew G. Keeler. 1996. "Neighborhood Exposure to Toxic Releases: Are There Racial Inequities?" *Growth and Change* 27 (4): 479–99.

Massey, Douglas, and Nancy Denton. 1994. *American Apartheid: Segregation and the Making of the Underclass*. Cambridge, MA: Harvard University Press.

McKinnish, Terra, Randall Walsh, and T. Kirk White. 2010. "Who Gentrifies Low-Income Neighborhoods?" *Journal of Urban Economics* 67 (2): 180–93.

Mohai, Paul, and Robin Saha. 2006. "Reassessing Racial and Socioeconomic Disparities in Environmental Justice Research." *Demography* 43 (2): 383–99.

Morello-Frosch, Rachel, Manuel Pastor, and James Sadd. 2001. "Environmental Justice and Southern California's 'Riskscape': The Distribution of Air Toxics Exposures and Health Risks among Diverse Communities." *Urban Affairs Review* 36 (4): 551–78.

National Environmental Justice Advisory Council (NEJAC). 2006. *Unintended Impacts of Redevelopment and Revitalization Efforts in Five Environmental Justice Communities.* Final Report. http://www.epa.gov/compliance/ej/resources/publications/nejac/redev-revital-recomm-9-27-06.pdf.

Pastor, Manuel, Jim Sadd, and John Hipp. 2001. "Which Came First? Toxic Facilities, Minority Move-In, and Environmental Justice." *Journal of Urban Affairs* 23 (1): 1–21.

Ringquist, Evan J. 1997. "Equity and the Distribution of Environmental Risk: The Case of TRI Facilities." *Social Science Quarterly* 78 (4): 811–29.

Sadd, James L., Manuel Pastor Jr., J. Thomas Boer, and Lori D. Snyder. 1999. "'Every Breath You Take . . .': The Demographics of Toxic Air Releases in Southern California." *Economic Development Quarterly* 13 (2): 107–23.

Schelling, Thomas C. 1969. "Models of Segregation." *American Economic Review* 59 (2): 488–92.

———. 1971. "Dynamic Models of Segregation." *Journal of Mathematical Sociology* 1 (2): 143–86.

———. 1972. "A Process of Residential Segregation: Neighborhood Tipping." In *Racial Discrimination in Economic Life*, edited by A. Pascal. Lexington, MA: Lexington Books.

Sieg, Holger, V. Kerry Smith, H. Spencer Banzhaf, and Randy Walsh. 2004. "Estimating the General Equilibrium Benefits of Large Changes in Spatially Delineated Public Goods." *International Economic Review* 45 (4): 1047–77.

Smith, V. Kerry, Holger Sieg, H. Spencer Banzhaf, and Randy Walsh. 2004. "General Equilibrium Benefits for Environmental Improvements: Projected Ozone Reductions under EPA's Prospective Analysis for the Los Angeles Air Basin." *Journal of Environmental Economics and Management* 47 (3): 559–84.

Tiebout, Charles. 1956. "A Pure Theory of Local Expenditures." *Journal of Political Economy* 64 (5): 416–24.

Turner, Margery Austin, Fred Freiberg, Erin Godfrey, Carla Herbig, Diane K. Levy, and Robin R. Smith. 2002. *All Other Things Being Equal: A Paired Testing Study of Mortgage Lending Institutions.* Urban Institute report prepared for the Office of Fair Housing and Equal Opportunity, US Department of Housing and Urban Development, Washington, DC. http://www.urban.org/UploadedPDF/1000504_All_Other_Things_Being_Equal.pdf.

Walsh, Randall P. 2007. "Endogenous Open Space Amenities in a Locational Equilibrium." *Journal of Urban Economics* 61 (2): 319–44.

Wu, JunJie, and Seong-Hoon Cho. 2003. "Estimating Households' Preferences for Environmental Amenities Using Equilibrium Models of Local Jurisdictions." *Scottish Journal of Political Economy* 50 (2): 189–206.

Household Behavior and Land Markets

Empirical Explorations

THIS SECTION CONTINUES the theme of Section I on the role of land markets in allocating environmental quality to different groups, turning now to specific empirical explorations.

In Chapter 5, Brooks Depro and Christopher Timmins consider residential mobility in San Francisco, California. Matching housing sales to households over time, Depro and Timmins present a unique opportunity to explore the mobility patterns of specific households as they move from one house to another. They find that when poorer households "trade up" to bigger homes, blacks and Hispanics tend to move into neighborhoods with more ozone pollution than do whites. Furthermore, they provide preliminary evidence that this may be a consequence of the fact that minorities face a higher cost of finding similarly sized houses in clean communities than do whites. This, in turn, may be because of discrimination in the housing market or because minorities are prioritizing other public goods over ozone.

Trudy Ann Cameron, Graham Crawford, and Ian McConnaha continue this discussion in Chapter 6, with a detailed examination of migration patterns around seven Superfund sites, from 1970 to 2000, including periods of remediation. They find a wide range of changing demographic patterns at the various sites but few definitive patterns across sites. It appears that there is little evidence of groups "coming to the nuisance" (or differentially fleeing the nuisance) in these data. As they discuss, one possible reason for this finding is that households may have had different perceptions about the environmental hazards of the sites, and these perceptions may have changed over time in unpredictable ways. For example, the sites may be perceived to be improving if they are remediated, or, alternatively, the sites may be permanently stigmatized.

In Chapter 7, Douglas Noonan concludes the empirical inquiry in this section with a case study of a brownfield-to-greenfield project in Atlanta, Georgia, known as the BeltLine. Because the project provides desirable amenities such as greenspace, it might be expected to cause gentrification, including price increases. However, Noonan cautions against jumping to this conclusion. He points out that projects like the BeltLine also encumber future residents with debt. When such projects are financed locally in this way rather than from outside, there is less scope for gentrification. Furthermore, the project frees up land for development and changes zoning laws to allow denser development in the area. This supply effect might offset the demand effect driven by the amenities. Consistent with these factors, Noonan finds little evidence of pure price effects but does find that additions and other renovations occurred more often in the area of the project, reflecting this supply effect. As with Vigdor's earlier point about vacant housing, these supply effects must play an important role in our understanding of gentrification.

5 Residential Mobility and Ozone Exposure

Challenges for Environmental Justice Policy

Brooks Depro and Christopher Timmins

Introduction

A variety of studies suggest that minority and low-income households often live in areas with poor environmental quality (Wernette and Nieves 1992; Institute of Medicine 1999). Annual data also show that 14 percent of the US population, or 40 million people, move to a new residence each year (US Bureau of the Census 2004). Together, these facts raise questions about residential mobility and the observed correlation among race, income, and pollution. For example, when people move to a bigger house, does their ozone exposure go up or down? Do minorities tend to take on more pollution for similar housing upgrades? If so, is it because the rates at which ozone and housing services trade in the marketplace differ or do minorities simply choose to spend less money for upgrades by moving into neighborhoods with more ozone pollution?

We offer a new assessment of these questions using data for home buyers in the San Francisco Bay Area of California that combines individual real estate transactions with buyer attribute information. Since we can observe individual choices and home buyer economic circumstances on multiple occasions, we can test selected environmental justice hypotheses in a new and more direct way that avoids many of the modeling assumptions that are typically required without these data. As a result, we build on existing analyses that draw conclusions about sorting-induced exposure.

We look for direct evidence that poor/minority homeowners who bought more housing services also got more ozone exposure when they moved, whereas other homeowners did not. This is an important addition to the environmental justice literature, because previous analyses that have looked for verification of the sorting explanation for environmental injustice used indirect evidence (i.e., do the percentages of poor and minority residents in a neighborhood rise when pollution increases?). However, this type of indirect evidence can be consistent with alternative explanations. For example, individuals could move near pollution not because of cheaper housing but because of proximate job opportunities. As a result, one cannot address the housing/pollution trade-off question directly without seeing the house the individual bought and the house he or she sold.

Our unique data set helps solve the problem because we are able to follow buyers as they move from one house to another; we directly observe whether ozone exposure increases when particular homeowners buy more housing services. Using the move outcomes data for homeowners who chose to buy more housing services, we find ozone exposure goes up for all groups as a result of the move. The positive relationship between housing services and ozone exposure is also stronger for low-income black/Hispanic homeowners than it is for low-income white homeowners. We also measure the rate at which each group (whites and minorities) are able to trade housing services for ozone pollution, holding total housing expenditure fixed. The results suggest that minorities' best housing choices lead them to take on more pollution in order to upgrade housing because the costs they face to obtain more housing services in neighborhoods with clean air are much higher than they are for white homeowners.

Related Literature

A large number of articles in the environmental justice literature have provided information to policy makers and stakeholders concerned about environmental justice policy questions. One group of studies documents the correlation between pollution and community characteristics (e.g., Freeman 1972; Asch and Seneca 1978; US General Accounting Office 1983, 1995; United Church of Christ 1987; Brooks and Sethi 1997; Bullard 2000). Houston et al. (2004); Kim et al. (2004); Fisher, Kelly, and Romm (2006); and Pastor, Sadd, and Morello-Frosch (2007) are notable recent examples of such analyses. A second group of articles in the literature investigates the siting decisions of polluting firms to better understand correlation patterns between pollution and community characteristics (e.g., Hamilton 1995; Arora and Cason 1999; see also Chapter 8). The last group suggests the observed correlation between pollution and demographics could be explained in part by a complex sequence of housing market changes and residential mobility decisions that occur over time (e.g., Oakes, Anderton, and Anderson 1996; Been 1997; Pastor, Sadd, and Hipp 2001; Morello-Frosch et al. 2002; Banzhaf and Walsh 2008; see also Chapter 4).

Correlation between Pollution and Community Characteristics

Pastor, Sadd, and Morello-Frosch (2007) also focus on a similar geographic area of interest—the San Francisco Bay Area. These authors were motivated to perform their analysis after finding that no existing empirical studies had addressed the overall distribution of air pollution exposure in this region. Titled "Still Toxic after All These Years: Air Quality and Environmental Justice in the San Francisco Bay Area," the study uses a single-year cross-sectional design.

Pastor, Sadd, and Morello-Frosch leveraged two data sets to compute census tract–level measures of hazardous air pollutant exposure and compared these to contemporaneous socioeconomic characteristics of the tracts. The first data set (EPA's Toxics Release Inventory [TRI]) is commonly used in the environmental justice literature and includes the location of and emissions information on large industrial facilities. Using this data set, the authors specified a binary logit model where the dependent variable describes a census tract's proximity to a TRI facility (1 if less than 1 mile, 0 if greater than 1 mile). After controlling for selected factors (i.e., race, population density, and share of manufacturing employment), their analysis found that census tracts with low per capita incomes and homeownership rates were more likely to be close (i.e., within 1 mile) to stationary TRI facilities with air releases. Although the income and homeownership coefficients have intuitive (negative) signs, their magnitudes and standard errors were not reported; therefore, it is not possible to assess whether the coefficients were large or small. However, the authors were able to reject the hypothesis that these coefficients were 0 at the 5 percent level. In addition to examining the influence of economic resources and proximity to toxic releases, the authors also found that black and Hispanic populations were more likely to live within a mile of a TRI facility with air releases after controlling for income and other tract-level characteristics.

The second data set used in the report (the 1999 National Air Toxics Assessment [NATA]) is unique because it considers mobile source emissions as well as large industrial facilities covered by the TRI. In addition, procedures can be applied to the NATA data to describe a census tract's potential cancer and respiratory hazards. Regressing these tract-level estimates of cancer and respiratory risk on income and share of homeownership shows that, after controlling for race, population density, and percentage of industrial/commercial/transportation land use, census tracts with lower incomes and homeownership rates appear to be at a higher risk for cancer and other respiratory hazards.[1]

Although Pastor, Sadd, and Morello-Frosch (2007) present compelling visual evidence of the correlation between Bay Area TRI facility locations and minority populations, analogous conclusions cannot necessarily be drawn for a criteria pollutant like ozone since ozone concentrations are influenced by a variety of factors unrelated to the source of the emissions. Winds tend to push ozone away from the coastal areas to the mountains in the east and southeast portions of the San Francisco Bay Area Air Basin.

There are high concentrations of Hispanic or Latino populations in the east and southeast basin, which is where ozone tends to be transported.[2] However, the overall mean ozone concentrations taken from our housing sample actually show slightly higher concentrations for white homeowners: white homeowners had the highest house-specific maximum annual one-hour ozone concentrations (96.0 parts per billion [ppb]), Hispanics were next (95.3 ppb), followed by Asians (94.8 ppb) and blacks (94.6 ppb). Census tracts in the east and southeast do have populations with lower median incomes, and evidence from our housing sample also suggests income is negatively correlated with house-specific ozone pollution (−0.10); lower incomes are associated with higher ozone concentrations. Homeowners in the lowest income quartile (less than $60,000) also had a higher mean house-specific concentration (95.9 ppb) compared to the upper quartile (greater than $200,000) mean concentration (93.7 ppb). However, it is difficult to make definitive conclusions about minority populations, income, and ozone pollution relationships using only information about ozone transport and geography-based summary statistics.

Siting Decisions of Polluting Firms and Pollution Exposure

Hamilton (1995) used contemporaneous community attributes to explain the planning decisions of commercial hazardous waste facilities. He tested three theories: (1) pure discrimination, (2) Coasian bargaining (i.e., that plants are sited in places where the potential costs of compensating affected residents are low because their demand for environmental quality is weak), and (3) collective action/political economy (i.e., that firms site plants in communities that are less likely to organize to collect compensation). Hamilton found that commercial hazardous waste facilities did avoid sites where potential compensation costs were high and areas were more likely to mobilize against plans for expansion. Arora and Cason (1999) compared 1993 TRI data to 1990 neighborhood attributes in an attempt to limit reverse causality in correlation (i.e., 1990 neighborhood attributes could not be caused by 1993 TRI emissions). They performed tests similar to Hamilton's and found that race, income levels, and unemployment influenced release patterns from TRI facilities. Community mobilization variables also influenced the level of TRI releases. In contrast, Wolverton (Chapter 8) examined TRI plant location decisions for two Texas cities and found little support for collective action and discriminatory siting theories; the best explanations of the plant location decisions in these cities were profit-maximizing location decisions (i.e., production and transportation costs). Although all the studies offer interesting hypotheses and empirical tests, siting explanations for exposure inequities are less relevant for ozone because cars and other mobile sources, rather than specific sites (e.g., TRI plants), are a substantial contributor to air quality problems.

Residential Mobility and Pollution Exposure

Only a few empirical studies have focused on the connection between household mobility and pollution exposure patterns. In one of several versions of the story, declines in environmental quality cause households to leave and property values to fall. In response, low-income minority households may find these communities attractive because they are more willing to trade higher rates of exposure in exchange for a bigger (and now less expensive) house. This process has been referred to as "housing market dynamics" (Been 1997), "white flight" (Oakes, Anderton, and Anderson 1996), and "minority move-in" (Morello-Frosch et al. 2002). However, three early longitudinal studies examining this question find limited or no evidence of community demographic changes after the siting of hazardous waste storage and disposal facilities (Oakes, Anderton, and Anderson 1996; Been 1997; Pastor, Sadd, and Hipp 2001).

Banzhaf and Walsh (2008) provide one of the most direct tests of migratory responses with the entry/exit of polluting facilities and emissions of air toxics. Using differences-in-differences and matching program evaluation methods, they find strong evidence of migration patterns that are consistent with the earlier work of Kahn (2000); communities in which the air becomes cleaner see population gains, while communities in which the air becomes dirtier experience population declines. In addition, they also find evidence of environmental gentrification similar to that found in Sieg and colleagues' (2004) statistical simulations of household responses to air quality changes. Increases in air pollution levels appear to encourage rich households to exit a community, while poor households are more likely to enter. However, in follow-up work, Banzhaf, Sidon, and Walsh (see Chapter 4) find little evidence of such effects by racial categories. See also Chapter 6.

One of Banzhaf and Walsh's important contributions is their attempt to better control for unobserved local factors that determine residential location decisions. Many previous studies have not considered the role these amenities play in household sorting because so many potential factors need to be considered; even if one were successful in developing a comprehensive and agreeable list, complete data would be too difficult and costly to collect. To overcome this challenge yet still address this issue, Banzhaf and Walsh used school district and zip code fixed effects in addition to other demographic controls. We follow their lead and use zip code fixed effects to control for unobserved spatially distributed amenities.

The evidence presented by Banzhaf and Walsh suggests that people migrate in response to environmental quality changes, and this evidence may help explain pollution exposure patterns that emerge over time. From a public policy perspective, this migration evidence suggests a very different policy response than would, for example, evidence of disproportionate siting.

However, research to date has not addressed an important question about the types of constraints movers face, the consequences these constraints may have in terms of pollution exposure, and the differences in the trade-offs they make in return for dirtier air (e.g., bigger houses, improved local amenities besides air quality). Well-known social advocate Robert Bullard argued that these mobility constraints are an important concern and that "poor whites and poor blacks do not have the same opportunities to 'vote with their feet'" when it comes to environmental quality choices (Bullard 2000, chap. 6). Mobility constraint differences (e.g., wealth effects associated with a previous home sale or marketplace ozone and housing service trade-offs that differ for whites and minorities) have not been addressed to date in this empirical literature.

Data

Our analysis uses a sample of 794,162 housing sales obtained from previous data work related to Bay Area real estate transactions (Bayer et al. 2008; Bishop and Timmins 2011). The commercial and public data sources include the following:

- *DataQuick real estate transactions.* Purchased from a national real estate company, these data provide actual transaction (instead of self-reported) prices and include information about housing characteristics (structural characteristics and geographic coordinates).
- *Home Mortgage Disclosure Act of 1975 (HMDA).* The HMDA data provide key demographic information about the home buyers.
- *California Air Resources Board (CARB) air quality data.* CARB provides the latest 27 years of monitor-level air quality data (1980 to 2006).

DataQuick includes a rich set of real estate transactions for 1990 to 2006, covering six key counties of the San Francisco Bay Area (i.e., Alameda, Contra Costa, Marin, San Francisco, San Mateo, and Santa Clara). Transaction variables for the analysis include a unique parcel identifier, sales price, sales date, and geographic information (e.g., census tract, latitude, longitude). DataQuick also provides several useful housing characteristics observed at the last transaction: lot size, square footage, number of bathrooms, and number of bedrooms. To ensure consistency of zip codes across time, we used geographic information system (GIS) software and *ESRI Data: U.S. Zip Code Areas: 2000* to add a five-digit US zip code to each house.

The complete DataQuick database was reviewed, and observations were selected for the study using the following criteria. First, we restricted the analysis to houses that sold one to three times during the sample period. These houses are more likely to be representative of typical residential housing transactions versus houses that may be bought and "flipped" for investment purposes or other unusual reasons. For similar reasons, we dropped properties within this group that sold multiple times on the same day or the same year. Next, we screened properties for land-only sales or rebuilds and dropped all transactions for which the year built was missing or the transaction date was prior to the year built. To compute distances between houses and air quality monitors, we needed the property's geographic coordinates. Therefore, we dropped properties for which the latitude and longitude were missing or miscoded (i.e., outside of the six counties). We also eliminated transactions without a sales price and dropped 1 percent of observations from each tail of the price distribution to minimize the effect of outliers. Finally, we restricted the sample to include only properties with the following ranges of attributes: only one housing unit, lot size (i.e., 1,000 to 70,000 square feet), square footage (i.e., 500 to 5,000 square feet), bathrooms (i.e., 1 to 5), and bedrooms (i.e., 1 to 5).[3]

For the empirical analysis, we use a single measure of each house's "size." Using the housing sample discussed above, hedonic regression models for each year were used to create *year-specific* housing service indices. In the models, the log of housing price is regressed on housing structural characteristics related to size (i.e., lot size, square footage, number of baths, and number of bedrooms), ozone concentration, and zip code indicators. This approach takes advantage of all housing sales observations in each year and allows the parameters in the regression to vary by year; as a result, it provides the most flexible calculation of the housing service indices possible. For each year t, we estimate the following model with ordinary least squares (OLS):

$$\ln P_{ijt} = Z_j' \phi_t + H_{ij}' \lambda_t + Ozone_{ijt}' \alpha_t + \eta_{ijt}, \tag{5.1}$$

where P_{ijt} is the price of home j purchased by buyer i in year t, Z_j is the zip code indicator for home j, H_{ij} are housing structural characteristics related to the size of the home consumed by household i, $Ozone_{ijt}$ is the ozone concentration measure for the house, and η_{ijt} represents the effect of unobserved factors.

Repeat Purchases by the Same Buyer

Another feature of the DataQuick/HMDA match process is that the same buyer can be linked to other housing purchases that occurred during the sample period (Bishop and Timmins 2011). As a result, a buyer's purchase decision can be observed on more than one occasion. For our analysis of repeat purchases, the initial set of housing sales was restricted to observations in which the same buyer makes only two purchases during the sample period.[4]

Next, a new variable was calculated and added that compares the price the buyer paid at the first observed purchase in the sample with the house's subsequent selling price when the buyer moved (i.e., the home appreciation rate experienced for the first home [*Sales price*$_2$/*Sales price*$_1$ − 1]). The appreciation variable allows us to examine whether residential mobility behavior might be influenced by the size of the previously owned home's appreciation rate. Using the result from the hedonic regression, we also added two other variables that allow us to compare the two houses bought by the buyer. To do this, we use the appropriate year's estimated housing coefficients (i.e., λ_t) to compare housing size (i.e., $H_{ij}' \lambda_t$) for the new home and old home *in the year of the second purchase* (t'). After making the calculation, we can measure the difference in the size between the new house and the old house *had the buyer decided not to move.* The difference between the two indices for buyer i in the year of the second purchase t' is calculated as

$$\Delta Housing\ services_{it'} = H'_{ij'}\lambda_{t'} - H'_{ij}\lambda_{t'}. \tag{5.2}$$

Similarly, we use the house-specific pollution measure (three-year simple moving average of maximum annual one-hour ozone concentration) for the new house and old house in the year of the second purchase to calculate the difference in ozone pollution between the new house (j') and the old house (j) *had the buyer decided not to move.* The difference between the pollution levels for buyer i in the year of the second purchase t' is calculated as

$$\Delta Ozone_{it'} = Ozone_{ij't'} - Ozone_{ijt'}. \tag{5.3}$$

In the last step, observations with no race information for either purchase and observations missing real income (in 2000 dollars) for the second purchase were excluded. One percent of observations from each tail of the real income (in 2000 dollars) and home appreciation rate distributions were dropped to minimize the effect of outliers for these two variables. In cases where conflicting race information was provided for the first and second purchases, the reported race in the second purchase was used. If race information for the second purchase was not available, the reported race for the buyer's first purchase was used.

As noted above, the repeat-purchase sample uses only a very small share of the initial housing sample ($N = 23,156$, or 3 percent of the housing sample). In order to assess whether the sample restrictions raise any selection issues with respect to the demographic variables (i.e., race and income), the repeat-purchase sample statistics were compared with earlier versions of the matched DataQuick/HMDA transactions reported by Bayer et al. (2008) and directly with the metro data for San Francisco–Oakland–Vallejo, California (id = 736) and San Jose, California (id = 740) included in the 2000 Integrated Public Use Microdata Series (IPUMS) 5 percent sample (Ruggles et al. 2010). Using the comparisons, the restricted sample can be considered representative of the complete sample and the metro-area IPUMS sample.

Additional buyer sample statistics are available by race/ethnicity. White and Asian buyers have similar income and rates of appreciation from the previously owned home. In contrast, black and Hispanic homeowners had lower average incomes and their home appreciation rates were higher (84 and 75 percent, respectively) than white and Asian households (69 and 67 percent, respectively).

Air Quality Data: Time and Spatial Variation in Ozone Concentration

The San Francisco Bay Area Air Basin has cleaner air relative to the other California air basins because of its coastal climate (CARB 2007). However, the basin continues to deal with air quality issues; federal and state governments have designated the Bay Area as a nonattainment area for ground-level ozone. Figure 5.1 depicts the time path of ozone pollution in the Bay Area. The early 1990s saw the implementation of several policies that would influence air quality trends over time:[5] the Clean Air Act Amendments of 1990, which included a pollution permit program for over 100 major polluting facilities; adoption of the first district Clean Air Plan; and public information programs designed to help reduce emissions from motor vehicles. The mid-1990s provided mixed results for these programs. In 1995, the Bay Area reached attainment under the federal ozone standard based on improvements in the preceding years, and the area experienced its worst air quality in 10 years. Two years later, the Bay Area rebounded and saw the best air quality on record. However, the improvement was not enough to overcome the poor air quality measures in 1995 and 1996. The EPA reclassified the Bay Area as being in nonattainment under federal ozone standards.

To meet these new challenges, several clean air initiatives (e.g., clean-burning gasoline, vehicle and lawn mower buyback programs, new-vehicle

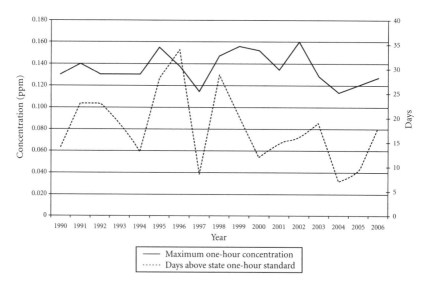

Figure 5.1 San Francisco Bay Area Air Basin ground-level ozone pollution, 1990–2006. Data from CARB (2007), Table 4-18.

smog-testing requirements, and bans on the use of garden and utility equipment during high pollution days) were adopted with some success. Since 2000, monitors measured ozone concentrations that exceeded the federal or state air quality standards on fewer than 20 days.

The spatial distribution of ozone within the air basin is influenced by west-to-east wind patterns and the mountains surrounding the Bay Area. Winds tend to push pollution away from the coast, and the mountains trap pollution within the region. Air pollution also escapes the Bay Area through certain mountain gaps and reaches other California air basins (CARB 2001, 38). CARB (2001) has identified the two routes in the west—the Carquinez Strait, which carries air pollution to the Sacramento Valley, and the Altamont Pass, which carries pollution into the San Joaquin Valley. The only outside air basin that CARB has classified as a contributor to San Francisco Bay Area ozone pollution is the broader Sacramento area (CARB 2001). The CARB classification ranges from "inconsequential to significant" because northern winds occasionally switch to a westerly direction and carry ozone to eastern parts of the San Francisco Bay Area (CARB 2001, 26). Figure 5.2 provides visual patterns of the spatial distribution of pollution for the first and last years of the data set (1990 and 2006). As shown, the patterns are consistent with descriptions of ozone transport described by CARB (2001).

Thirty-eight monitors in the San Francisco Bay Area Air Basin provide maximum annual one-hour ozone concentration statistics. The monitors are part of a statewide system of over 250 monitors that collect pollution measurements (CARB 2007).

With the house and monitor geographic information (latitude and longitude coordinates), house-specific maximum ozone concentrations (1990 to 2006) were calculated using an inverse distance-weighted average of all 38 San Francisco Bay Area Air Basin monitors with at least 60 percent coverage for a given year. For example, consider a hypothetical set of five monitors at distances of 5, 10, 15, 20, and 25 kilometers from a house. Suppose the maximum annual one hour concentrations recorded by the monitors in 1995 are 95, 110, 115, 96, and 102 ppb. The 1995 house-specific ozone measure calculated as an inverse distance-weighted average of all the monitor values is

Average ozone =

$$\frac{\frac{1}{5} \times 95 + \frac{1}{10} \times 110 + \frac{1}{15} \times 115 + \frac{1}{20} \times 96 + \frac{1}{25} \times 102}{\frac{1}{5} + \frac{1}{10} + \frac{1}{15} + \frac{1}{20} + \frac{1}{25}} = 101.90 \text{ ppb.} \qquad (5.4)$$

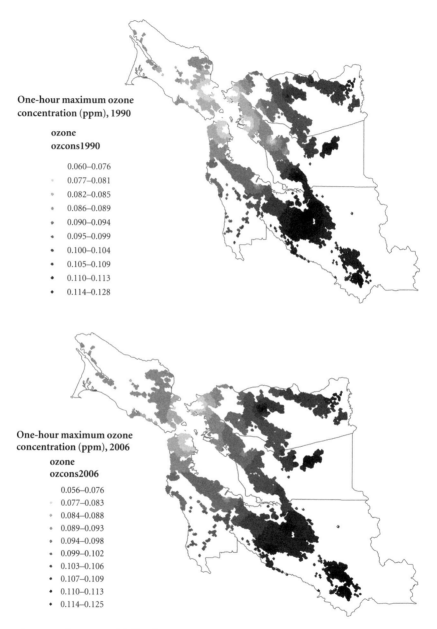

One-hour maximum ozone concentration (ppm), 1990

ozone
ozcons1990

   0.060–0.076
· 0.077–0.081
· 0.082–0.085
· 0.086–0.089
· 0.090–0.094
· 0.095–0.099
· 0.100–0.104
· 0.105–0.109
· 0.110–0.113
· 0.114–0.128

One-hour maximum ozone concentration (ppm), 2006

ozone
ozcons2006

   0.056–0.076
· 0.077–0.083
· 0.084–0.088
· 0.089–0.093
· 0.094–0.098
· 0.099–0.102
· 0.103–0.106
· 0.107–0.109
· 0.110–0.113
· 0.114–0.125

Figure 5.2 Ozone spatial distribution, 1990 and 2006. Authors' calculations using data from CARB (2008).

Since pollution levels tend to fluctuate from year to year and buyers may take into account recent pollution trends, a simple three-year lagged moving average of each house-specific measure ($[Ozone_t + Ozone_{t-1} + Ozone_{t-2}]/3$) was also calculated.

Did Bay Area Home Buyers Who Upgraded Housing Services Take on More Ozone Pollution?

If homeowners decide to upgrade houses, they can pay for the upgrade in two ways: (1) they can pay for these services with additional money (giving up other goods), or (2) they can "pay" for them by moving to a neighborhood with more ozone pollution. To illustrate the choice, consider Figure 5.3, where the quantity of housing services is shown on the x-axis and the quantity of ozone pollution is shown on the y-axis. Within the space, we can trace the original housing expenditure line ($\$E_{original}$). A homeowner who wants a new service level (H') *without* getting more ozone pollution has to spend more money and give up other goods (point A on the new expenditure line $\$E_{new}$). Alternatively, a homeowner could stay on the original housing expenditure line and get the same new service level by taking on more ozone pollution (point B) (i.e., move along the original expenditure line).

Our buyer repeat-purchase sample allows us to track individuals, observe the housing choice, and determine the ozone exposure consequence associated with that choice. Since we are interested in the exposure consequences for homeowners who buy more housing, we focus on the subset of homeowners who bought more housing services (over 75 percent of the buyer panel). Initially, we measure the economic and statistical significance of the linear relationship between the two differenced variables ($\Delta Housing\ services$ and $\Delta Ozone$ *concentration*) using Pearson's correlation coefficient (r). If a group has a high correlation, it means that when they get more housing, they tend to "pay for it" by taking on more ozone. If a group has a low correlation, it means that when they get more housing, they tend to pay for it with money (or by sacrificing other amenities).

As shown in Table 5.1, the black/Hispanic homeowner's housing service/ozone correlation coefficient (0.06) is approximately 1.5 times higher than the white homeowner's correlation coefficient (0.04), and the Asian homeowner's correlation coefficient (0.08) is approximately two times higher. However, hypothesis tests show that the minority correlation coefficients are not statistically different from each other at the 10 percent level.

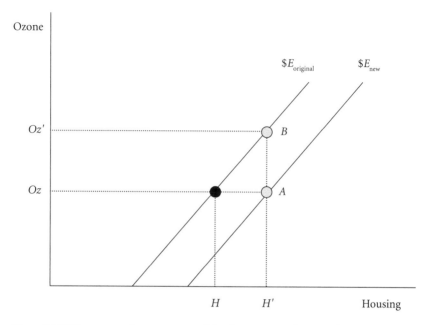

Figure 5.3 Different ways homeowners might choose to pay for more housing services

Next, we looked more closely at the real income differences to see what role (if any) income plays in mobility-induced exposure patterns. To do this, we divided the buyers in each race/ethnicity group into two income groups in each year: buyers with real income (in 2000 dollars) above the median value (taken from the set of all home buyers) and buyers with real income (in 2000 dollars) equal to or below the median value. As shown in the middle panel of Table 5.1, black/Hispanic households are the only low-income racial group in which the conditional correlation is positive and statistically different from 0. In addition, their correlation coefficient is higher than and statistically different from low-income whites. At the same time, high-income whites and Asians also have a positive correlation between housing upgrades and ozone purchases.

We also considered whether changes in homeowner housing wealth (measured by large and small house appreciation rates for the previously owned home) influence the correlation coefficients. The idea is that households that make more money from the previous home sale relative to the initial purchase price may be in a better position to minimize additional ozone exposure. Additional resources may be especially beneficial for lower-income homeowners because the resources can expand the available affordable housing options.

Table 5.1 Correlation coefficients (conditional on buying more housing services)

Racial/ethnicity group	Correlation coefficient	Statistically different from white homeowners?
Black/Hispanic	0.06[a]	No
Asian	0.08[a]	No
White	0.04[a]	—

By income and race/ethnicity group

	Black/Hispanic	White	Absolute difference (row)
Above the median income	0.05	0.07[a]	−0.02
Below or equal to the median income	0.09[a]	0.02	0.07[a]
Absolute difference (column)	−0.04	0.05[a]	

	Asian	White	Absolute difference (row)
Above the median	0.12[a]	0.07[a]	0.05
Below or equal to the median	0.05	0.02	0.03
Absolute difference (column)	0.07	0.05[a]	

By appreciation rate, income, and race/ethnicity group

	Above median income	Below median income
White		
Above the median appreciation rate	0.00	0.06[a]
Below or equal to the median appreciation rate	0.04	0.07[a]
Absolute difference (column)	−0.05	0.00
Black/Hispanic		
Above the median appreciation rate	0.09[a]	0.02
Below or equal to the median appreciation rate	0.09[a]	0.07
Absolute difference (column)	0.00	−0.05
Asian		
Above the median appreciation rate	−0.02	0.11[a]
Below or equal to the median appreciation rate	0.12[a]	0.13[a]
Absolute difference (column)	−0.14[a]	−0.02

Note: For each buyer, the new home's housing services and ozone concentration are compared with the previous home's housing services and ozone concentration had the buyer decided not to move.

[a]Denotes that the correlation coefficients conditional on buying more housing services are statistically different from 0 at the 0.10 level.

To analyze the effects of house appreciation rates within each racial/ethnic group, we further subdivided the buyers into two additional house appreciation rate groups in each year: buyers with large appreciation rates (i.e., above the median) and buyers with small (or negative) appreciation rates (equal to or below the median). As shown in the bottom panel of Table 5.1, the only statistically different conditional correlation coefficient between high and low appreciation group is for low-income Asian homeowners. For the remaining race/ethnicity and income groups, differences cannot be distinguished from 0.

Why Did Poor Minorities Take on More Ozone Pollution?

One limitation of the correlation analysis is that we don't know whether (poor) minorities took on more pollution in exchange for more housing because they face a different constraint (i.e., ozone and housing services were traded in the marketplace at different rates for poor minority homeowners relative to white homeowners) or because they face the same constraint but simply choose to spend less money. Alternatively, we could ask how much more the minority home buyer would have to spend (i.e., how much income would have to be taken away) to get to the same consumption of housing services (H) and ozone as the white home buyer. Paying this extra amount would presumably force the home buyer to consume less of other goods, leading him or her to choose to optimally end up with more ozone than the white home buyer (conditional upon the increase in H being the same).

To better understand the reason minorities took on more pollution, consider a function in which total housing expenditure is a function of two independent variables: ozone pollution and housing services:

$$E = f(Ozone, H). \tag{5.5}$$

The total differential dE measures the change in total housing expenditure brought on by a move with small changes in ozone pollution ($dOzone$) and housing (dH):

$$dP = f_{Ozone} dOzone + f_H dH, \tag{5.6}$$

where f_{Ozone} and f_H are the partial derivatives of P with respect to ozone pollution and housing services. Holding expenditure constant ($dE = 0$), we can see how ozone and housing services are traded (i.e., the slope of an iso-expenditure function):

$$\frac{dOzone}{dH} = -\frac{f_H}{f_{Ozone}}.$$
(5.7)

Since houses with more services are more expensive $\left(f_H > 0\right)$ and houses with more ozone are cheaper $\left(f_{Ozone} < 0\right)$, the slope is positive; a homeowner can get more housing services without spending additional money by taking on more pollution.

For the empirical analysis of the trade-offs made by different demographic groups, we switch from a simple correlation analysis to an estimator whereby the total expenditure of individual i for house j (i.e., sales price) is determined by ozone pollution and housing services and unobserved factors (v_{ij}):

$$P_{ij} = Ozone_{ij} + f(H_{ij}) + v_{ij}.$$
(5.8)

Other unobserved factors (v_{ij}) can be broken into two groups: a fixed component that is specific to the buyer (a_i) and an idiosyncratic error (u_{ij}):

$$v_{ij} = a_i + u_{ij}.$$
(5.9)

One of the strengths of our repeat-purchase sample is that we observe the same buyer who bought two homes. We have information (e.g., sales prices, ozone, $f[H]$) on the first home purchase, the first home's subsequent sale, and the second home purchase. As a result, we can control for an unobserved buyer fixed effect (a_i) by estimating a differenced equation. In this approach, we subtract the variables associated with the buyer's new house and the old house had the buyer decided to stay. We take the values of the variables based on the year of the second purchase (t') and estimate the following differenced equation using OLS:

$$P_{ij_{new}} - P_{ij_{old}} = \beta_1 \left(Ozone_{ij_{new}} - Ozone_{ij_{old}}\right) + \beta_2 \left(f(H_{ij_{new}}) - f(H_{ij_{old}})\right) + \left(u_{ij_{new}} - u_{ij_{old}}\right).$$
(5.10)

The ratio of the coefficients on housing services and ozone (β_2/β_1) reveals the constraint faced by the individual (i.e., the slope of the iso-expenditure function). We rerun this procedure for both whites and minorities in an effort to determine whether the constraints faced by these two groups are different. Results of this procedure are described in Table 5.2.

Table 5.2 Regression results for ozone and housing service trade-offs in the marketplace

Variable		White	Black/Hispanic	Asian
β_2	Change in housing services (dH)	327,351	370,838	448,926
β_1	Change in ozone (dOzone)	−3,672,208	−2,543,142	−5,126,330
Ratio: $-\left(\dfrac{\beta_2}{\beta_1}\right)$		0.09	0.15	0.09
R^2		0.075	0.109	0.117
Observations		5,793	1,224	1,977

Note: β_1 and β_2 were statistically different from 0 at the 0.01 level for each demographic group.

The results of these regressions indeed indicate that white and black and Hispanic home buyers do face different trade-offs between housing services and pollution in the housing market. In contrast, whites and Asians appear to face similar trade-offs. For some reason (e.g., more predominantly white and Asian neighborhoods offering higher housing service alternatives), whites and Asians are able to increase housing consumption without having to take on as much additional ozone. Holding the increase in ozone concentration constant across the two racial groups, the black/Hispanic home buyer has to increase expenditure by more to get the same increase in housing services (Figure 5.4; point X to point Y). This suggests that blacks and Hispanics may be incurring more ozone exposure because they are unwilling to pay to avoid it, given the higher price they face. For the same increase in expenditure, the minority home buyer has to take on more additional ozone than his or her white counterpart, for an identical increase in housing services (point Z versus point Y). These higher opportunity costs may be a consequence of discrimination in the housing market. Alternatively, they may indicate a priority for other locational amenities omitted from the model.

Conclusion

We offer a new assessment of environmental justice questions in the San Francisco Bay Area using a unique data set that combines individual real estate transactions with home buyer information. A correlation analysis shows that homeowners who buy more housing services also take on more ozone pollution as a result of the move. In addition, the positive relationship between housing services and ozone exposure is statistically stronger for low-income black and Hispanic homeowners than it is for low-income white homeowners, suggesting that (at least at low income levels) race may force some individuals into a worse

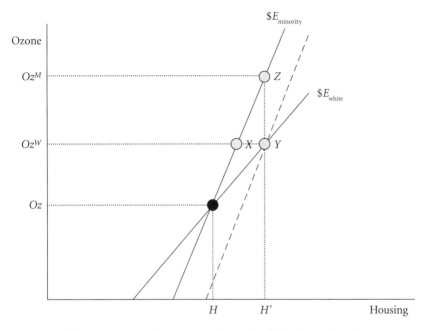

Figure 5.4 Different ozone and housing service trade-offs in the marketplace

trade-off. These findings are consistent with sorting-induced exposure stories and can help explain observed correlation patterns between race and pollution. That said, they cannot determine whether minorities are simply less willing to give up other consumption to get additional housing services, choosing rather to pay this premium in the form of increased ozone consumption. Alternatively, they may face different trade-offs in the marketplace. We go on to test this hypothesis by running a series of regressions that measure the rate at which each group (whites and minorities) are able to trade housing services for ozone pollution, holding total housing expenditure fixed. These results suggest that blacks and Hispanics do face a very different (and disadvantageous) trade-off compared with whites. This speaks to the mechanism underlying observed patterns of environmental injustice—minorities find it optimal to take on more pollution in exchange for more housing services because the cost of getting those services without doing so is greater than for whites.

Although our analysis finds that wealth taken from appreciating housing stocks can increase the ability of lower-income Asian homeowners to avoid the conventional sorting story (e.g., pay for more housing services with money versus taking on more pollution), these gains do not seem to help other low-income groups. This finding has two implications. First, certain house-holds living in a declining neighborhood that want to improve their housing situation could be at a significant disadvantage; they own a house that will not appreciate by as much as a house in an improving neighborhood. Second, policies designed to increase homeowner housing wealth and expand access to mortgages may not enhance all homeowners' ability to move to cleaner neigh-borhoods in the same way. Policy makers could consider this as they weigh the many other benefits and costs of these policies.

Notes

1. The authors' use of NATA shows how the environmental justice literature has evolved from simple distance calculations to actual estimates of risks (Viscusi and Hamilton 1998; Hamilton 1999; Hamilton and Viscusi 1999).

2. See Figures A.5.1 to A.5.4 in the online appendix at http://www.sup.org/envi ronmentaljustice.

3. The sample statistics (e.g., mean and standard deviation) for over half a million houses (grouped by number of sales) are reported in Tables A.5.1 to A.5.3 in the online appendix at http://www.sup.org/environmentaljustice.

4. Although there are cases in which the same buyer appears to make more than two home purchases, people who bought only two houses were selected because they may be more representative of a "typical" buyer. In contrast, buyers who made three or more purchases in the sample period may have faced unusual and unobserved cir-cumstances that led to more frequent moves.

5. As part of the Bay Area Air Quality Management District's 50th anniversary celebration, the district published a history of significant events. Additional details can be found at http://www.baaqmd.gov.

References

Arora, Seema, and Timothy N. Cason. 1999. "Do Community Characteristics Influence Environmental Outcomes? Evidence from the Toxics Release Inventory." *Southern Economic Journal* 65 (4): 691–716.

Asch, Peter, and Joseph J. Seneca. 1978. "Some Evidence on the Distribution of Air Qual-ity." *Land Economics* 54 (3): 278–97.

Banzhaf, H. Spencer, and Randall P. Walsh. 2008. "Do People Vote with Their Feet? An Empirical Test of Tiebout's Mechanism." *American Economic Review* 98 (3): 843–63.

Bayer, Patrick, Robert MacMillan, Alvin Murphy, and Christopher Timmins. 2011. "A Dynamic Model of Demand for Houses and Neighborhoods." NBER Working Paper

17250, National Bureau of Economic Research, Cambridge, MA. http://ideas.repec
.org/p/nbr/nberwo/17250.html.

Been, Vicki, with Francis Gupta. 1997. "Coming to the Nuisance or Going to the Barrios? A Longitudinal Analysis of Environmental Justice Claims." *Ecology Law Quarterly* 24 (1): 1–56.

Bishop, Kelly, and Christopher Timmins. 2011. "Hedonic Prices and Implicit Markets:
Estimating Marginal Willingness to Pay for Differentiated Products without Instrumental Variables." NBER Working Paper 17611, National Bureau of Economic Research, Cambridge, MA. http://www.nber.org/papers/w17611.

Brooks, Nancy, and Rajiv Sethi. 1997. "The Distribution of Pollution: Community
Characteristics and Exposure to Air Toxics." *Journal of Environmental Economics and
Management* 32 (2): 233–50.

Bullard, Robert D. 2000. *Dumping in Dixie: Race, Class, and Environmental Quality*, 3rd
ed. Boulder, CO: Westview Press.

California Environmental Protection Agency, California Air Resources Board (CARB).
2001. "Ozone Transport: 2001 Review." http://www.arb.ca.gov/aqd/transport/as
sessments/assessments.htm.

———. 2007. "The California Almanac of Emissions and Air Quality: 2008 Edition."
http://www.arb.ca.gov/aqd/almanac/almanac08/almanac08.htm.

———. 2008. California air quality data available on DVD-ROM. http://www.arb
.ca.gov/aqd/aqdcd/aqdcddld.htm.

Fisher, Joshua B., Maggi Kelly, and Jeff Romm. 2006. "Scales of Environmental Justice:
Combining GIS and Spatial Analysis for Air Toxics in West Oakland, California."
Health and Place 12 (4): 701–14.

Freeman, A. Myrick. 1972. "Distribution of Environmental Quality." In *Environmental
Quality Analysis*, edited by A. Kneese and B. Bower, 243–80. Baltimore: Johns Hop-
kins University Press.

Hamilton, James T. 1995. "Testing for Environmental Racism: Prejudice, Profits, Political Power?" *Journal of Policy Analysis and Management* 14 (1): 107–32.

———. 1999. "*Exercising Property Rights to Pollute: Do Cancer Risks and Politics Affect
Plant Emission Reductions?*" *Journal of Risk and Uncertainty* 18 (2): 105–24.

Hamilton, James T., and W. Kip Viscusi. 1999. *Calculating Risks? The Spatial and Political
Dimensions of Hazardous Waste Policy*. Cambridge, MA: MIT Press.

Houston, Douglas, Jun Wu, Paul Ong, and Arthur Winer. 2004. "Structural Disparities
of Urban Traffic in Southern California: Implications for Vehicle-Related Air Pollution Exposure in Minority and High-Poverty Neighborhoods." *Journal of Urban Affairs* 26 (5): 565–92.

Institute of Medicine. 1999. *Toward Environmental Justice Research, Education, and
Health Policy Needs*. Washington, DC: National Academy Press.

Kahn, Matthew E. 2000. "Smog Reduction's Impact on California County Growth." *Journal of Regional Science* 40 (3): 565–82.

Kim, Janice, Svetlana Smorodinsky, Michael Lipsett, Brett C. Singer, Alfred T. Hodgson, and Bart Ostro. 2004. "Traffic-Related Air Pollution near Busy Roads: The East Bay Children's Respiratory Health Study." *American Journal of Respiratory and Critical Care Medicine* 170 (5): 520–26.

Morello-Frosch, Rachel, Manuel Pastor, Carlos Porras, and James Sadd. 2002. "Environmental Justice and Regional Inequality in Southern California: Implications for Future Research." *Environmental Health Perspectives* 110 (Suppl. 2): 149–54.

Oakes, John Michael, Douglas L. Anderton, and Andy B. Anderson. 1996. "A Longitudinal Analysis of Environmental Equity in Communities with Hazardous Waste Facilities." *Social Science Research* 25 (2): 125–48.

Pastor, Manuel, Jim Sadd, and John Hipp. 2001. "Which Came First? Toxic Facilities, Minority Move-In, and Environmental Justice." *Journal of Urban Affairs* 23 (1): 1–21.

Pastor, Manuel, James Sadd, and Rachel Morello-Frosch. 2007. "Still Toxic after All These Years: Air Quality and Environmental Justice in the San Francisco Bay Area." Center for Justice, Tolerance, and Community, University of California, Santa Cruz. http://cjtc.ucsc.edu/docs/bay_final.pdf.

Ruggles, Steven, J. Trent Alexander, Katie Genadek, Ronald Goeken, Matthew B. Schroeder, and Matthew Sobek. 2010. Integrated Public Use Microdata Series: Version 5.0 [machine-readable database], University of Minnesota, Minneapolis.

Sieg, Holger, V. Kerry Smith, H. Spencer Banzhaf, and Randall P. Walsh. 2004. "Estimating General Equilibrium Benefits of Large Changes in Spatially Delineated Public Goods." *International Economic Review* 45 (4): 1047–77.

United Church of Christ. 1987. *Toxic Wastes and Race in the United States: A National Report on the Racial and Socio-Economic Characteristics of Communities with Hazardous Waste Sites.* New York: Public Data Access.

US Bureau of the Census. 2004. *Geographic Mobility: 2002 to 2003. P20-549.* http://www.census.gov/prod/2003pubs/m01as-1.pdf.

US General Accounting Office (GAO). 1983. *Siting of Hazardous Waste Landfills and Their Correlation with Racial and Economic Status of Surrounding Communities.* Washington, DC: GAO.

———. 1995. *Hazardous and Nonhazardous Waste Demographics of People Living near Waste Facilities: Report to Congressional Requesters.* Washington, DC: Government Printing Office.

Viscusi, W. Kip, and James T. Hamilton. 1999. "*Are Risk Regulators Rational? Evidence from Hazardous Waste Cleanup Decisions.*" *American Economic Review* 89 (4): 1010–27.

Wernette, D. R., and L. A. Nieves. 1992. "Breathing Polluted Air." *EPA Journal* 18 (March/April): 16–17.

6 Superfund Taint and Neighborhood Change

Ethnicity, Age Distributions, and Household Structure

Trudy Ann Cameron, Graham D. Crawford, and Ian T. McConnaha

Introduction

Are there systematic *time-varying* spatial patterns in the sociodemographic characteristics of populations in the vicinity of major environmental hazards? We investigate the existence of such patterns around seven different Superfund sites over the 31-year period spanned by census years 1970, 1980, 1990, and 2000. Superfund sites, of course, are environmental problem areas that the US Environmental Protection Agency (EPA) has deemed sufficiently hazardous to warrant major remedial actions. The EPA uses Hazard Ranking System (HRS) scores as a rough quantitative measure of the risk posed by each site. One would expect that populations surrounding a site with either a high HRS score or plenty of media exposure would be most likely to respond systematically over time in expected ways to these risks, and there is some evidence that they do. However, populations around sites with lower HRS scores also respond systematically over time but sometimes less predictably. Our study is explicitly descriptive: We do not construct or intend a causal model in this chapter. Instead, it is our goal to establish some of the stylized facts that should probably be accommodated by future studies of environmental justice and land markets.

Advocates for environmental justice (EJ) have long been concerned that snapshots of the demographics surrounding environmental hazards often reveal a disproportionate share of low-income and minority groups living in these areas. However, the degree to which we should be concerned about this fact depends on the dynamic process that leads to this result. If some types of households are adequately compensated (subjectively, in the form of cheaper housing) for the disutility they experience by living closer to the site, they may be inclined to move closer to the site than would otherwise be optimal. This has sometimes been called "coming to the nuisance," a phenomenon also noted by Banzhaf and McCormick in Chapter 2.[1] A number of researchers have explained that we need to understand how neighborhoods change over time, both close to environmental disamenities and elsewhere, in order to understand the dynamics of neighborhood adaptation to the presence of environmental hazards.[2]

We address this need with an empirical model that reveals how an array of sociodemographic variables shifts, across time, as a function of distance from Superfund sites. Households in the United States relocate frequently for a variety of reasons. The overall median time spent in a particular dwelling is only about 4.7 years (Schachter and Kuenzi 2002); as noted by Depro and Timmins (see Chapter 5), about 14 percent of the US population moves to a new residence each year. We hypothesize that households that receive relatively less disutility from proximity to an environmental disamenity (or a relatively greater utility from the depressed housing prices, if applicable) will tend to locate closer to the site. Those with relatively more disutility from the environmental hazard will locate farther away. For instance, lower-income groups may receive relatively greater incremental utility from depressed housing prices. Or, if households fear the greater risk of environmental contaminants to children, we might expect that households with young children might be more responsive to neighborhood environmental threats than other households when making the types of periodic relocation decisions that most households face.

Two distinct scenarios regarding group movement are possible. If the total population close to the site is constant or increasing, and the relative concentration of a particular group is increasing near the site over time, this is consistent with that particular group's "coming to the nuisance." If the total population is decreasing near the site and the relative concentration of a group near the site is increasing, it is possible that other groups are instead leaving the area and the group in question is simply "failing to flee the nuisance." Either of these scenarios can produce the result that relative concentrations of some groups increase near the site. We are interested solely in changes in *relative* concentrations, nearby and farther away, of various sociodemographic variables over time. We hypothesize that these population shifts and their net effects on neighborhood composition are the result of the various groups' heterogeneous perceived risks and the associated net utility changes prompted by revelation of the presence of an environmental hazard.

Studies regarding risk from environmental hazards typically focus on either actual risk or perceived risk. Some studies argue that *actual* risks, reported in a quantitative manner, should be used in assessing changes in housing prices around an environmental disamenity. However, there is a general lack of direct exposure measurement, which greatly complicates the use of actual risks (see the review by Vrijheid [2000] concerning the health effects of residence near hazardous waste landfill sites). In this chapter, we focus on the observed reactions of the public to an environmental hazard rather than on scientific risk assessments. It is likely that local housing demands are generated by subjective views of a variety of factors, including perceived risk levels influenced by media and community attention, rather than simply a quantitative measurement of the actual risk level.[3]

Earlier empirical studies related to EJ, even those focusing on the possibility of "coming to the nuisance," have tended to discriminate only between neighborhoods that are "near" or "far" from an environmental disamenity. Generally, the data used in such studies are census tract–level data. When using such data, the choice of an appropriate comparison group of census tracts is a key consideration in attempting to model the effects of environmental disamenities on neighborhood composition over time. The best census tracts to use as controls will be other tracts, in the same locality, at greater distances from the same disamenity. This strategy allows the researcher to control implicitly for a host of other unobserved local conditions that could affect the sociodemographic mix near a site. Using randomly drawn census tracts from around the country, as in a number of existing studies, does not adequately control for these unobserved local conditions.[4]

The greatest benefit from using other local census tracts as controls, however, is that the continuously measured *distance* of a tract from the site of the environmental disamenity is a particularly valuable variable to use in explaining changes in local spatial patterns for sociodemographic characteristics over time. Rather than asking whether there are significant differences in differences (across time, between "near" and "far" census tracts), we can examine continuous local distance profiles for selected sociodemographic characteristics.

While the EJ literature does not seem to have taken advantage of the opportunity to consider continuous distance profiles, this modeling strategy has been used routinely in the hedonic property value literature, which relates property values to locational attributes such as nearby pollution.[5] However, the hedonic literature generally fails to consider adequately the neighborhood dynamics that may accompany variations in the level of a point-source environmental disamenity when attempting to discern the effect on housing prices of changes, over time, in the level of that disamenity. When sociodemographic variables are considered, they have generally been treated as exogenous.[6] The possibility of joint determination of housing prices and neighborhood sociodemographics appears to be emphasized in just a couple of cases.[7]

One purpose of this chapter is to question the maintained hypothesis in the hedonic property value literature that sociodemographic characteristics are merely exogenous control variables to be taken into account when modeling housing prices as a function of environmental characteristics. However, our model is not itself a hedonic model but rather a descriptive model that strongly suggests that sociodemographic characteristics are also endogenously determined, since these variables, too, appear to depend on perceived environmental quality.

First, we describe the data available for our analysis, both sociodemographic and spatial, and outline the empirical specifications we will use to examine changes in distance profiles for group proportions over time. Then we review our results and their interpretation, focusing on just the key results concerning changes in distance profiles over time, for the more than 150 regression models involved. Detailed numeric parameter estimates and other relevant comments on each model are offered in the online appendix.[8] Finally, we outline some directions for future research and present some concluding remarks.

Data

For our analysis, we require instances of significant environmental contamination that should be readily apparent to the population in a particular local area. We have selected a set of seven Superfund sites on the presumption that the inclusion of a site on the National Priorities List (NPL) is likely to be better recognized in the local community than less significant sites and that knowledge of a site's existence should be available to realtors and property managers as well as to a larger share of homeowners, home buyers, and renters.

We limit our analysis to Superfund sites that were listed in the interval between the census years of 1980 and 1990 and had not been cleaned up completely as of 2000.[9] The analyses we report are limited to a 12-kilometer radius around each Superfund site, which should be more than sufficient to exhaust any proximity effects.[10] One selection criterion for our seven sites is their presence in highly urbanized areas so that the surrounding census tracts are relatively small in area, ensuring a large number of tracts within the 12-kilometer radius of each site. Thus, we assume that the areas surrounding each of the sites were more or less fully "built out" in 1970. Our seven sites are also distinguished by the relative absence of certain potentially confounding geographical features, such as major rivers or lakes and other nearby Superfund sites. Table 6.1 provides a brief description of each site, its important dates, site details, specific contaminants, site location, and site status and risks.

We use geographic information system (GIS) software to locate each Superfund site and the centroid of each census tract for which any portion of the tract lies within our predefined distance from the local Superfund site. We also employ Esri's available shapefiles to identify a number of other major geographic features that may be perceived as either amenities or disamenities: we use point data for the nearest major or minor central business district(s) and retail centers (malls), lines for major roads and railroad tracks, and polygons for airports and transit terminals. We use Esri's ArcMap software to compute the distance, in kilometers, from each census tract centroid to the nearest entity in a particular class.[11] Three of our sites are landfill sites or involve landfills: Old Bethpage Landfill (Oyster Bay, New York), Sayreville Landfill (Sayreville, New Jersey), and Cinnaminson Landfill (Burlington County, New Jersey). Four are predominantly non-landfill sites, being mostly cases of industrial waste leading to contaminated groundwater: Montrose Chemical (Torrance, California), CTS Printex Inc. (Mountain View, California), Chem Central (Wyoming, Michigan), and Havertown PCP (Haverford Township, Pennsylvania).

Detailed summary statistics regarding changes in overall average population density from census to census are presented in Appendix A.6A in the online appendix.[12] These changes may reflect either new construction on empty lots, or changing occupancy rates for existing dwellings or the replacement of single-family units by multifamily structures. Across all tracts in each area, data on the decennial average tract populations reveal continuous increases over the four census years for the 12-kilometer areas around the Sayreville, CTS Printex, Montrose, and Chem Central sites. Areawide population declined continuously for the Havertown site. For the Cinnaminson and Old Bethpage landfill sites, areawide populations fell through 1990 and then increased again in 2000. The areawide averages, however, cannot reveal any specific depopulation in the tracts closest to each Superfund site versus those farther away. Summary

Table 6.1 Site description, public knowledge, and risk

Site name	Public knowledge	Site details	Specific contaminants	Site location	Site status and risk
Old Bethpage Landfill (operating from 1957 to 1986)	Proposed NPL: 10/1/1981 Final NPL: 9/1/1983 HRS score: 58.83 Media exposure:[a] 1970s: 139 1980s: 7,567 1990s: 674 Total words: 8,380 Total articles: 11	65-acre inactive municipal landfill that is part of a sanitary landfill complex; primarily used for disposing incinerator residue, then accepted garbage, trash, solid industrial process wastes, damaged drums.	Groundwater: heavy metals (including iron and manganese), VOCs. Leachate: same heavy metals as above.	Located in Oyster Bay, New York; situated above the Magothy Aquifer, which supplies many public wells; approximately 10,000 residents live within a mile of site.	Initial risk: contamination of drinking water with VOCs. Risk as of 2005: in 1993, site cleanup was considered complete, and the site was deleted from the NPL; potential exposure considered fully controlled.
Sayreville Landfill (operating from 1970 to 1977)	Proposed NPL: 12/1/1982 Final NPL: 9/1/1983 HRS score: 37.05 Media exposure:[a] 1970s: 526 1980s: 8,635 1990s: 150 Total words: 9,311 Total articles: 15	Municipal landfill covering about 30 acres; received municipal and light industrial waste; allegedly received hazardous waste during operations and after closure.	Soil/sediment: toluene, TCE, benzene, arsenic, chloroform. Groundwater: phenol, heavy metals, VOCs, PAHs, cadmium, lead.	Located in Sayreville, New Jersey; along tidal South River; part of site is in a wetland adjacent to South River; nearest resident is 0.5 mile away; municipal wells are in the vicinity.	Initial risk (early 1980s): contaminated groundwater migration into the South River, in addition to potential hazards for those in direct contact with site. Risk as of 2005: remedial activities began in 1998 and were completed in the same year; human exposure to risk considered under control.
Montrose Chemical (operating from 1947 to 1982)	Proposed NPL: 10/15/1984 Final NPL: 10/4/1989 HRS score: 32.10 Media exposure:[a] 1970s: 0 1980s: 1,353 1990s: 17,090 Total words: 18,443 Total articles: 31	13-acre plant property, manufactured technical-grade pesticide (DDT).	Soil: DDT, chlorobenzene, BHC. Groundwater: DDT, chlorobenzene.	Located in city of Torrance, California; within the Harbor Gateway between Los Angeles proper and the Los Angeles Harbor.	Initial risk: Montrose Chemical manufactured DDT until 1982. Threat of DDT exposure from contamination in soil, surface water, and sediment. More than 3,000 people live within 0.25 mile of the site. Risk as of 2005: some areas having DDT-contaminated sediments have been removed or capped; site studies are ongoing; final cleanup activities being planned; the area is considered at risk.

Site	NPL / HRS / Media exposure	Description	Contaminants	Location	Risk
Cinnaminson Landfill (operating from 1950s to 1980)	Proposed NPL: 10/1/1984 Final NPL: 6/1/1986 HRS score: 37.93 Media exposure:[a] 1970s: 0 1980s: 85 1990s: 69 Total words: 154 Total articles: 2	400-acre site consisting of landfill, residential, light to heavy industrial properties; municipal, institutional, and industrial wastes, including hazardous substances, were deposited.	Groundwater: arsenic and VOCs, including chloroform, benzene, tetrachloroethylene, and vinyl chloride.	Located in Cinnaminson and Delran townships of Burlington County, New Jersey; the Delaware River is located approximately 5,000 feet to the northwest.	Initial risk: potential ingestion of arsenic and VOCs through groundwater. Risk as of 2005: groundwater pumping began in 2000 and is still under way; no remedial action was undertaken in the time frame of this study.
CTS Printex Inc. (operating from 1966 to 1985)	Proposed NPL: 6/24/1988 Final NPL: 2/21/1990 HRS score: 33.62 Media exposure:[a] 1970s: 0 1980s: 0 1990s: 117 Total words: 117 Total articles: 1	5.5-acre site, manufactured printed circuit boards.	Soil: copper, lead. Groundwater: VOCs, heavy metals.	Located in city of Mountain View, California; 2.5 miles south of San Francisco Bay.	Initial risk: more than 188,000 people live within 3 miles of the site and use potentially contaminated groundwater as a source of drinking water; potential contamination of bay. Risk as of 2005: cleanup considered complete in 1992, although groundwater treatment is ongoing; EPA is analyzing site for health risks, and has yet to reach a conclusion.
Chem Central (operating since 1957)	Proposed NPL: 12/30/1982 Final NPL: 9/8/1983 HRS score: 38.20 Media exposure:[a] 1970s: 0 1980s: 0 1990s: 0 Total words: 0 Total articles: 0	2-acre facility, distributed industrial chemicals.	Soil: phthalates, VOCs, PCBs. Groundwater: VOCs and semi-VOCs.	Located in city of Wyoming, Michigan; 0.5 mile south of Plaster Creek; 0.10 mile from the nearest residence.	Initial risk: groundwater contamination spilling into Plaster Creek, causing health risk to the approximately 15,000 residents located within 1 mile of the site. Risk as of 2005: five-year review completed in 1999 found that remedy is protective of human health and environment.

(continued)

Table 6.1 (*Continued*)

Site name	Public knowledge	Site details	Specific contaminants	Site location	Site status and risk
Havertown PCP (operating from 1947 to 1981)	*Proposed NPL:* 12/30/1982 *Final NPL:* 9/8/1983 *HRS score:* 38.34 *Media exposure:*[a] 1970s: 0 1980s: 0 1990s: 0 *Total words:* 0 *Total articles:* 0	Wood treatment facility; reportedly disposed primarily oil contaminated with PCP into a well leading to the groundwater under the plant; spilled liquid wastes on surface.	*Soil/groundwater/surface water:* PCP, arsenic, dioxins, VOCs, petroleum hydrocarbons.	Located near Haverford Township in Delaware County, Pennsylvania; situated along Naylor's Run, a small stream that flows through a residential area and eventually into the Delaware River.	*Initial risk:* groundwater PCP contaminants leaching into Naylor's Run and subsequently into the Delaware River. *Risk as of 2005:* soils are now clean and safe; groundwater treatment plant constructed; treatment ongoing.

Note: BHC, benzene hexachloride; DDT, dichlorodiphenyltrichloroethane; PAH, polycyclic aromatic hydrocarbon; PCB, polychlorinated biphenyl; PCP, pentachlorophenol; TCE, trichloroethylene; VOC, volatile organic compound.

[a]Number of words in articles about the site in question in major national and regional newspapers during each decade.

statistics for all of the distance variables used in this study are given in Appendix A.6A, Table 2, in the online appendix.[13]

Relatively high population densities within a few miles of our Superfund sites are crucial to our analysis, since we need many nearby observations to be able to identify distance profiles within a 12-kilometer radius. Spatially aggregated census data offer the only broad-based and reliable information on local-scale changes in demographics available (outside a Census Research Data Center). We use a data set made available by GeoLytics, called the CensusCD Neighborhood Change Database (NCDB). In the NCDB, at the time this research was undertaken, "short form" census data at the level of census tracts had been linked across the last four decennial censuses.

An important feature of the NCDB is that it conforms tract boundaries across time; thus, we have consistent spatial boundaries for our analysis.[14] We use the distance from the centroid of each year 2000 census tract to the Superfund site as a proxy for perceived risk from Superfund contaminants. The expected effect of this perceived risk will depend on the nature of the contamination, so we do not anticipate that the effect of distance on the demographic mix of neighborhoods (census tracts) will be the same across all types of Superfund sites. Thus, we will model the dynamics of neighborhood change separately for each locality.

Empirical Models

We wish to examine what happens, over time, to the distance profile for the proportion of each census tract's population in each of a number of categories. We have data for local census tracts $I = 1, \ldots, N$ and for census years 1970 through 2000, denoted by $t = 0, 1, 2, 3$. The impact of differences in proximity to a Superfund site on the characteristics of a census tract should diminish with distance from the Superfund site. Thus, we model the proportion of the population in a particular category, $\%X_{it}$, as a function of the *natural logarithm* of distance from the site, $\ln(d_{it})$. The baseline distance profile is

$$\%X_{it} = \beta_0 + \beta_1 \ln(d_{it}) + \varepsilon_{it}. \tag{6.1}$$

The magnitude of the β_1 coefficient determines how quickly or slowly the profile flattens out.

If we were simply looking for current-period patterns around our Superfund sites in the percentages of census tract populations in particular sociodemographic groups (such as the percentage of African Americans or Hispanics, or the percentage of children or seniors), we would look for nonzero estimates of the simple scalar parameter β_1. However, we wish to know how these spatial patterns *change* over time in response to *changes* in the (perceived) level of an environmental risk. This question requires spatial data collected over time as perceived risks change.

We have noted that each of our Superfund sites was listed on the NPL during the 1980–1990 interval. If one imagines that this interval corresponds to the first publicly available information about the hazard associated with the site, one would expect that there should be little movement of a particular group relative to the site prior to its listing. However, local area residents may have been well aware of the hazards prior to listing, and environmental advocacy groups in each area may have publicized the need to have the site listed. We use the number of words in major newspapers devoted to each site in a given decade as a proxy for public information (see column 2 of Table 6.1). While it would have been beneficial to measure coverage by local news media, this information is, unfortunately, not available to us. The Old Bethpage Landfill had the highest HRS score, indicating especially high toxicity, and Old Bethpage Landfill, Sayreville Landfill, and Montrose Chemical sites had significantly more major media exposure than the other sites. Thus, observed mobility patterns around these three sites are more likely to be responses to perceived risks than patterns around sites with less media exposure.

None of the Superfund sites in our sample had been delisted by the year 2000. Officially, therefore, all of these sites were technically still contaminated at the time of the 2000 census. However, cleanup will have been proceeding to different degrees at each site, and people may have begun making longer-term housing decisions in anticipation of delisting at some time in the near future. Thus, we need to allow for bidirectional, not just unidirectional, shifts in our distance profiles over time.

The model in (6.1) implies that the distance profile is constant across all four decades in our sample. We wish to explore the possibility that the coefficient β_1 is not a simple constant but rather a nonlinear function of time t (where $t = 0$, 1, 2, and 3) that has the flexibility to both increase and then decrease (or vice versa) over the census years in our study. By allowing the intercepts to differ as well, via the year indicators D_{80t}, D_{90t}, and D_{00t}, we can generalize the slope parameter to a quadratic function of t:

$$\%X_{it} = \beta_{00} + \beta_{01}D_{80t} + \beta_{02}D_{90t} + \beta_{03}D_{00t} + \left[\beta_{10} + \beta_{11}t + \beta_{12}t^2\right]\ln(d_i) + \varepsilon_{it}. \qquad (6.2)$$

Given our definition of t, the coefficient β_{10} dictates the shape of the distance profile in 1970, since $t = t^2 = 0$ for that year. The key feature of the distance profile, for our research questions, may be summarized by the derivative of Equation (6.2) with respect to the log of the distance: $\beta_{10} + \beta_{10}t + \beta_{12}t$.

A special case of the model in Equation (6.2) allows the log-distance coefficient to change only monotonically over time, so that the model is simply

$$\%X_{it} = \beta_{00} + \beta_{01}D_{80t} + \beta_{02}D_{90t} + \beta_{03}D_{00t} + \left[\beta_{10} + \beta_{11}t\right]\ln\left(d_i\right) + \varepsilon_{it}. \qquad (6.3)$$

This is the minimal model wherein we can test statistically for any pattern of "coming to the nuisance." If $\beta_{11} > 0$, the distance profile is becoming more positively sloped over time (i.e., the profile that describes the proportion of the population in this category, as a function of distance from the site, is rotating *counterclockwise*. This change in slope means that our quantity of interest, the *relative* concentration of X_i nearer the site as opposed to farther away, is falling). If $\beta_{11} < 0$, the distance profile is becoming less positively sloped over time (i.e., the profile is rotating *clockwise* so that the relative concentration of X_i near the site is increasing). If this parameter is 0, the distance profile is unaffected by the passage of time. While we cannot track the movement of individuals, these changes in relative concentration suggest the overall *net* effect of geographic mobility by different sociodemographic groups in this locality.

In the more general quadratic-parameter specification in Equation (6.2), the sign of β_{12} determines whether the distance profile suggests a relative concentration near the site that is first falling and then rising over time or vice versa. There is likely to be considerable heterogeneity across our seven Superfund sites in terms of what probably happened to the subjective risks posed by the sites over time. In some cases, the hazards of the site were well known prior to its listing, and the process of listing may have increased optimism about the long-term prospects of healthier conditions near the site. In other cases, the hazards represented by the site may have been less well known prior to listing, and the process of listing the site may have created public information that sparked considerable fear about the site's hazards.

Our dependent variables are proportions. They are census tract averages of $(0, 1)$ variables that capture whether each individual (or household) in the population has a certain characteristic, X_i. When using an average as a dependent variable, it is important to reflect the size of the sample used to compute that average. The variance of an average depends inversely on the size of the sample used to compute it. We therefore weight the data for each census tract by the number of individuals (or households) in the census tract, as appropriate.[15] The number of tracts within a 12-kilometer radius varies between 89 for Chem Central and 271 for Montrose Chemical.

If data on proportions are regressed linearly on a range of explanatory variables, it is possible that some of the fitted proportions may fall outside the $(0, 1)$ range. To preclude this outcome, researchers often use a log-odds transformation of the dependent variable: $\log\left(\%X_i / [1 - \%X_i]\right)$. In our case, however, the observed proportions in a handful of cases are either 0 or 1. Given the extreme minority of cases where this is a concern, we adjust the data by first converting each proportion according to $\%X_i^* = 0.9998\,(\%X_i) + 0.0001$.[16]

The information for each of our seven Superfund localities constitutes panel data with four time-series observations per census tract. Models with fixed or random effects are often appropriate when panel data are available, since these models are so valuable for controlling for unobserved sources of heterogeneity across groups (where the groups, in this application, are census tracts). However, models with tract fixed effects cannot be used to estimate the effects of variables that are constant over time within each cross-sectional group. The key variable—distance of the census tract from the Superfund site—is such a variable. Dummy variables for each census tract (fixed effects) are therefore inappropriate in this model.

Nevertheless, there are still a number of stochastic considerations relevant to cross-sectional/time-series data. The number of time-series observations for each tract is very small, and the number of tracts is large relative to the overall number of observations. Thus, we are limited to specifications that employ timewise fixed effects (dummy variables for each census year), heteroskedasticity across census tracts, and a common AR(1) error process shared by all census tracts. This appears to be the greatest level of generality for the error structure permitted by the quantities of data we have available.[17] Note that besides accommodating the simple difference over time in slopes with respect to distance, our timewise fixed effects (i.e., the indicator variables D_{80t}, D_{90t}, and D_{00t}) implicitly control for any type of areawide differences across census years, including differences in the levels of average housing prices and average incomes.

We generalize the basic quadratic model with timewise heterogeneity in Equation (6.2) to include the logs of the distances to a number of other geographic features that may represent local amenities or disamenities:

- Primary regional central business district
- Secondary regional central business district, if applicable
- Nearest retail center
- Nearest airport, if applicable
- Nearest railroad
- Nearest major road
- Nearest transit terminal

We denote these variables generically as $\ln(d_{ki})$. We also allow for monotonic changes over time in the effects of proximity to these other features by including the interaction terms $t\ln(d_{ki})$, resulting in a set of up to 14 additional coefficients in our models (γ_{k0}, γ_{k1}, $k = 1, \ldots, 7$), depending on which subset of these seven distance variables is relevant for a particular locality.

Finally, Cameron (2006) describes how failure to recognize directional heterogeneity in distance effects can obscure what might otherwise be statistically significant distance effects. The distance effect may be systematically larger in one direction than in another, say, if the pollutant in question produces an odor that travels farther downwind than upwind. Ignoring direction amounts to collapsing all distance effects into a single direction. The resulting relationship may then exhibit heteroskedasticity and potentially larger standard errors than could be achieved if directional effects were accommodated.

In order that the models used in this chapter are minimally sufficient to allow us to consider directional effects as we assess changes in the distance profiles of various sociodemographic characteristics over time, we restrict the directional effects to be constant over time. Let θ_i be the direction, in radians, from the Superfund site to the centroid of census tract i. With timewise fixed effects, controls for other time-varying distance effects, and directional heterogeneity, the model in Equation (6.2) can be generalized to achieve the specification that produces the empirical results we discuss in the next section:

$$
\begin{aligned}
\log\left[\frac{\%X_{it}^{*}}{1-\%X_{it}^{*}}\right] = {} & \beta_{00} + \beta_{01}D_{80t} + \beta_{02}D_{90t} + \beta_{03}D_{00t} \\
& + \left[\beta_{10} + \beta_{11}t + \beta_{12}t^{2}\right]\ln(d_i) \\
& + \sum_{k=1}^{7}\left[\gamma_{k0}\ln(d_{ki}) + \gamma_{k1}t\ln(d_{ki})\right] \\
& + \left[\gamma_{1}\cos(\theta_i) + \gamma_{2}\sin(\theta_i)\right]\ln(d_i) + \varepsilon_{it}.
\end{aligned}
\tag{6.4}
$$

Results and Interpretation

In this chapter, we focus on just the two key parameters in Equation (6.4)—β_{11} and β_{12}—and their implications for changes over time in the relative concentration of different sociodemographic groups near the Superfund site versus farther away. We distill these core results from a very large number of distinct regressions, which are reported in detail in Appendix A.6C in the online appendix.[18] Specifically, we have multiple categories within three classes of sociodemographic variables to consider (ethnicity, age, and household structure). These are captured by population shares. For ethnicity, we consider "White," "Black," and "Hispanic" population shares. For age, our shares are for "Under 6," "Kids 6–17," "Adults 18–64," and "Seniors (>65)." Household structure will be divided into two categories—those with children present and those without children. In the category with children, we look at shares for "Married & kids," "Male head & kids" (e.g., single dads), and "Female head & kids" (e.g., single moms). Finally, for households without children, we consider the shares for "Married, no kids," "Male head, no kids," "Female head, no kids," and "Nonfamily households" (e.g., roommates). Thus, there are 14 share variables for each of our seven sites, for a total of 98 unique dependent variables. Means and standard deviations in each of these proportions (across census tracts and time, for each site) are given in Appendix A.6A, Table 3, in the online appendix.[19]

It is worth noting that the Montrose site is somewhat anomalous in several respects. Across all time periods, the areawide proportions of blacks and Hispanics are markedly higher for the Montrose site (at 22 and 32 percent, respectively) than for any of the other sites (where between 2 and 13 percent is more common). The areawide proportion of "Female head, no kids" households, across all periods for Montrose, is between two and three times higher (at over 10 percent) than for the other sites. These female heads could be single, divorced, or widowed. The areawide proportion of "Male head, no kids" households for Montrose is about 8 percent, rather than just 1 to 2 percent for other sites, and the areawide proportion of "Male head & kids" is around 11 percent, rather than close to 1 percent. In contrast, the areawide proportion of "Married & kids" households for Montrose is only about 22 percent, rather than the 30 to 40 percent for most other sites, and the areawide proportion of "Married, no kids" households is less than 16 percent, rather than the 23 to 33 percent observed elsewhere. These unusual features of the Montrose site may partially explain some of the estimated effects for this site.

Our three classes of sociodemographic variables do not include income and education, although there will certainly be some correlations between these variables and ethnicity, age, and household structure. It is generally accepted that minority groups, on average, tend to have lower income levels and less education than nonminorities, for example, and that female-headed households with children have, on average, lower incomes than households with children where both parents are present. For this study, however, we have data only for ethnicity, age, and household structure shares.

Recall that if the slope of the distance profile for a particular socioeconomic variable *increases* over time, then the group in question is becoming *relatively less* concentrated nearer the site. We will describe this as "moving out," although we recognize that this is actually just the net effect of several mobility processes: people moving out of the area entirely, people moving into the area from outside our study radius, and people moving locally within our study radius. In contrast, if the slope of a distance profile for a population share *decreases* over time, the group has become *relatively more* concentrated nearer the site. An increasing concentration near a particular site is consistent with members of that group moving closer to the site over time, on net. We will describe this as "coming to the nuisance" (although it could also reflect "failing to flee the nuisance").

Table 6.2 begins by reporting simple changes in population patterns as a function of distance from the site. These are the results for specifications that are identical to Equation (6.4) but with simple tract populations as the dependent variable. We wish to know whether tract populations nearer the Superfund site change over time relative to the populations of more distant tracts. Area-wide population changes over time are reported in Appendix A.6A, Table 2, in the online appendix, but the first set of results in the first panel of Table 6.2 reveal *relative* population changes within the 12-kilometer radius in each case.[20] In this first set of results in Table 6.2, the "/" symbol indicates an increase in relative population, while a "\" symbol indicates a decrease in relative population in the vicinity of the Superfund site as opposed to farther away. For the Old Bethpage Landfill, Chem Central, and Havertown PCP sites, nearby tract populations have declined steadily over time relative to those in more distant tracts. For these sites, therefore, increasing relative concentrations of certain groups over the same time period might be more aptly characterized as "failing to flee the nuisance" instead of "coming to the nuisance." For the Montrose site, however, nearby tract populations have increased steadily over time relative to

Table 6.2 Population and relative concentrations of different groups near Superfund site

Panel 1: Total population; race/ethnicity

Site	State	Population[a] Quad.	Population[a] Linear	White[b] Quad.	White[b] Linear	Black[b] Quad.	Black[b] Linear	Hispanic[b] Quad.	Hispanic[b] Linear
Old Bethpage Landfill	NY	⟋	–	–	⟍	–	⌒*	⟋	⟍
Sayreville Landfill	NJ	–	–	⌒*	(–)	–	⌒*	–	⟍
Montrose Chemical	CA	–	⟍	⌒	–	⟍	⟍	–	⟍
Cinnaminson Landfill	NJ	–	–	⟍	–	⟍	⌒*	⌣	⟋
CTS Printex Inc.	CA	–	–	–	⟍	⌣	⟍	⌣	⟍
Chem Central	MI	–	⟋	⌣	⟋	⌒*	(–)	–	⌒
Havertown PCP	PA	⟋	⟍	–	⟋	–	⟍	⌒	–

Panel 2: Age groups

Site	State	Under 6[b] Quad.	Under 6[b] Linear	Kids 6–17[b] Quad.	Kids 6–17[b] Linear	Adults 18–64[b] Quad.	Adults 18–64[b] Linear	Seniors (>65)[b] Quad.	Seniors (>65)[b] Linear
Old Bethpage Landfill	NY	⌣	–	⌣	–	⌒	⟍	–	⟍
Sayreville Landfill	NJ	–	⟋*	–	–	⌒*	⌒	–	–
Montrose Chemical	CA	⌣	–	⌣	–	⌒	–	⌒	–
Cinnaminson Landfill	NJ	–	–	–	⟍*	–	⟍	⌣	–
CTS Printex Inc.	CA	–	–	⌒*	(–)	⌣	⟍	–	⟍
Chem Central	MI	–	–	⟍*	–	–	–	–	⟋
Havertown PCP	PA	⟋	–	⌣*	⌒	–	⟋	–	⟍

Panel 3: Households with children

Site	State	Married & kids[b]	Male head & kids[b]	Female head & kids[b]
Old Bethpage Landfill	NY	⌣	-	-
Sayreville Landfill	NJ	-	∪	-
Montrose Chemical	CA	╱	-	∪
Cinnaminson Landfill	NJ	-	∪*	-
CTS Printex Inc.	CA	╱	(-)	╲* (-)
Chem Central	MI	-	-	-
Havertown PCP	PA	∪	∪	∪

Panel 4: Households without children

Site	State	Married, no kids[b]	Male head, no kids[b]	Female head, no kids[b]	Nonfamily[b] households
Old Bethpage Landfill	NY	⌢	-	⌢	⌣
Sayreville Landfill	NJ	⌢	-	⌢* (╱)	∪
Montrose Chemical	CA	-	⌢	⌣	⌢
Cinnaminson Landfill	NJ	⌢	╱* (╲*)	⌢	∪
CTS Printex Inc.	CA	∪	╲	-	╱
Chem Central	MI	-	-	-	-
Havertown PCP	PA	⌢	-	-	╲

[a]Key regression results for population trends as a function of distance from the site are summarized in symbolic form. ∪ = quadratic coefficient not statistically significant; - = linear coefficient in linear specification not statistically significant, either. Change in tract population near the Superfund site versus farther away: ╲ = quadratic or linear, declining over the four census years; ╱ = increasing over the four census years.

[b]Symbols show change over time in relative concentration of the indicated sociodemographic group near the site (versus farther away). Positive coefficient on quadratic term in time interacted with distance variable: ╲, ∪, ⌢, ╱ = fitted maximum relative concentration of group near site occurs during pre-1970, 1970s, 1980s, 1990s, or post-2000 period. Negative coefficient on quadratic term in time interacted with distance variable: ╱, ╲, ∪, ⌣, ⌢ = fitted minimum relative concentration of group near site occurs during pre-1970, 1970s, 1980s, 1990s, or post-2000 period. - = quadratic term not significant, whereupon in "Linear" column: ╱, ╲ = when linear term in time interacted with distance is statistically significant and negative or positive, respectively; - = no significant change over time even in linear specification. The asterisk (*) means that the effect is statistically significant only at the 10% level. When this is the case in the quadratic specification, we check the corresponding linear version to determine whether a statistically significant linear effect is present. These additional results are enclosed in parentheses.

more distant tracts. This is therefore another way in which the Montrose site is somewhat anomalous. Any increase in the relative concentration of a particular group near the Montrose site is more likely to represent a net pattern of "coming to the nuisance."

We now turn to consider our 98 basic regression models (14 sociodemographic characteristics for each of seven Superfund sites). To reiterate, the results that we summarize in this section come from regressions that also control for the effects of distances to/from other locational amenities and disamenities and allow these other effects to vary systematically over time. Each regression also controls for timewise fixed effects to accommodate overall shifts in the dependent variable over time that are common to all census tracts in each area (and also to accommodate the changing slopes with respect to the distance variable). The Superfund site distance effects are also allowed to vary systematically with *direction* from the Superfund site in a fashion that is constant across census years, which means, for example, that prevailing winds are assumed not to change over this time period.

For each sociodemographic share variable and for each site, the first model we estimate in each case allows the derivative of the transformed share, with respect to the log of distance to the site, to take the quadratic form $\beta_{10} + \beta_{11}t + \beta_{12}t^2$. If the coefficient β_{12} on the quadratic term in that model is not statistically significantly different from 0, we drop the quadratic time-interaction term by restricting β_{12} to 0 and revert to a simpler specification where the "distance effect" derivative is simply linear: $\beta_{10} + \beta_{11}t$. We refer to this model as the "Linear" model because the distance profile is linear (in time). This model is estimated *only* when β_{12} turns out to be statistically insignificant, and its results supplant the "Quad." (quadratic in time) model in that case. If the coefficient β_{11} turns out *also* to be statistically insignificant, we confirm this result by reporting that outcome explicitly as well.

It is important to be very clear about what we are looking for in our fitted models. We wish to know whether particular groups are becoming *relatively* more concentrated, or *relatively* less concentrated, near a Superfund site over time. In answering this question, we are not concerned with whether the distance profile itself is positively or negatively sloped at any specific point in time. Single time-specific slopes correspond to the "snapshot" sociodemographic patterns, mentioned in the introduction, that EJ advocates find so provocative. What matters for our question is the *change over time* in the slope of the distance profile, since any systematic change in slope corresponds to a change

in the relative concentration of a particular group near the site relative to farther away.[21] The key indicators for the "coming to the nuisance" hypothesis are
the β_{11} and β_{12} coefficients on the implied time-and-distance interaction terms:
$t\ln(d_i)$ and $t^2\ln(d_i)$.

Besides the very first set of results in Table 6.2 for population changes, the
other sets of symbols in the four horizontal panels of Table 6.2 present sum-
maries of the key results from our 98 "Quad." (quadratic in time) regressions,
as well as for the 55 additional "Linear" variants examined when the coefficient
on the squared term of the quadratic-in-time distance effect model is statistically insignificant. We use symbols as a shorthand method to summarize the
different types of statistically significant time patterns in the distance profiles
that we find in our data. If there is no statistically significant effect, we convey
this result using a horizontal line. In the quadratic-in-time models, a longer
horizontal line signifies no statistically significant *quadratic* time effect (i.e., β_{12}
is not significantly different from 0). When this result causes us to revert to a
simpler linear-in-time model, a shorter horizontal line depicts no statistically
significant *linear* time effect (i.e., even β_{11} alone is not significantly different
from 0).

If the quadratic-in-time specification reveals statistically significant quadratic effects, we identify five possible classes of outcomes for each of the two
possible signs on β_{12} according to the time interval wherein the minimum or
maximum of the fitted quadratic-in-time effect lies. The five intervals include
pre-1970, 1970–1980, 1980–1990, 1990–2000, and post-2000. Again, we focus
on the relative concentration of the group in question near the Superfund site
(as opposed to farther away). For example, if the quadratic-in-time term that
shifts the distance profile is *positive* and statistically significant at the 5 percent
level, this implies that the slope of the distance profile, over time, is first decreasing and then increasing. Correspondingly, the relative concentration of
the group in question nearer the Superfund site is first increasing and then
decreasing. We summarize the time pattern in the near-site relative concentrations as one of "＼," "⌐＼," "⌐⌐," "⌐／," or "／" according to whether the implied
maximum of the near-site relative concentration occurs in each of these five
time intervals defined by the four census years.

In a set of intermediately detailed tables of results presented in Appendix
A.6B in the online appendix, we report the key parameter estimates, β_{11} and
β_{12} (along with their standard errors), as well as the directional coefficients, for
each of the population shares that make up our set of dependent variables.[22]

We suppress the detailed results for the other regression parameters for each specification, but note the number of other slope coefficients that are statistically significant at the 5 and 10 percent levels, as well as the extent of the multicollinearity between all of the different distances employed in each model. This statistic is the R^2 value for an auxiliary regression of the variable measuring the distance to the nearest Superfund site on the levels of the other distance variables used in each model, and is labeled "Distance Aux-R^2."[23]

Note that the three most publicized sites were the Old Bethpage Landfill, the Sayreville Landfill, and Montrose Chemical. These sites were proposed for listing in 1981, 1982, and 1984, respectively. There was media exposure even during the 1970s for the first two but not until the 1980s for the third. The Cinnaminson site was proposed for listing in 1984 and publicized only during the 1980s and 1990s. CTS Printex was proposed later, in 1988. Chem Central and Havertown PCP were listed relatively early but had little if any media exposure.

Race/Ethnicity

If "white flight" and minority move-in occur when a neighborhood develops a well-publicized environmental problem, we might expect to see white households moving out and minorities replacing them. If local knowledge of the environmental problems associated with each site sufficiently preceded the NPL listing event, the relative near-site concentration for whites might be expected to decrease over the period of greatest perceived risk (e.g., "\\" if environmental risk was perceived throughout the period spanned by the four census years; "⌐\\," or at least "⌐\\," if risk became apparent only during or after the decade of listing; or "_/" or "_/" if risk was perceived in the prelisting period but the prospect of cleanup made the area more attractive after listing). In contrast, we would expect the relative near-site concentrations for the two nonwhite groups to increase (e.g., "/" or "_/," or at least "_/," if risk became apparent only during or after the decade of listing; or "⌐\\" or "⌐\\" if risk was perceived in the prelisting period but the prospect of cleanup made the area more attractive after listing).

Expectations concerning changes in the relative concentrations of different groups near our seven Superfund sites are driven mostly by the presumption that as an area becomes less desirable because of perceived environmental risks, then those who can best afford to live elsewhere and those who face the fewest housing market constraints (e.g., the least discrimination) will be inclined to move away in order to occupy housing that does not have this accompanying threat. However, the findings of Flynn et al. (1994) suggest that minorities and white females have roughly comparable perceptions of risk, but white males have a systematic tendency to view risks as smaller and much more acceptable than do other people. Finucane et al. (2000) reaffirm the "white male" effect but emphasize that the reasons for this effect may be complex. They find that whites rate risks lower than do nonwhites and that nonwhite females often gave the highest risk ratings. Relevant to the current analysis, they find that white males, compared to the rest of their sample, were less sensitive to potential stigmatization of communities from hazards. All this might suggest that white households whose location decisions are dominated by a male head might be more inclined to remain in the vicinity of an environmental hazard while female-headed households and minority households might be more inclined to move away. "Move back" decisions might be similarly influenced by these different risk perceptions.

In Table 6.2, the second through fourth sets of results in panel 1 show only occasional evidence of the types of local migration patterns for various ethnicities that typically cause concern for EJ researchers. Although it is possible to discern at least some evidence of the EJ-type hypothesized patterns for one or more groups around several sites, these trends are far from uniform across all sites. The variety of results may stem from differences across groups in the perceived risks associated with each site.

We can use the first panel of Table 6.2 to look site-by-site for evidence of the types of race/ethnicity patterns that have concerned EJ researchers. For the Old Bethpage Landfill, with an HRS almost twice as high as the other sites, nearby census tracts became relatively less populated over the entire time interval, and all three focal racial/ethnic groups ("White," "Black," and "Hispanic") declined in their relative concentrations near the site versus farther away, implying that other types of minority groups may have stayed or even moved in.

For the Sayreville Landfill, there is some evidence that whites were moving in but began to move away after the site was listed, but the relative populations of blacks and Hispanics continued to increase. Against a backdrop where minorities and women may be more concerned than white males about environmental risks, however, the net increase in concentrations of blacks and Hispanics near the site is notable.[24] The Montrose Chemical case is similar to Sayreville for whites and blacks but not for Hispanics, who have decreased in concentration nearer this site relative to farther away. Unfortunately, the spatial distribution of the growing Asian population in this area cannot be assessed because of the lack of conformable data on this group. Furthermore, important changes in the distribution of Hispanics throughout Southern California over this time period may confound these results, especially if areas of net Hispanic in-migration, for other reasons, coincidentally happen to be near the fringe of the (rather atypical) study area for the Montrose site.

For the Cinnaminson Landfill, however, the pattern seems to be at odds with typical EJ concerns. Whites have tended to move toward the landfill over the entire time period and blacks to move away. However, Hispanics moved closer in the prelisting period but farther away in the postlisting decade. For CTS Printex, whites have also tended to increase in relative concentration nearer the site. In this case, however, the relative concentrations nearer the site of blacks and Hispanics appear to have decreased prior to listing but have increased postlisting—consistent with "net minority move-in."

The Chem Central site shows whites becoming relatively less numerous in the vicinity of the site over the first two intercensal intervals, although in the final interval, this trend moderates, perhaps reflecting the effects of the cleanup process ensuing from listing. The pattern for blacks, although statistically significant only at the 10 percent level, is the opposite, so some net minority move-in may have been occurring here.

Finally, for the Havertown PCP site, whites have moved systematically farther away from the site, on net, and blacks have moved systematically closer to the site, suggesting minority move-in along these dimensions. Hispanics, however, have moved farther from the site, on net, at least over the last two intercensal decades. Thus, there may be important differences across nonwhite groups.

Admittedly, we do not have the whole picture. Blacks and Hispanics do not constitute the entire spectrum of minority groups in all cases, and we do not incorporate income heterogeneity within each of these groups. This chapter addresses only sociodemographic variables, rather than economic variables, and our analysis is limited by the subset of variables that can be conformed across these four census years. For the variables we have, however, there are statistically significant changes in relative concentrations near the site in 20 of the 21 race/ethnicity cases. We see some evidence of minority move-in during at least a portion of the time interval (in five of seven cases for blacks, and in perhaps three of seven cases for Hispanics), although these findings are not generalizable across all sites.[25]

Children

If these Superfund sites were known during the decade of the 1970s, we can infer that children were being protected if their relative concentrations nearer the site during that period were declining. If listing of the site and the commencement of cleanup activities reduced the perceived risks, we might expect that households with children would begin to move back, leading to increased relative concentrations nearer the Superfund site as cleanup progressed during the decade of the 1990s. We might expect to see a U-shaped profile in cases where this has occurred. In Table 6.2, children are featured in two cells in panel 2 (in the categories "Under 6" and "Kids 6–17"). Children also appear in all three cells in panel 3.

Across the five child-related cells in Table 6.2, a statistically significant U-shaped profile (either symmetric or asymmetric) is identified in 12 of the 35 cases, which suggests that children are being protected in the prelisting period in these cases. However, statistically significant *increasing* relative concentrations nearer the site, over the entire time period, are observed for the child-related groups in 9 of these 35 cases. In only two cases does the child-related group continuously decline in relative concentration nearer the site (Cinnaminson for "Kids 6–17", and Montrose Chemical for "Married & kids"). An inverted U-shaped profile is observed only for "Kids 6–17" for CTS Printex, where this group was increasing in relative concentration prior to the listing decade, then decreasing afterward. But this site was only proposed for listing in 1988 and listed in 1990, with relatively little coverage in the press, so it may have been relatively unknown prior to 1985, compared to the other sites. The "protection effect" may not have been activated until later on in this case.

Among the three cells in panel 3, only 14 of the 21 cases exhibit any statistically significant pattern in the relative concentration of the group in question near the site versus farther away. Of these 14 cases, the 5 cases that display uniformly increasing relative concentrations near the Superfund site are in the "Married & kids" and "Male head & kids" categories. For no site does the relative concentration of "Female head & kids" increase during the prelisting period or uniformly over the entire period. It is possible—to the extent that white male heads of household dominate locational decision making in "Married & kids" or "Male head & kids" households—that the lower risk perceptions of white males lie behind these tendencies. There is some evidence that single mothers keep their children away from these sites, at least until the site has been listed, implying that cleanup is under way.

For all of the child-related groups, however, it would be helpful to know which racial or ethnic groups tend to lead the net return of households with children to the vicinity of listed Superfund sites. In cases where child-related groups begin to return after listing, but the relative concentration of whites declines over this period (such as Old Bethpage and Havertown PCP), there may be cause for concern that nonwhite children are being returned sooner to the vicinity of Superfund sites that are not yet completely remediated.

The Elderly and Households without Children

For the more publicized sites of the Old Bethpage Landfill and Montrose Chemical, and for the less publicized Havertown PCP site, the data suggest that the relative concentration of seniors nearer the site is increasing (at least over the first two decades in the case of Montrose). Given the tendency for seniors to be less mobile, this probably reflects a "failure to flee the nuisance." However, the relative concentration for the seniors group at the Cinnaminson site mimics the predominant U-shaped pattern of child-related groups, and at the Chem Central site, the relative concentration of seniors falls steadily across periods. This mirrors Chem Central's atypical pattern for all three of the statistically significant child-related groups, for which the relative concentration rises steadily across periods. This pattern may reflect minimal media exposure for this site, although the declining relative concentration of whites and increasing relative concentration of blacks over the time period is reversed only in the final census period.

Among the four cells of panel 4 in Table 6.2, only 18 of the 28 cases have statistically significant changes in relative concentrations over time. In 9 of these 18 cases, the pattern is an *inverse* U-shape (either symmetric or asymmetric), implying that the group in question became relatively more concentrated near the site in the prelisting period but relatively less concentrated afterwards. This is the inverse of the dominant pattern for child-related groups, which is plausible.

Among the exceptions, a U-shaped pattern is present in five cases. The CTS Printex case may again be anomalous because of its later listing and minimal media exposure. Except for the "Female head, no kids" group where there is no discernible pattern, the relative concentrations of these types of households without children are either declining through all but the last census period or declining overall (whereas the "White" and "Married & kids" groups were increasing in relative concentration near the site throughout this period). This evidence for CTS Printex appears to go against the expected pattern based on the EJ literature, except for the fact that the relative populations of the black and Hispanic groups began to increase in the decade of proposed listing.

Among the exceptions, a U-shaped pattern is present in four other cases besides the "Married, no kids" group for CTS Printex. As for so many of the child-related groups, a U-shaped pattern is observed for "Male head, no kids" for Cinnaminson, for "Female head, no kids" for Montrose, and for the "Non-family households" group for both Sayreville and Cinnaminson. To the extent that these groups constitute young singles still in their reproductive years, it may be unsurprising that their patterns mimic those for the child-related groups. Again, however, there is considerable variability, and it is still difficult to generalize across all sites.

Directions for Related and Future Research

This chapter does not consider any economic variables, since the census data available from GeoLytics at the time this study was undertaken included only "short form" variables. In contrast, Cameron and McConnaha (2006) consider some economic variables in a related study of four Superfund sites (including three high-profile sites that have been studied elsewhere in the literature— Love Canal [Niagara Falls, New York], RSR Corporation's lead smelter [Dallas, Texas], and the Tacoma copper smelter and Commencement Bay Superfund site [Tacoma, Washington]—but also the high-HRS Old Bethpage Landfill site that is one of the seven sites considered in this chapter).[26] In- or out-migration from a Superfund area will also be mediated by the time pattern of housing prices and rental rates near those areas, as opposed to farther away. These changes in market prices of housing will interact with the demand elasticity for housing of these different sociodemographic groups. Individual households will assess their marginal disutility from changes in proximity to a Superfund site relative to their marginal utility from differences in housing prices to be obtained from moving toward or away from the site.

Each of the Superfund sites in our current sample is located in an urbanized area, so there are assumed to be many jobs and other attractions that might lead individuals to wish to live in the vicinity of the Superfund site, had there been no environmental hazard at that location. If housing prices and the types of local jobs were uniform across this region, we would assume that households would prefer to live farther away.

Conclusion

The seven Superfund sites we examine in this chapter are just a small fraction of all the sites on the NPL, yet they represent an important subset of these sites. They are located in heavily populated areas, so they may contribute a relatively large share to aggregate Superfund human exposure.

Our current empirical models describe what has happened to different population subgroups, over time, in the vicinity of these seven urban Superfund sites. Our empirical specifications are descriptive models, rather than models that attempt to reveal causality or the mechanisms underlying these changes. These models have been designed to contribute to the set of stylized facts to be accommodated by researchers who are concerned with modeling the spatial distribution of different sociodemographic groups in light of the processes that accompany the discovery and cleanup of hazardous waste sites.

We conclude that there is likely to be no widespread and pervasive standard pattern over time of different socioeconomic groups "coming to the nuisance" with respect to all urban Superfund sites. Time patterns are statistically significant in many cases, but vary rather widely in their direction and magnitude. No doubt this heterogeneity accounts, at least in part, for the difficulty that even very careful researchers have had in establishing any single overall tendency for the sociodemographic mix to change in any particular way when an environmental threat emerges.

Our hypotheses regarding group movement hinge on a supposition of changing public knowledge and perceptions regarding each site. One would expect the Old Bethpage and Sayreville landfills and the Montrose Chemical site, with their relatively greater media exposures, to produce the most reliable results. Sayreville and Montrose show some evidence of white flight and minority move-in, but the Old Bethpage site seems dominated by an overall decline in population near the site and a decrease in relative concentration near the site for all three focal groups (relative to "other racial/ethnic groups"). In looking at our collection of seven sites as a whole, however, it is difficult to conclude that there is a "standard" pattern of movement that is common across all sites.

Our work also draws attention to the competing forces that may be acting to deliver some of the observed patterns over time in the spatial allocation of different groups. Housing market constraints in the form of income levels and housing market discrimination can be expected to lead to decreases in the relative concentrations near the site of higher-income white households, at least prior to the commencement of cleanup operations. At the same time, however, the "white male" effect that is associated with systematically lesser perceptions of risk implies that white households with male decision makers are less likely to want to move away from an environmental hazard. If groups who perceive greater risks (female-headed households and minority households) are relatively more inclined to move farther away, we might expect increases in the relative concentrations nearer the site of higher-income white households. Which of these two effects dominates, in the face of different types of risks, is likely to account somewhat for the observed patterns of residential mobility.

This chapter constitutes a very thorough study of the spatial movement of sociodemographic groups surrounding environmental disamenities where the environmental threat changes in its perceived severity over time. However, additional data would, in principle, allow for a more detailed examination of sociodemographic movements around each site. For instance, yearly (rather than decennial) data would, of course, enhance the resolution of our study and allow us to track population movements by the year for each of the sites listed on the NPL. The growing availability of samples from the American Communities Survey, at yearly intervals, might facilitate such analysis in the future. In addition, more specific data concerning local public knowledge regarding each site would help, as our hypotheses are based on these types of risk perceptions. Unfortunately, data on actual risk perceptions are not widely available.

Our results make it clear that it is difficult to generalize about the results from any particular site. Had our study involved solely the Old Bethpage site, for example, and had we considered only those groups consisting of "Whites," "Married & kids," and "Married, no kids," we might have been tempted to conclude that whites and couples with children tend to decrease in relative concentration in the vicinity of Superfund sites, while couples without children increase in relative concentration around the site, at least until remediation is under way. Alternatively, if we had considered only the CTS Printex site, we may have concluded that whites and couples with children increase in relative concentration near the site, while couples without children tend to decrease in relative concentration near the site, at least until remediation is under way. Thus, depending on which sites are studied and which population measures are considered, it is possible that nearly any result could be obtained.

The original impetus for an investigation of the time patterns in distance profiles for sociodemographics around Superfund sites stemmed from concerns about articles that attempt to estimate "rebound" patterns in housing prices, such as Kiel and Zabel (2001) and Dale et al. (1999). In some cases, distance profiles for housing prices seem to recover completely when the Superfund site is remediated. In other cases, the price recovery is incomplete. In yet others, it might be termed "overcomplete," as for the McMillen and Thorsnes (2003) study of Tacoma. Vigdor (see Chapter 3) also notes that there is not much consensus about whether remediation of an environmental hazard leads to increases in housing prices. Our current results, pertaining to changes in the sociodemographic mix near the site, may help to explain these seemingly inconsistent findings.

The stigma from environmental contamination can be a potentially important factor in housing markets, as addressed in Messer et al. (2006). In some areas, the property "taint" associated with identification and cleanup activities at a Superfund site appears to be accompanied by changes in sociodemographic patterns in the vicinity of the site. In some cases, younger families, minorities, or other housing-market-constrained groups, such as single parents, may be attracted by what are likely to be lower housing prices, but this tendency may be confounded by the tendency of white males to perceive lesser risk from environmental hazards than do other groups. Ceteris paribus, we would expect remediation to eliminate the taint on properties. To the extent that the presence of different groups, as a result of environmentally induced migration, also decreases housing prices (as suggested by the work of Kiel and Zabel 1996), remediation of the Superfund site may not be enough to immediately restore pretaint housing prices.

Notes

This research was funded in part by the US Environmental Protection Agency (CR 824393-01) through a cooperative agreement with Cornell University (29067-5808, PI: William D. Schulze) and a subcontract to the University of California at Los Angeles. Support from research funds accompanying the R. F. Mikesell Chair in Environmental and Resource Economics at the University of Oregon is also gratefully acknowledged. Helpful comments have been received from participants at the 2003 AERE Workshop in Madison, Wisconsin.

1. See Cooter and Ulen (1997). Whether a group *moves* near the site, or simply chooses to *stay* near the site when other groups are leaving, is not relevant for this study. We are interested in changes in *relative* population shares for a variety of groups. Greenberg and Schneider (1996) present evidence from interviews of residents in the proximity of a Superfund site that suggests that depressed property values allowed them to move into the neighborhood. In other cases, groups with more limited housing market opportunities may remain in a degraded neighborhood while other groups move out.

2. Bowen (2002) offers a critical review of the existing EJ literature. Been (1994, 1997) and Liu (1997) explain the need to understand neighborhood change over time. Been (1997) studies the demographics of 544 different communities that contained active commercial hazardous waste treatment, storage, and disposal facilities (TSDFs)

in 1994. Their analysis "provides little support for the theory that market dynamics following the introduction of the TSDF into a neighborhood might lead it to become poorer and increasingly populated by racial and ethnic minorities."

3. Hamilton and Viscusi (1999) generate Lifetime Excess Cancer Risk (LECR) scores for environmental hazards as a means of quantifying actual risk. Such data, however, are unavailable in a systematic manner for the sites that we consider in this study.

4. As discussed in Been (1997), there are advantages and limitations to census tracts as the geographical unit of analysis. Additional work on the siting of TSDFs has been conducted for Los Angeles County, California, by Pastor, Sadd, and Hipp (2001). In contrast to Been, however, they consider "near" to consist of all census tracts within one-quarter mile, or within one mile, of the TSDF. They limit their analysis to Los Angeles, which is helpful, but they pool their data across all TSDFs in this region, which suppresses information about heterogeneity across sites.

5. Rosen (1974) is the seminal paper on hedonic models. In this literature, Michaels and Smith (1990) and Kohlhase (1991) find that distance from Superfund sites has a positive effect on house prices. Kiel and her coauthors control for distances to Superfund sites or hazardous waste incinerators (Kiel 1995; Kiel and McClain 1995; Kiel and Zabel 2001). Dale et al. (1999) emphasize housing prices over time as a function of distance from a lead smelter, focusing explicitly on what happens to housing prices following cleanup of toxic sites. These authors find evidence of market rebound, but emphasize that "a continuous price/distance relationship fails to capture the entire effect of proximity to the smelter." McMillen and Thorsnes (2003) investigate the effect on housing prices of Superfund listing and cleanup for a copper smelter. They find that prices rebound more than completely, while Dale et al. (1999) uncover an anomaly in that "proximity to the [site] in 1987–1990 is actually desirable, *ceteris paribus.*" We suspect that these results may reflect, in part, the endogeneity of sociodemographic characteristics around Superfund sites during the cleanup phase.

6. Kiel and Zabel (2001) use only the proportion of unemployed workers and the log of median household income for the relevant census tract "from decennial censuses," citing their importance based on Kiel and Zabel (1996). They do not, however, use any of the other sociodemographic neighborhood characteristics explored in that earlier study. Dale et al. (1999) control for just three census tract sociodemographic variables: percentage below the poverty line, percentage Hispanic, and percentage African American, all assumed to be exogenous.

7. Graham et al. (1999) explore the siting of coke plants and oil refineries. These authors cite "market dynamics theory" as predicting, over time, that hazardous or unattractive residential areas will lose some types of residents and attract others (because of the relatively depressed property values in these areas). Greenberg and Schneider (1996) also consider neighborhood dynamics and price effects.

8. The online appendix can be found at http://www.sup.org/environmental justice.

9. The set of sites on the initial Superfund NPL was announced in 1983.

10. Maps of the census tracts surrounding each of these sites are included in Appendix A.6A in the online appendix at http://www.sup.org/environmentaljustice.

11. We do need to assume that the characteristics of these other geographic features have remained essentially constant over the 1970–2000 time period, since detailed historical data on these features is not available.

12. The online appendix can be found at http://www.sup.org/environmental justice.

13. The online appendix can be found at http://www.sup.org/environmental justice.

14. For each census, the geographic definition of a number of tracts in any local area will change. Most commonly, a tract is split into two or more tracts as the population it contains increases. In the NCDB, larger census tracts active in the 1970, 1980, and 1990 census windows have been apportioned according to documented formulas to conform to the smaller year 2000 census tracts whenever splitting has taken place.

15. We discard any tract for which the population is less than 100 in any of the four census years on the grounds that this appears to provide insufficient precision in calculating the shares of different sociodemographic groups. In these heavily urbanized areas, tracts with fewer than 100 people are probably anomalous in a number of ways.

16. The transformed proportions lie between 0.0001 and 0.9999, so that they can be subjected to a log-odds transformation without difficulty. As log-odds transformations of slightly attenuated proportions, the dependent variables used in our estimations are free to range over the entire real line and could therefore be approximately conditionally normally distributed.

17. We rely on the xtgls command in Stata, with weights to reflect the different sizes of each census tract ([aweight=trctpop]), i(trct) t(year) panels(h) and corr(a). We do not pursue corrections for spatially autocorrelated errors. This decision may have milder consequences in the case of census tract data than in the case of individual hedonic property value data, for example, but we treat the "spatial error" issue as a second-order problem in this chapter. Subsequent research may pursue this aspect of the empirical problem.

18. The online appendix can be found at http://www.sup.org/environmental justice.

19. The online appendix can be found at http://www.sup.org/environmental justice.

20. The online appendix can be found at http://www.sup.org/environmental justice.

21. This subtlety is especially important since we entertain models with directional heterogeneity in distance effects. For particular values of the γ_1 and γ_2 coefficients, the overall coefficient on $\ln(d_i)$ may well be negative in some directions, even though its "average" value—using the assumption of zero means for $\cos(\theta)$ and $\sin(\theta)$—may be positive. It is therefore of no real consequence for our specific research questions if the actual distance profile in some directions is negatively sloped, even when it is positively sloped in the "average" direction.

22. The online appendix can be found at http://www.sup.org/environmental justice.

23. Full regression results are relegated to Appendix A.6C in the online appendix at http://www.sup.org/environmentaljustice.

24. Been (1997) finds that noxious facilities are more likely to be sited in areas that are disproportionately Hispanic at the time of siting, but little evidence of substantial changes in a neighborhood's racial or ethnic composition following siting. Note that the designation "Hispanic" in the present study includes whites and blacks, so our three categories are not mutually exclusive. Likewise, conformable data on other ethnic groups are not available all the way back to the 1970 Census, so we cannot model other groups, such as Asian/Pacific Islanders. In contrast, Depro and Timmins (see Chapter 5) are able to explore the sorting outcomes for lower-income Asian homeowners in the San Francisco Bay Area of California because their analysis does not rely upon consistently reported race/ethnicity census data back to 1970, but mainly on their buyer-based panel of home purchases.

25. The "short form" census variables from GeoLytics do not include income, house values, or rental rates.

26. For the sites studied in Cameron and McConnaha (2006), we had access to GeoLytics data that included later census tract "long form" data on median house values, median gross rents, and household incomes by census tract, converted to a panel across the four census years.

References

Been, Vicki. 1994. "Locally Undesirable Land Uses in Minority Neighborhoods: Disproportionate Siting or Market Dynamics?" *Yale Law Journal* 103:1383–1422.

Been, Vicki, with Francis Gupta. 1997. "Coming to the Nuisance or Going to the Barrios? A Longitudinal Analysis of Environmental Justice Claims." *Ecology Law Quarterly* 24 (1): 1–56.

Bowen, William M. 2002. "An Analytical Review of Environmental Justice Research: What Do We Really Know?" *Environmental Management* 29 (1): 3–15.

Cameron, Trudy Ann. 2006. "Directional Heterogeneity in Distance Profiles in Hedonic Property Value Models." *Journal of Environmental Economics and Management* 51 (1): 26–45.

Cameron, Trudy Ann, and Ian T. McConnaha. 2006. "Evidence of Environmental Migration." *Land Economics* 82 (2): 273–90.

Cooter, Robert, and Thomas Ulen. 1997. *Law and Economics*, 2nd ed. Reading, MA: Addison-Wesley-Longman.

Dale, Larry, James C. Murdoch, Mark A. Thayer, and Paul A. Waddell. 1999. "Do Property Values Rebound from Environmental Stigmas? Evidence from Dallas." *Land Economics* 75 (2): 311–26.

Finucane, Melissa L., Paul Slovic, C. K. Mertz, James Flynn, and Theresa A. Satterfield. 2000. "Gender, Race, and Perceived Risk: The 'White Male' Effect." *Health, Risk and Society* 2 (2): 159–72.

Flynn, James, Paul Slovic, and C. K. Mertz. 1994. "Gender, Race, and Perception of Environmental-Health Risks." *Risk Analysis* 14 (6): 1101–8.

Graham, John D., Nancy Dean Beaulieu, Dana Sussman, March Sadowitz, and Yi-Ching Li. 1999. "Who Lives near Coke Plants and Oil Refineries? An Exploration of the Environmental Inequity Hypothesis." *Risk Analysis* 19 (2): 171–86.

Greenberg, Michael R., and Dona Schneider. 1996. *Environmentally Devastated Neighborhoods: Perceptions, Policies, and Realities.* Piscataway, NJ: Rutgers University Press.

Hamilton, James T., and W. Kip Viscusi. 1999. *Calculating Risks? The Spatial and Political Dimensions of Hazardous Waste Policy.* Cambridge, MA: MIT Press.

Kiel, Katherine A. 1995. "Measuring the Impact of the Discovery and Cleaning of Identified Hazardous Waste Sites on House Values." *Land Economics* 71 (4): 428–35.

Kiel, Katherine A., and Katherine T. McClain. 1995. "The Effect of an Incinerator Siting on Housing Appreciation Rates." *Journal of Urban Economics* 37 (3): 311–23.

Kiel, Katherine A., and Jeffrey E. Zabel. 1996. "House Price Differentials in US Cities: Household and Neighborhood Racial Effects." *Journal of Housing Economics* 5 (2): 143–65.

———. 2001. "Estimating the Economic Benefits of Cleaning Up Superfund Sites: The Case of Woburn, Massachusetts." *Journal of Real Estate Finance and Economics* 22 (2–3): 163–84.

Kohlhase, Janet E. 1991. "The Impact of Toxic Waste Sites on Housing Values." *Journal of Urban Economics* 30 (1): 1–26.

Liu, Feng. 1997. "Dynamics and Causation of Environmental Equity, Locally Unwanted Land Uses, and Neighborhood Changes." *Environmental Management* 21 (5): 643–56.

McMillen, Daniel P., and Paul Thorsnes. 2003. "The Aroma of Tacoma: Time Varying Average Derivatives and the Effect of a Superfund Site on House Prices." *Journal of Business and Economic Statistics* 21 (2): 237–46.

Messer, Kent D., William D. Schulze, Katherine F. Hackett, Trudy Ann Cameron, and Gary H. McClelland. 2006. "Can Stigma Explain Large Property Value Losses? The

Psychology and Economics of Superfund." *Environmental and Resource Economics* 33 (3): 299–324.

Michaels, R. Gregory, and V. Kerry Smith. 1990. "Market Segmentation and Valuing Amenities with Hedonic Models: The Case of Hazardous Waste Sites." *Journal of Urban Economics* 28 (2): 223–42.

Pastor, Manuel, Jim Sadd, and John Hipp. 2001. "Which Came First? Toxic Facilities, Minority Move-In, and Environmental Justice." *Journal of Urban Affairs* 23 (1): 1–21.

Rosen, Sherwin. 1974. "Hedonic Prices and Implicit Markets: Product Differentiation in Pure Competition." *Journal of Political Economy* 82 (1): 34–55.

Schachter, Jason P., and Jeffrey J. Kuenzi. 2002. "Seasonality of Moves and the Duration and Tenure of Residence: 1996." Working Paper Series 69, Population Division, US Census Bureau, Washington, DC.

Vrijheid, Martine. 2000. "Health Effects of Residence near Hazardous Waste Landfill Sites: A Review of Epidemiologic Literature." *Environmental Health Perspectives* 108 (Suppl. 1): 101–12.

7 Amenities Tomorrow

A Greenbelt Project's Impacts over Space and Time

Douglas S. Noonan

Introduction

The distribution of people and local amenities—and how changes in the system can affect that distribution—is often the focus of heated debate. This chapter considers these themes generally and in an analysis of a particular local development project. The urban renewal project is particularly compelling because it features an important temporal dimension, along with the standard spatial dimension, and attempts to harness market forces to finance a brownfield-to-greenfield project. Not only does the project affect the spatial distribution of investment and local greenspace, it does so by encumbering future residents with public debt to finance the improvement. In this case, an increasingly common public finance instrument—tax increment financing (TIF)—is employed to finance the renewal of blighted areas. The first half of this chapter discusses basic economic models of how current and future local amenity values are capitalized into property values. When debt leaves tomorrow's residents paying for today's benefits, temporal or "intergenerational" equity concerns arise. Of course, some residents may have better access to new local amenities than others. Understanding the distributional impacts of such a project requires appreciating how market forces operate—especially the difference between renters and owners. Even "self-financing" TIF projects raise the possibility of funding (and capturing the value from) local improvements by diverting *ongoing* development from other areas or increasing the burdens faced by *future* residents.

The second half of this chapter discusses the particular project, the BeltLine in Atlanta, Georgia, as a bold, in-development urban amenity. The BeltLine marks a massive, multibillion-dollar effort to revitalize much of Atlanta's core and targets future property value gains as the source of funding for the renewal. Implementing the BeltLine project poses especially interesting challenges because of its temporal dimension, market forces, and its dependence on gentrification. The background information on the BeltLine is supplemented with a hedonic price analysis of housing sales in Atlanta before and after the BeltLine proposal originated. The hedonic analysis allows an investigation of some of the impacts of the BeltLine proposal on welfare, as revealed through property markets. The case of the BeltLine lets us examine the critical roles of speculation, uncertainty, spillovers, renters and landlords, and the broader housing market.

Conceptual Model

Of interest here is how city residents respond to changes in localized environmental quality, how property markets govern those responses, and how future assets and taxes affect markets today. Banzhaf, Sidon, and Walsh (see Chapter 4) discuss environmental gentrification and sorting in much greater detail, as do Banzhaf and McCormick and Vigdor (see, respectively, Chapters 2 and 3). Equilibrium prices are expected to reflect the value of access to different environmental amenities. That housing prices capitalize amenity values is common to a host of standard models such as the Alonso-Muth-Mills urban economic model (Diamond and Tolley 1982), Roback's (1982) model for compensating differentials, and Brueckner's (2001) model of improving local public services. These approaches model the connection between local amenity values and housing prices, although formal links between implicit or "hedonic" prices and welfare measures are more complex (Epple 1987; Palmquist 1988). The vast hedonic literature following Rosen (1974) generally estimates the capitalized value of (or marginal willingness to pay for) varying environmental quality. Hedonics has been used recently to explore the sorting that occurs in response to environmental changes (e.g., Smith et al. 2004; Bayer, Keohane, and Timmins 2009; see also Chapter 5). This analysis focuses on market responses *before* the local environment actually changes.

Residential Location

For a simple approach initially, imagine a world of renters who must rent in one of three locations: neighborhood A, neighborhood B, or outside of the city.[1] Renters try to get the best combination of neighborhood quality (E) and consumption goods (x) that they can afford, given their income and the rents

(r) in the three areas. Renters are trading off between E and x. In equilibrium, market rents maintain the equilibrium where nobody can be made better off by relocating. We expect the neighborhood with higher E to have higher rents (otherwise, renters could get more E and x by moving). Renters keep moving into neighborhood A, with its higher amenities, until the rent premium rises such that the "last" renter in is indifferent about moving. Thus, rental premiums (Δr) reflect the welfare gains from higher amenity values *for the marginal renter*.

How this equilibrium adjusts to exogenous shocks gives a sense of the balance in the system. Consider a change to amenity levels in one neighborhood. Increasing E^j will attract marginal renters to neighborhood j until r^j rises to restore equilibrium. If the improvement occurs in neighborhood A, where E^A was initially higher than E^B, then migration to neighborhood A follows, and the initial rent premium must increase (by raising r^A). Conversely, improving E^B instead will induce migration to neighborhood B, and the rent premium must decrease by increasing r^B. Either way, neighborhood rents track with changes in that neighborhood's amenity level, and the other neighborhood's rents are unaffected. For an improved E, presumably all movers are better off from moving. For a marginal improvement in E^A, if those with stronger tastes for E had already sorted into neighborhood A, the new Δr necessary to restore equilibrium will leave natives in neighborhood A better off because they have already revealed that they were willing to pay more for better E than residents of neighborhood B. (For nonmarginal changes in E and when willingness to pay for those changes is heterogeneous, this may not hold.[2]) If the improvement is in neighborhood B, conversely, rents can rise in neighborhood B more than the natives—who don't especially value the amenity—are willing to pay, and thus they are harmed by the improvement.

Ownership

Ownership adds an interesting wrinkle. A standard economic model treats homeownership from a user cost of capital perspective (Smith, Rosen, and Fallis 1988), where owner-occupiers pay themselves an implicit rent. The value of owning a home derives from the stream of rent payments received. (I abstract from factors like depreciation, maintenance, and income taxes for simplicity here.) Future events and speculation now come into play. If rents remains constant at r, the value of owning that property is given by $p = r/\delta$, where δ is the discount rate. Introducing a tax τ on property value, akin to Brueckner's (2001) property tax, leads to a modification where $p = (r - \tau p)/\delta$. The present value of the rental payments (r) minus the tax payments (τp) constitutes the asset value. Rearranging this expression yields

$$p = r/(\delta + \tau).$$

Obviously, the sales price of homes is rising in rent and falling in tax and discount rates. If rents will rise in the future, sales price today rises to reflect the increase in asset value. As discussed above, when E changes, the rents follow. The intertemporal model allows for future changes in r to affect current sales price even when they do not affect current rents. Rents do not rise until the change in E actually occurs. This means that in the current period (i.e., after the improvement is expected but before it is completed), the rents are insufficient to cover the cost of capital. A major concern, cited by Immergluck (2007) and others, arises after a speculation-induced price bubble bursts when property tax assessments lag behind market prices. When assessed values and property taxes are rising but real home values are falling, homeowners may suffer from a higher effective property tax rate even with a constant τ. The bubble might burst for exogenous reasons or because of overly optimistic expectations about future E, possibly leaving poorer and credit-constrained homeowners to suffer from the increased taxes.

To summarize up to this point, a shock to E is expected to be accompanied by a shift in rents to restore equilibrium. The new equilibrium leaves entrants better off but might harm native renters. Owners immediately enjoy wind-fall gains (losses) from current *or future* improvements (degradations) in E as prices mirror the changes in the expected stream of rental rates. Unless there is friction in the system (e.g., mobility or liquidity constraints, transaction costs), future changes in E do not affect renters.

Tax Increment Financing

Finally, consider tax increment financing (TIF), a widespread tool for financing local amenity improvements using future tax revenues.[3] The popularity of TIF comes partly from its helping local governments finance economic development through the issuance of (tax-exempt) bonds (Immergluck 2007). TIF projects essentially fund improvements in E from the increased property tax revenue that they generate. Brueckner (2001) emphasizes the political advantages offered by TIF, where tax rates are untouched, thereby dampening political opposition from outside the host neighborhood. A primary and contentious distinguishing feature of TIF mechanisms involves overlapping tax jurisdictions (e.g., school districts). Instituting a TIF project freezes the tax base of a designated district at pre-project levels, and for the life of the TIF project (typically around 25 years), the various taxing jurisdictions continue to receive their pre-project tax receipts. If the project grows the tax base, as intended, all additional tax revenues are earmarked for funding the TIF project or servicing its debt. Thus, if a city and a school district were splitting the tax revenues before the improvement in E, the school would continue to get its share of the pre-TIF tax base, and all increases in tax revenues would accrue to the TIF project instead of being split between the overlapping jurisdictions.

In light of the previous housing market discussion, several observations about TIF projects warrant highlighting. First, gentrification not only is expected here but is nearly a prerequisite of the TIF project's being self-financed from property values being bid up. Second, the capitalization into property values of expected changes to E should be effectively instantaneous. This makes the timing of establishing or "freezing" the tax base critical. Expectations of TIF impacts might be reflected in the property prices even before the TIF is enacted or authorized. If expected improvements are capitalized before the tax base is established (and assessed values reflect market values), the TIF tax base should be expected to generate *no* incremental tax revenues. In this case, the viability of the TIF hinges on luck or friction in the property markets. The timeliness of assessed values used for taxation is a critical component of the viability of TIF; a fast tax assessor might undermine the TIF. Third, insofar as TIF projects target "blighted" neighborhoods where the housing market is slack (i.e., many undeveloped or vacant parcels exist), prices will not rise even while the amount of housing supplied increases (see Chapter 3). Total property value in the TIF district would rise even though existing housing values remain relatively constant.

Fourth, there may be other (non-TIF) reasons for price changes that affect the tax increment available to the project. Secular trends in property values, costs of amenity provision, or even inflation could greatly affect the viability of TIF proposals. Unless the trends in property prices are matched by trends in the costs of providing improvements and the tax increments due to secular trends in property values are returned to the overlapping jurisdictions, the TIF project could effectively grab more tax increment than it actually creates. The windfall gains from loosely defining the increment give city managers reason to institute TIF zones in areas expected to experience robust appreciation independently of the TIF project. (Conversely plummeting housing prices throughout the market can eliminate funding for a TIF project that, conditional on the secular decline in prices, actually improves values.) With a frozen tax base, school districts may be unable to continue providing the same level of amenities if their costs rise after the TIF is instituted. Such a shift in amenities would alter the equilibrium prices and location patterns in ways that are difficult to predict.

Fifth, and relatedly, the TIF project might essentially redirect development that would have simply gone elsewhere in the city. Improved amenities likely attract new investment and improved capital stock (Diamond and Tolley 1982). TIF projects signal commitment for future investment, possibly lowering developers' risk and spurring additional investment. The concern here is with using TIF to reallocate resources from one neighborhood to another (rather than from one taxing authority to another). Dye and Merriman (2006) examine these kinds of effects, noting that the reallocation might even be a negative-sum game.

Equity Implications

The discussion thus far has emphasized how environmental amenity changes—actual or anticipated—can affect equilibrium locations of residents, housing prices, and welfare. Equity concerns appear along several dimensions. Owners differ from renters in their ability to capitalize improvements (degradations), obtaining windfall gains (losses) *regardless* of their residential location (Sieg et al. 2004; Fullerton 2008). Generally, those benefiting from, paying for, and experiencing changes in environmental quality might not be the same. For TIF projects, as discussed above (and in Dye and Sundberg 1998), the financing mechanisms presume or depend on the capitalization of amenity improvements as well as shifting tax revenues or development activities from other services (e.g., schools) or locations. Anticipated benefits should be capitalized immediately. This market response signals the magnitude and location (but not the timing) of expected benefits. Some neighborhoods will benefit more than others.

This discussion gives rise to several conjectures about how an anticipated TIF project would affect an urban housing market:

Hypothesis 1. Better access to urban amenities is reflected in higher home prices.
  1a. Expected access to urban amenities is reflected in higher home prices.
  1b. Changes in expectations will be reflected in that premium.

Hypothesis 2. TIF districts will receive more private investments, even before project implementation.
2a.   Housing stock shifts (more renovation, turnover) along with gentrifying neighborhoods.
2b.   Change will be greater in high-risk areas of TIF districts.

The BeltLine Context

In the sprawling metropolis of Atlanta, an effort to redirect the city's development trajectory has risen to the fore: the Atlanta BeltLine project. The BeltLine is a large urban renewal project built around transforming an old 22-mile ring of rail rights-of-way into a greenbelt with enhanced public transit opportunities and subsidized workforce housing. The brownfield-to-greenbelt project aims to catalyze a revitalization of Atlanta's urban core, attract greater density and mixed-use development, and stem the tide of sprawl in the metropolitan area. It would install a 6,500-acre greenbelt that connects trails (33 miles of new biking and walking pathways), open space and new parks (1,200 new acres), and new mixed-use development and workforce housing (5,600 new units). The project was to be funded by a tax allocation district (TAD)—the equivalent of a TIF zone in Georgia. The Atlanta Development Authority expects the TAD to generate approximately $1.7 billion in bonds over its 25-year life (Atlanta Development Authority 2005). These bonds would cover about 60 percent of the project's overall cost. The city has issued supplemental zoning rules for the BeltLine Overlay District, which occupies roughly a half-mile buffer on either side of the BeltLine TAD corridor and aims to guide future development in ways consistent with the BeltLine vision. Approximately 100,000 people live inside the overlay district.

The BeltLine has garnered support from public and private entities and has encountered some controversy. Its supporters view the BeltLine as a rare opportunity to fundamentally reimagine and transform the landscape of Atlanta. Their ambitions are considerable. Some legal opposition has emerged because the primary funding mechanism for the BeltLine (a TIF) would deprive schools of future funding streams. Political and technical complexities associated with assembling scattered land holdings into a new greenbelt, dealing with holdout landowners, and the current housing market crisis have stalled—but not derailed—the BeltLine project. The momentum behind the project is strong. Numerous subprojects are already under way, without major public funding, and the city council in October 2008 approved a $117 million bond for the BeltLine even without TIF.

The TAD itself is entirely within the city of Atlanta (and Fulton County). The TAD is composed largely of parks, rights-of-way, and other derelict industrial lands. It is large, is close to the city center, and goes near other major employment centers in Atlanta. In Figure 7.1, the dark shaded area indicates the TAD, the light shaded area denotes the city area, and the lines are the major expressways.

The BeltLine idea was born out of the thesis of a graduate student at the Georgia Institute of Technology's city and regional planning program. Ryan Gravel's 1999 thesis caught the attention of city leaders and by early 2003 city council president, Cathy Woolard, wrote an editorial in the *Atlanta Journal-Constitution* advocating for the BeltLine. After intermittent press coverage in 2003, the BeltLine proposal gathered steam, and support (from public officials and private donors) grew steadily during 2004 and 2005. Land acquisition by the city and organizations like the Trust for Public Land accompanied the planning and debates. In November 2005, the city council approved the TIF for the

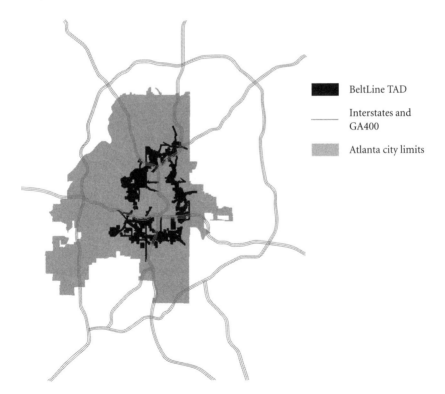

Figure 7.1 Atlanta and the BeltLine TAD

BeltLine, and by February 2007, the BeltLine Overlay District was approved. (The property tax base was set in 2005 at $546,360,280.) A year later, however, the Georgia Supreme Court ruled that the school district's share of the tax increment (about 54 percent of 2007's levy) must remain the school district's. In November 2008, Georgians approved a statewide referendum to amend the state constitution to permit school districts to opt into the TIF.

It is still early in the BeltLine's long-term plan. Only a small amount of the BeltLine vision has been achieved. At the end of 2006 (the most recent data used in this study), the outlook for the BeltLine was quite favorable, with enormous public support partially offset by a high-profile holdout and the start of a legal challenge (whose later success would result in the constitutional amendment). Although most legal challenges have been settled in the BeltLine's favor, the recession and foundering housing market pose new challenges. The next section highlights how the market has responded to the BeltLine proposal, its approval, and more recent challenges.

Empirical Model and Data

The central question here is how property values vary with distance to an urban amenity. As access to the amenity is scarce and travel is costly, land prices fall with distance from an amenity. The standard, downward-sloping "bid-rent curve" shows how prices or rents decline as the distance to the city's central business district (CBD) increases. Like elevation decreasing as one moves away from a mountain's summit, prices fall with distance to the CBD. Local amenities like the BeltLine cause wrinkles within this broader landscape. Set against the general downward slope of prices, a price "submountain" is expected around the local amenity, just as a price crater would be expected for a disamenity. The amenity is "local" in that its influence on prices is small relative to the city's radius. (For a much richer discussion, see Grimes 1982.)

To assess the impact of the BeltLine proposal on property prices, several hedonic price models are estimated. The data used here come from several sources. The Fulton County Tax Assessor's Office collects data on property sales and provides an extract of its data on single-family housing sales from 2000 to 2006. Sales are excluded from consideration in this analysis if they do not represent arm's-length market transactions.[4] These observations are then matched to a parcel map of Fulton County, which contains limited information on every lot in the county. Unfortunately, structure characteristics (e.g., quality grade, age, square footage) are available only from 2004 to 2006.[5] The georeferenced parcels also enable the construction of various geographic indicators, many of which are provided by the Atlanta Regional Commission (2002). Variables from the 2000 Census are available for each parcel's block group. Most importantly, the parcels are mapped onto maps of the BeltLine TAD and Overlay District (provided by the city of Atlanta). Computing distances between parcel centroids and geographic features (e.g., the BeltLine, transit stations, rivers) allows measures of proximity to a variety of other amenities.

The models estimate the hedonic price functions in the Fulton County housing market under different assumptions or using different variables and samples. Model A has the general form:

$$\ln P = \alpha + \beta X + \delta T + \gamma G + \mu GT + \epsilon. \tag{7.1}$$

A least squares estimator predicts the log of the price (Cropper, Deck, and McConnell 1988) using a number of variables.[6] X includes housing attributes, specifically the lot size in square feet. T includes indicators of the timing of the sale, specifically indicators for whether the sales occurred after February 14, 2003 (the date of Woolard's editorial), and November 1, 2005 (the date the city council passed the BeltLine ordinance), plus 28 quarterly dummy variables from 2000 through 2006. G represents a host of geographic attributes, including the percentage of the residents in the property's 2000 census block group who are white and who are below (150 percent of) the poverty line; distance to the CBD, the closest park, the closest hydrography feature, the closest expressway, the closest subway station, the closest manufacturing plant; a dummy variable for being north of the CBD, dummy variables for lying within each of 37 tax districts, and a measure of how far north (i.e., latitude); the shortest distance to the BeltLine TAD and a dummy variable for lying within the TAD; and likewise the distance to the BeltLine Overlay District and a dummy variable for lying within that district. ϵ is an error term.

Finally, the vector GT represents interactions between certain geographic and time variables, which allows for trends in amenity prices. This includes interactions between the two milestone dates and each of the TAD and overlay district dummies and the distances to the TAD and overlay district. This cross-sectional model uses only the most recent sale of a property if it appears multiple times in the data set.

Column 1 of Table 7.1 reports an estimation of Model A. The full set of quarterly dummy variables is included to control for time trends in sales price, and a large G vector picks up geographic and neighborhood effects. This

Table 7.1 Hedonic price model estimates

Variable	Model A	Model B1	Model B2	Model B3
ln($land\,ft^2$)	0.2925***			0.1258***
Δ ln($land\,ft^2$)		−0.1628*	−0.1688**	−0.2342***
%White	0.7442***		−0.3956***	−0.3063***
%Poverty	0.4227***		0.9568***	0.6903***
ln($Income$)	0.4074***		0.1650***	0.0372
ln($DistCBD$)	−0.2126***		−0.1305***	−0.1541***
ln($DistPark$)	−0.0160***		−0.0130*	−0.0153**
ln($DistHydro$)	−0.0082***		−0.0307***	−0.0172**
ln($DistExwy$)	−0.0099***		0.0523***	0.0281***
ln($DistMARTA$)	−0.0136***		0.0757***	0.0462***
ln($DistMfg$)	−0.0184***		0.0127	−0.0064
latitude	0.0295***		0.0079***	0.0072***
North	0.1661***		0.0976***	−0.0564*
tax district dummies	Included			
quarter2	0.0364**	0.0363	0.0405*	0.0425*
quarter3	0.0157	0.0822***	0.0859***	0.0959***
quarter4	0.0289	0.1451***	0.1586***	0.1846***
quarter5	0.0694**	0.135***	0.1270***	0.0997***
quarter6	0.1182***	0.1541***	0.1433***	0.1269***
quarter7	0.1186***	0.2476***	0.2341***	0.2002***
quarter8	0.0886***	0.1622***	0.1769***	0.1684***
quarter9	0.1303***	0.0843**	0.0989**	0.1161***
quarter10	0.1495***	0.0715*	0.0834**	0.1054***
quarter11	0.1545***	0.0104	0.0527	0.0767**
quarter12	0.1062***	−0.0149	0.0388	0.0687**
quarter13	0.2057***	0.0350	0.0227	0.0285
quarter14	0.2188***	0.0657	0.0731	0.0672
quarter15	0.2236***	−0.0025	0.0173	−0.0129
quarter16	0.1850***	0.0252	0.0313	0.0179
quarter17	0.2838***	0.0225	0.0409	0.0226
quarter18	0.2856***	0.0236	0.0393	0.0285
quarter19	0.2816***	0.0299	0.0704	0.0579
quarter20	0.2935***	0.0444	0.0580	0.0561
quarter21	0.3295***	0.2210***	0.2067***	0.1383**
quarter22	0.3681***	0.1387***	0.1389***	0.0940
quarter23	0.3646***	0.1210***	0.1275***	0.0850
quarter24	0.3711***	0.1412***	0.1198**	0.1202
quarter25	0.3935***	0.3043***	0.2142***	0.1882**
quarter26	0.4088***	0.3013***	0.2276***	0.2135***
quarter27	0.3892***	0.2666***	0.1713***	0.1621**
quarter28	0.3264***	0.2952***	0.1685***	0.1431*

(continued)

Table 7.1 (*Continued*)

Variable	Model A	Model B1	Model B2	Model B3
DistTAD	−0.1715***		−0.0565	−0.0183
DistTAD × *2001*	0.1582***	0.0971*	0.0387	
DistTAD × *2002*	0.1084***	0.1288**	0.0311	
DistTAD × *2003*	0.1161***	0.1231**	−0.0135	
DistTAD × *2004*	0.0715**	0.1513***	0.0082	
DistTAD × *2005*	0.0695**	0.2282***	0.0757	
DistTAD × *2006*	0.1237***	0.3812***	0.1585**	
TAD	−0.1003		0.0689	0.0153
TAD × *2001*	0.1585	−0.0772	−0.0466	
TAD × *2002*	0.1632	0.0253	−0.0236	
TAD × *2003*	0.3429**	−0.0299	−0.0661	
TAD × *2004*	0.3455**	−0.1826	−0.2993	
TAD × *2005*	0.3503**	−0.1718	−0.2853	
TAD × *2006*	0.2854*	−0.0718	−0.2072	
DistOver	0.1418***		0.0504	0.0172
DistOver × *2001*	−0.1537***	−0.0989*	−0.0403	
DistOver × *2002*	−0.1037***	−0.1254**	−0.0295	
DistOver × *2003*	−0.1135***	−0.1238**	0.0128	
DistOver × *2004*	−0.0710**	−0.1496***	−0.0057	
DistOver × *2005*	−0.0702**	−0.2324***	−0.0753	
DistOver × *2006*	−0.1178***	−0.3872***	−0.1566**	
Overlay	−0.0869**		0.0708	0.0402
Overlay × *2001*	0.0467	0.0139	−0.0099	
Overlay × *2002*	0.1228***	0.1887***	0.1224*	
Overlay × *2003*	0.0829**	0.2594***	0.1943***	
Overlay × *2004*	0.0965**	0.2460***	0.1461**	
Overlay × *2005*	0.2085***	0.2603***	0.1263*	
Overlay × *2006*	0.2186***	0.2219***	0.0660	
milestone$_1$				0.0491
milestone$_2$				−0.0092
DistTAD × *milestone$_1$*				−0.0012
TAD × *milestone$_1$*				−0.1453
DistOver × *milestone$_1$*				0.0015
Overlay × *milestone$_1$*				0.1003**
DistTAD × *milestone$_2$*				0.1018**
TAD × *milestone$_2$*				0.1259
DistOver × *milestone$_2$*				−0.1016**
Overlay × *milestone$_2$*				−0.0661
Constant	−0.4911	0.4043***	−2.9103***	−1.7418***
N	88,916	20,733	20,687	20,697
R^2	0.5141	0.0313	0.1048	0.1205

*$p < 0.1$; **$p < 0.05$; ***$p < 0.01$.

should soak up countywide trends in the housing market and variations across 37 tax districts (i.e., neighborhood fixed effects). While data limitations restrict Model A to a few X variables, introducing a richer set of housing attributes for only 2004–2006 sales does little to affect the results of interest here. Of interest in Model A are year-specific BeltLine proximity variables. These allow the distance gradient and the price effect of being inside the TAD or the overlay district to vary over time.

The second set of models reported in Table 7.1 relies on a repeat-sales framework. Perhaps the most important advantage of the repeat-sales framework is its robustness to omitting unobserved property attributes (as long as their implicit price is time invariant), which are a serious problem with these limited data. Model B builds on Model A and recognizes that the same property might be sold multiple times in the data range. For any sale in period t,

$$\ln P_t = \alpha_t + \beta_t X_t + \delta T_t + \gamma_t G + \mu GT_t + \epsilon_t. \tag{7.2}$$

For sales in different periods, t and s, this equation can be estimated in differences, as in Model B2:

$$\ln P_s - \ln P_t = \Delta \ln P = \Delta\alpha + \Delta\beta X_s + \beta_t \Delta X + \delta\Delta T + \Delta\gamma G + \mu G\Delta T + \Delta\epsilon. \tag{7.3}$$

This model represents a "complex model" (Kiel and Zabel 1998), as it allows both housing characteristics and implicit prices to vary over time. Its primary advantage is controlling for all time-invariant unobservable attributes, assuming their implicit price is constant. Unfortunately, $\Delta\epsilon$ might not have zero mean and other desired properties because of selection issues in using only the repeat-sales subsample. By including changes in attributes (e.g., change in lot size, change in quarter of sale) to explain changes in sales price, implicit prices as in Model A can be recovered. When variables measured at the time of the most recent sale are included (e.g., distance to parks), their coefficients represent shifts in the hedonic prices of that attribute.

Table 7.1 reports estimates using the repeat-sales Model B for different sets of variables. All models control for quarterly time trends. Model B1 implicitly treats all hedonic prices β and γ as time invariant. Model B2 relaxes this assumption for γ. Models B1 and B2 include BeltLine proximity variables interacted with year of sale to detect how price gradients (or "submountains") vary over time. Model B3 resembles Model B2 except that year indicator variables (interacted with BeltLine proximity variables) are replaced by two indicator variables to detect shifts in price levels in repeat sales that occurred on either side of two milestone dates (e.g., the initial editorial about the BeltLine and the passage of the TAD). The uninteracted milestone and BeltLine proximity variables capture baseline price trends around those dates and locations. By interacting milestone variables with BeltLine proximity, Model B3 allows for the news of the BeltLine to have differential effects on property value appreciation near to or far away from the BeltLine. The early milestone (Woolard's initial editorial in the *Atlanta Journal-Constitution* on February 14, 2003) should capture initial changes in expectations, whereas the later event (the passage of the TAD in November 2005) should reflect additional information and certainty about the project.[7]

The simplest conception of the BeltLine predicts a price "submountain," in which Atlanta property values have their greatest peak downtown and gradually fall with distance with the exception of a local "bump" in prices around the BeltLine, because of its amenity values. To capture this, the G vector includes dummy variables to indicate whether or not a sale is inside the TAD or inside the overlay district, and it also includes a measure of proximity to the TAD. If the TAD is an amenity (or disamenity), *TAD* should have a positive (negative) coefficient as should *DistTAD*, at least after news of the project spreads. If the market values being near to the TAD without being in it, or if it anticipates the BeltLine rezoning's impact on development, then the *Overlay* coefficient should reflect this.

Results

The overall results in Table 7.1 show that the hedonic models explain the bulk of the variation in housing prices in this sample. Estimated with Huber-White robust errors, most of the attributes included reveal significant hedonic prices. As is common, data limitations require the estimation of either a larger sample with few variables or a richer array of covariates on a smaller sample. Other regressions (not reported here) suggest that omitting several X attributes does little to affect the estimated γ. (The variables of interest, proximity to the TAD and overlay district, tell very similar stories between 2004 and 2006.) Model A shows a substantial price premium for homes in the TAD starting in 2003—the year of the first BeltLine editorial. In Model A, sales prices in the TAD (overlay district) are noticeably lower (higher) in 2006 than in the previous two years, and the downward-sloping TAD price gradient flattens significantly in 2006. It seems that the TAD's amenity level fell in the year following the approval of the TAD (even before the state supreme court upheld the legal challenge). Conversely, the amenities of the BeltLine Overlay District appeared to improve in recent years: prices inside the overlay district rose in 2005 to 2006. Although not yet enacted at the time of sales, the *Overlay* dummy captures spillover effects from the TAD. While countywide prices climbed, prices in the TAD (overlay district) generally did not rise significantly faster until 2003 (2005)—about the time that the BeltLine gained prominence and took shape.

Figure 7.2 helps interpret the array of BeltLine geographic variables (*G*) and their trends (*GT*). The graph depicts the price trends for otherwise similar homes over time, normalizing prices to equal 100 in 2002 (roughly just prior to *milestone*$_1$). Homes in different locations with respect to the BeltLine experienced different price trends. Four different scenarios are estimated, plus a "baseline" estimate. First, the "TAD" line represents a home inside the TAD. Second, the "Overlay–inside edge" line represents a home inside the overlay district just outside the TAD. Third, the "Overlay–outside edge" line represents a home inside the overlay district but 0.5 mile away from the TAD. Fourth, the

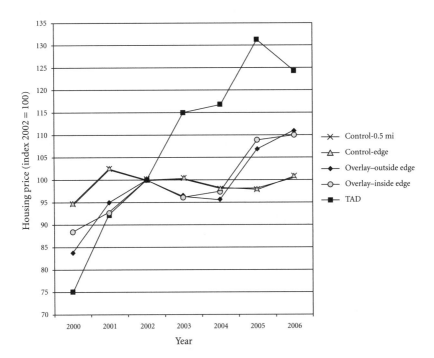

Figure 7.2 Price trends, from Model A

"Control-edge" line represents a home just outside the overlay district but still 0.5 mile from the TAD. Fifth, the "Control–0.5 mi." line represents a baseline or "control" home that is 0.5 mile away from the overlay district (and 1 mile from the TAD). If the BeltLine is expected to improve local amenities, homes with better access should have higher prices—implying that the TAD line should be above the inside edge line, which should be above the outside edge line, which should be roughly the same as the control edge line, and the control line the lowest. If being in or near the overlay district is expected to be valuable, of course, this will affect the relative prices for those homes.

Figure 7.2 shows a few interesting things. First, note that the two control (i.e., outside of the overlay district) homes have nearly identical prices. The nearly opposite gradients for the TAD and the overlay district for linear distances effectively cancel each other for distances *away* from the overlay district (and also, by design, away from the TAD).[8] Thus, the premium to be nearer to the TAD applies only nearby (i.e., within the overlay district). Second, the TAD properties were relatively low value in 2000 but experience great price growth between 2000 and 2005. Positive price trends in the TAD predate the advent of the BeltLine (suggesting that perhaps the TAD boundaries might have been influenced by market trends) and continue until 2005, even though the overlay district premiums did not appear until 2005. Trends in 2005 and 2006 point to a possible shift in expectations in which the BeltLine benefits are increasingly accruing to neighborhoods nearby but not necessarily within the TAD.[9] Overall, Figure 7.2 paints a fairly favorable picture for the amenity effects of the BeltLine project. Unfortunately, Model A rests on an assumption that unobserved housing attributes are uncorrelated with time trends. The possibility that recent years saw nicer homes being brought to market around the TAD, rather than recent years in the TAD raising the values of homes, suggests caution in interpreting the results in Figure 7.2.

Table 7.1 contains the results for the repeat-sales hedonic models (Model B). Whereas Model A implicitly restricts hedonic prices to be constant over time, Model B1 assumes that most housing attributes are time invariant. Model B1 explains appreciation using changes in lot size, (quarterly) time trends, and trends in the amenity value of being near the BeltLine. The strong countywide price growth (relative to the first quarter of 2000) is still evident. An overlay district "submountain" is apparent, starting in 2002, but there is no TAD premium and later sales even suggest that the TAD is a disamenity. Model B2 replicates Model B1 except that it allows the value of the underlying location (e.g., proximity to downtown or parks, neighborhood demographics) to vary. Rapid price growth has occurred in areas with more minorities and poor, higher income, closer to downtown, and farther from Metropolitan Atlanta Rapid Transit Authority (MARTA) rail lines. Moreover, controlling for the underlying appreciation rates in the TAD and overlay district, the amenity value of being in the overlay district is seen to peak in 2003 and fade considerably after 2005. In recent years, proximity to the TAD appears to be undesirable.

Figure 7.3 shows the price trends based on the more flexible Model B2, using the same comparison groups as in Figure 7.2. First, the two control comparison groups remain nearly identical as in Figure 7.2. The price impacts of the BeltLine do not seem to extend by the overlay district. Second, the TAD and overlay district exhibit relatively depressed property values in 2000–2001, also similar to Figure 7.2. The continued rise in TAD premiums evident in Model A, however, vanishes in Model B. Figure 7.3 shows very large discounts to property values in the TAD following 2003. The price growth evident in the overlay district in Model A is not evident here. The overlay district properties fare comparably to the control properties, with a possible downturn evident in 2006. Combined with the Model A results, the repeat-sales models indicate

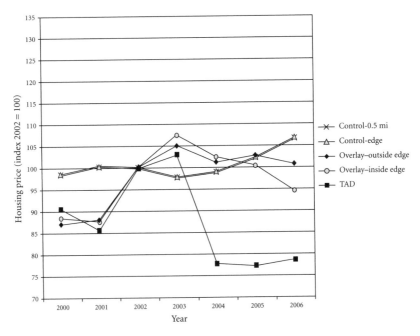

Figure 7.3 Price trends, from Model B2

that, even though TAD home sales are increasing in quality, homes in the TAD experienced substantial price declines after some initial price increases.

Finally, Model B3 tests whether the amenity values of the BeltLine changed following milestone events. This model is similar to Model B2 except that three time periods (pre-*milestone*$_1$, post-*milestone*$_1$ and pre-*milestone*$_2$, and post-*milestone*$_2$) are examined instead of seven (2000–2006, annually). Table 7.1 presents a few key results. Model B3 shows significant increases (roughly 10 percent) in home prices for sales after *milestone*$_1$ (the Woolard editorial in February 2003) in the overlay district, but that premium is not experienced inside the TAD. Sales following the city council's approval of the BeltLine TAD, on the other hand, exhibited lower prices in the neighboring overlay district, and prices in that district declined as one moved closer to the TAD. The post-*milestone*$_2$ price gradient described in Model B3 showed no premium for properties inside the TAD or the overlay district relative to similar properties outside the area. The disparity in results between Model B2 and Model B3 suggests that estimates of the price impact of the BeltLine are sensitive to the choice of break points in the time trend. Nonetheless, there is some evidence in Model B3 that market prices responded to the news of positive spillovers to nearby communities but mixed impacts in the district itself, and more time and information brought a sort of convergence in values after the BeltLine's approval.

At first glance, the results in Table 7.1 paint a mixed picture. Still, some messages come through consistently. First, the BeltLine area had depressed prices (relative to the rest of the county) in 2000, when the BeltLine idea was unknown. Those prices were already trending upward before the BeltLine news first broke. Second, being nearer to the BeltLine TAD but not in it—something that should reflect the advantages of proximity to the enhanced amenities but suffer fewer of the negative consequences (e.g., congestion, fiscal constraints)—does not command higher prices, especially after the BeltLine was passed. That said, third, properties in what would become the overlay district but *not* inside the TAD do appear to exhibit a price "submountain" during 2002 to 2005—in the initial and possibly optimistic phase of the BeltLine project. This general expectation of enhanced amenities in the area, not tied to the TAD or its current greenspace, could reflect uncertainty about the specific location of BeltLine projects.[10] Overall, the models in Table 7.1 show a rapidly fading amenity value to being inside the TAD after 2004. This result is consistent with growing expectations of major public transit lines in the BeltLine, which owners may see as bringing congestion or other disamenities. There is scant evidence in any model that property values inside the TAD have risen following the establishment of the tax year in 2005 for TIF purposes. This poses a serious problem for a project whose funding mechanism depends on appreciation inside the TAD.

In terms of the hypotheses presented earlier, some qualified support is found. Significant price effects are indeed evident, although expectations about the BeltLine are not consistently positive. First, significant price gradients do appear to reflect access to urban amenities (e.g., downtown, parks, rivers) and disamenities (e.g., transit rail lines, expressways). Market prices reflect expected access (Hypothesis 1a) as well, as the BeltLine benefits are captured in home values as the project is announced and takes shape. This is especially striking in Models A and B2, when prices in 2003 rose inside the TAD and the overlay district (neither of which would formally exist until years later). The market also reflects changes in the expectations about the amenity (Hypothesis 1b). Initial optimism was replaced by more caution (and even negative expectations), and prices for access to the BeltLine dipped in recent years as shown in both models. Model B3 highlights how a watershed event altered appreciation rates in and around the TAD. The market responses are in line with theoretical expectations, even if the market does not share the BeltLine advocates' optimism. Moreover, as the nature of the BeltLine project has evolved, the decline in prices around the BeltLine may be capturing the disamenity effect of expected BeltLine transit lines (note that people pay a premium to live *farther* from MARTA lines, per Model B).[11] This analysis highlights the important result that the project's expected benefits are captured immediately as windfall gains in property value to owners (owner-occupants or absentee landlords). Environmental improvements, once realized, alter owners' welfare only insofar as they deviate from expectations—and disappointment may be as likely as relief. Expected improvements affect renters far less, although realized improvements may leave them worse off (see Chapter 4).[12]

The complex reality of the BeltLine project leads to some ambiguity from theory because the BeltLine project is more than just an amenity. It is a TIF that will also include rezoning. Theory gives ambiguous predictions about the effects of new zoning rules as well. The BeltLine's rezoning to increase residential density should foster greater housing supply in the area and thus depress prices. If the zoning overlay achieves its other goals of promoting positive externalities and improving neighborhood quality, however, prices should rise following demand. Thus, even though the effect on quantity of housing provided

Table 7.2 Effects of proximity to the BeltLine on upgrading

Variable	Coefficient for dependent variable ΔCode	Coefficient for dependent variable Δ ln(bldg ft²)
years between sales	0.164***	0.011***
TAD	−0.058	−0.002
Overlay	−0.038**	−0.002
milestone₂	0.103***	−0.002
milestone₂ × TAD	−0.110	0.006
milestone₂ × Overlay	0.343***	0.009***
Constant	−0.016**	−0.0004
N	23,441	23,441
R²	0.0269	0.0083

*$p < 0.1$; **$p < 0.05$; ***$p < 0.01$.

unambiguously rises, the impact of the zoning overlay on prices is ambiguous in theory.[13]

The second set of expectations concerns changes in the housing stock around the BeltLine. More investment is expected, even in advance of the project (Hypothesis 2a). Some regressions using data on homes with multiple sales explore these issues and are reported in Table 7.2. Column 1 shows that homes sold in the overlay district experienced more renovations, measured by between-sales improvements in the county assessor's quality code measure for the property, and that disparity in renovations increased significantly after formal approval ($milestone_2$). Renovations inside the BeltLine TAD, however, were not greater than in the rest of the overlay neighborhood. That *Overlay* rather than *TAD* captures the bulk of the impact is not surprising, given the (price) results in Table 7.1. A second regression shows that homes in the overlay district tended to increase their building's square footage after $milestone_2$, more than other properties in the county or before the passage of the BeltLine TAD. The share of countywide annual home sales in the overlay district steadily rose every year between 2000 and 2006, from 6.9 to 10.7 percent. (The share in the TAD also rose, from 0.7 to 1.1 percent, but did so erratically.) Turnover and renovation appear to be on the rise around the BeltLine. Moreover, consistent with another conjecture (Hypothesis 2b), larger price gains from the BeltLine tended to occur in poorer neighborhoods, as discussed below.

Market responses to the BeltLine project affect groups of residents differently. The BeltLine loop traverses heterogeneous urban neighborhoods, and

its impacts are unlikely to be uniform. Table 7.3 displays some pairwise correlations between measures of price impacts and neighborhood demographics. For 59 census block groups in the overlay district, the observed increase
in the median sales price (ln P) from the first 10 months of 2005 (before the
BeltLine's approval) to the first 10 months of 2006 is uncorrelated with demographics (e.g., percent white, income).[14] Although the sales prices around the
BeltLine seem to be changing independently of the underlying demographics,
a better test of the impact of the BeltLine would be to assess its price effects
conditional on other housing attributes. The hedonic models estimated above
show different effects around the BeltLine, depending on proximity to the
TAD. The semi-log model also implies that impacts (measured in dollars) are
proportional to property values. To better assess the distribution of impacts,
Model B3 is used to predict how housing values would change if $milestone_2$ had
never occurred. This thought experiment identifies the impact of the BeltLine
approval on prices, holding all other home attributes fixed.[15] At the aggregate
level, the block-group median predicted price effect's correlations with key
demographics are not statistically significantly different from 0. Simple correlations between aggregate impacts and demographics are difficult to observe
in the diverse BeltLine landscape. Disaggregated, however, individual homes
experiencing larger (negative) percent price effects from $milestone_2$ tend to be
in block groups that have greater percentages of school-aged children, minorities, and poor residents (in the 2000 Census). The small but statistically significant correlations indicate the uneven impacts of the BeltLine project. Market
prices reflect how approval of TIF might adversely affect schools. As expected
(Hypothesis 2b), homes in lower-income and higher-risk neighborhoods experienced larger BeltLine-related price effects. Also, as expected, neighborhoods
with greater shares of owner-occupants experienced greater price changes in

Table 7.3 Selected correlations, overlay district observations only

Correlation	Variable				
	ln(Income)	*%White*	*%Renters*	*%Kids*	*N*
Block-group median of ΔP[a]	0.092	0.159	−0.065	−0.040	59
Block-group median of $\Delta \ln(\text{predicted } P)$[a]	0.149	0.078	−0.146	0.046	60
$\Delta \ln(\text{predicted } P)$[a]	0.053***	0.054***	0.021*	−0.088***	8,370
$\Delta(\text{predicted } P)$[a]	−0.082***	−0.098***	−0.021*	0.072***	8,370

[a]See text.

*$p < 0.1$; **$p < 0.05$; ***$p < 0.01$.

response to news of the BeltLine. Finally, as homes experiencing larger percentage changes in price after *milestone*$_2$ tended to be lower in value, Table 7.3 shows the correlations between impacts in gross dollar values and neighborhood demographics to be opposite that of those with percent price impacts.

Conclusion

The empirical evidence presented here raises some questions about the BeltLine's prospects and equity. The housing market quickly incorporates news of the BeltLine, adjusts as expectations change, and confers immediate windfall gains and losses on property owners well before the project itself is completed. From an environmental justice perspective, the dynamic nature of the property market plays a major role in allocating the benefits of an urban amenity—not just in space but also through time. Noonan (2008) expands on this discussion for environmental justice studies in general. Even a longitudinal environmental justice study might overlook how property markets capitalize future changes, thereby complicating efforts to link changes in welfare to changes in environmental quality. Promises to remediate brownfields into a greenbelt are quickly capitalized into property values. This confers immediate gains on property owners, who may or may not be among the residents who actually experience the improved environment. The incidence of the improvement falls largely on property owners at the time expectations are set. This group differs from the eventual residents at the time of completion insofar as newcomers (renters or owners), who pay full market rate for proximity to the amenity, bid up prices and move in.

As much as theory guides our expectations for a project like the BeltLine, the impacts are ultimately empirically observable, and this chapter offers a preliminary glimpse into these impacts. The price impacts, driven by speculation, are not consistently positive according to a variety of hedonic price models. As the BeltLine proposal was building momentum, prices likely experienced a surge—in the broader BeltLine area rather than in the area that was later to be designated part of the TAD—but this price premium largely vanished by 2006. The perception that the BeltLine was a mixed bag (with some enhanced greenspace amenities but also with some congestion, rail lines, and possible tax burdens) seems evident and, at least by the time the city council approved the TAD, the mix was apparently negative on balance. Homes just outside of the BeltLine area sold at a premium compared to those inside the zoning district. Properties in the TAD itself typically sold for even less.

Several possible explanations for this result come to mind. First, property owners' expectations about the BeltLine do not measure up to its lofty aims. Sufficient uncertainty about the project's benefits, belief that its implementation is so far in the (discounted) future, or pessimism about its feasibility (and legality) could account for the weak price impacts. Second, the benefits are not expected to be localized to the area while some of the costs are. The jobs, transit, and broader "transformation" benefit the broader city, but local home prices would not reflect that increased amenity level. Some costs are likely perceived to be local to residents—fiscal constraints associated with the TIF and some ills associated with increased density or congestion and proximity to new public rail lines—while access to many benefits may not significantly require local residence. Third, the slackness in the housing supply, possibly combined with increased housing supply spurred by the BeltLine transformation (and new zoning rules), is inhibiting the price change. The coincident increase in housing supply and upgrading evident in the data suggest that the BeltLine project entails more than just an increase in demand. The supply side of the story may matter just as much.

From a programmatic standpoint, this analysis also raises concerns about the viability of the BeltLine. Speculation should lead the BeltLine's future gains to be capitalized into property values immediately. Locking in the property tax base at the end of 2005—after any substantial price increases owing to the Belt-Line were observed—suggests that the tax base was frozen too late or optimism over the BeltLine's prospects was too dim for the market to reflect. The amenity value of proximity to the BeltLine faded after 2005. Whether this was in anticipation of legal and other challenges, a market correction for earlier exuberance, or something else is unclear. Ordinarily, this would not doom a project like the BeltLine because the TIF's increment can come from any source, such as broader upswings in the housing market or inflation. Unfortunately for the BeltLine, and perhaps other TIF projects, the tax base was established near the peak of a massive housing market bubble that has subsequently "popped."

The case of endogenous environmental improvements (see Chapter 2) poses even greater challenges. The power of markets to capitalize on changes in E and directly affect the welfare of owners, whether they experience or directly care about those environmental changes, provides incentives for owners to improve their environment. This long-time theme of free-market environmentalists has much to commend itself in theory. The efforts of planners in Atlanta to harness market forces for the BeltLine project attests to their faith in markets and residents to bid up prices and effectively gentrify the area. The next step is to better understand how changes in the environment in the BeltLine, population, and welfare vary *along with* one another (rather than innocently reacting to exogenous shocks).

Notes

1. For additional discussion of price and sorting effects from remediations, see Chapter 3.

2. In particular, it may not hold without the single-crossing property discussed in Chapter 4.

3. Recent empirical work on TIF implementation and impacts is mixed. The empirical research typically falls into one of two strands—investigations of designation processes or decisions (e.g., Man and Rosentraub 1998; Man 1999; Gibson 2003; Byrne 2005) or measurements of a designation's effects on prices (e.g., Man and Rosentraub 1998; Dye and Merriman 2000; Weber, Bhatta, and Merriman 2003, 2007; Byrne 2005; Smith 2006; Carroll 2008).

4. Multiparcel sales, government resales, sales not on the open market, sales combining other unrecorded parcels, "suspicious" sales, sales for properties that are to be demolished, and sales violating other technical criteria are dropped. Those with sales prices less than $5,000 are also excluded.

5. Hedonic analyses were conducted using these characteristics and only the latter three years of data, but are not reported here for brevity. The inclusion of additional property characteristics in the models does not substantively alter the basic conclusions, at least with respect to the trends in the final three years. The results are available from the author upon request.

6. A complete list of variables along with descriptive statistics can be found in Table A.7.1 in the online appendix at http://www.sup.org/environmentaljustice.

7. Other watershed dates in the history of the BeltLine were tested, but they were either insignificant or no different from the ones presented here. Future research would do well to use a break-point analysis to infer from the data when structural breaks in the BeltLine's amenity price might have occurred.

8. This owes partly to the design of the BeltLine as a ring around the CBD; hence, the distance-to-CBD control soaks up the effects of moving away from the TAD or the overlay district *and* downtown. Entering *DistCBD* as a quadratic produces no major changes in the model. A useful interpretation in Tables 7.2 and 7.3 is that there is no significant price gradient outside the overlay (other than the prevailing *DistCBD* gradient), but the *DistTAD* coefficients reveal a within-overlay gradient.

9. It seems plausible that, at least initially, investors believed that the BeltLine would be paid for by redistributing resources within the city. Later, as they learned,

the viability of the project hinged on not raiding other areas' tax revenues but instead on localized debt and diverting school funding. Still a positive idea, the BeltLine project is less appealing to property owners inside the TAD and more appealing to "free riders" on the outside.

10. When the regressions in Table 7.1 are estimated while allowing for trends in the price gradient for parks (various *TAD* and *DistPark* and time interactions), the results reported above do not appreciably change. Inside the TAD, there does not appear to be a significantly different price gradient for parks, at any point in time, than there is for the county in general.

11. Over time, the initial emphasis on brownfield-to-greenfield and rails-to-trails transformations has been replaced by discussions of more controversial and expensive components, namely, subsidized higher-density housing and mass-transit rail lines.

12. The TAD surrounds downtown Atlanta and has higher rentership (63 percent) and poverty rates than the countywide average (47 percent), based on the 2000 Census. The high share of renters, especially in the southern half of the BeltLine loop, raises concerns about environmental gentrification.

13. This ambiguity is central to many urban redevelopment projects that aim to simultaneously raise property values and either density or affordable (i.e., subsidized) housing. The Atlanta BeltLine project has these primary goals. Funding for the project relies on increased property values from improved amenities, yet much of the project expenses come from subsidizing housing and the zoning overlay aims to increase housing density. Simultaneously promoting demand *and* supply even in the simplest economic models will have an ambiguous impact on prices (and unambiguous increases for quantity).

14. The correlations are statistically insignificant when block groups are weighted by the number of households.

15. Specifically, for overlay homes, the Model B3 coefficients from $milestone_2$ interactions are used to predict the price effects of moving *TAD* and *Overlay* to 0 and increasing *DistTAD* to 0.5 mile to 0 *after* the BeltLine approval date. I use the Kennedy (1981) correction for the *TAD* and *Overlay* dummy variables. The TAD properties suffer an 8.8 percent price drop, while elsewhere in the overlay district the price drop ranges from 9.0 to 13.7 percent.

References

Atlanta Development Authority. 2005. *Atlanta BeltLine Redevelopment Plan.* http://www.atlantada.com/adaInitiatives/BeltLineRedevelopmentPlanA.jsp.

Atlanta Regional Commission. 2002. "Atlanta Region Information System." CD, vol. 1b.

Bayer, Patrick, Nathaniel Keohane, and Christopher Timmins. 2009. "Migration and Hedonic Valuation: The Case of Air Quality." *Journal of Environmental Economics and Management* 58 (1): 1–14.

Brueckner, Jan K. 2001. "Tax Increment Financing: A Theoretical Inquiry." *Journal of Public Economics* 81 (2): 321–43.

Byrne, Paul F. 2005. "Strategic Interaction and the Adoption of Tax Increment Financing." *Regional Science and Urban Economics* 35 (3): 279–303.

Carroll, Deborah A. 2008. "Tax Increment Financing and Property Value: An Examination of Business Property Using Panel Data." *Urban Affairs Review* 43 (4): 520–52.

Cropper, Maureen L., Leland Deck, and Kenneth E. McConnell. 1988. "On the Choice of Functional Forms for Hedonic Price Functions." *Review of Economics and Statistics* 70 (4): 668–75.

Diamond, Douglas B., and George S. Tolley. 1982. "The Economic Roles of Urban Amenities." In *The Economics of Urban Amenities*, edited by Douglas B. Diamond and George S. Tolley, 3–54. New York: Academic Press.

Dye, Richard F., and David Franklin Merriman. 2000. "The Effects of Tax Increment Financing on Economic Development." *Journal of Urban Economics* 47 (2): 306–28.

———. 2006. "Tax Increment Financing: A Tool for Local Economic Development." *Land Lines* 18 (1): 2–7.

Dye, Richard F., and Jeffrey O. Sundberg. 1998. "A Model of Tax Increment Financing Adoption Incentives." *Growth and Change* 29 (1): 90–110.

Epple, Dennis. 1987. "Hedonic Prices and Implicit Markets: Estimating Demand and Supply Functions for Differentiated Products." *Journal of Political Economy* 95 (1): 59–80.

Fullerton, Don. 2008. "Distributional Effects of Environmental and Energy Policy: An Introduction." NBER Working Paper 14241, National Bureau of Economic Research, Cambridge, MA. http://ideas.repec.org/p/nbr/nberwo/14241.html.

Gibson, Diane. 2003. "Neighborhood Characteristics and the Targeting of Tax Increment Financing in Chicago." *Journal of Urban Economics* 54 (2): 309–27.

Grimes, Oliver, Jr. 1982. "The Influence of Urban Centers on Recreational Land Use." In *The Economics of Urban Amenities*, edited by Douglas B. Diamond and George S. Tolley, 143–64. New York: Academic Press.

Immergluck, Daniel. 2007. "The BeltLine and Rising Home Prices: Residential Appreciation near the BeltLine Tax Allocation District and Policy Recommendations to Minimize Displacement." Study prepared for Georgia Stand-Up, Atlanta, GA. http://www.gastandup.org/pdfs/Full Report FINAL.pdf . Last accessed: 9 September 2008.

Kennedy, Peter E. 1981. "Estimation with Correctly Interpreted Dummy Variables in Semilogarithmic Equations." *American Economic Review* 71 (4): 801.

Kiel, Katherine A., and Jeffrey E. Zabel. 1998. "Evaluating the Usefulness of the American Housing Survey for Creating House Price Indices." *Journal of Real Estate Finance and Economics* 14 (1–2): 189–202.

Man, Joyce Y. 1999. "Fiscal Pressure, Competition and the Adoption of Tax Increment Financing." *Urban Studies* 36 (7): 1151–67.

Man, Joyce Y., and Mark S. Rosentraub. 1998. "Tax Increment Financing: Municipal Adoption and Effects on Property Value Growth." *Public Finance Review* 26 (6): 523–47.

Noonan, Douglas S. 2008. "Evidence of Environmental Justice: A Critical Perspective on the Practice of EJ Research and Lessons for Policy Design." *Social Science Quarterly* 89 (5): 1153–74.

Palmquist, Raymond B. 1988. "Welfare Measurement for Environmental Improvement Using the Hedonic Model: The Case of Nonparametric Marginal Prices." *Journal of Environmental Economics and Management* 15 (3): 297–312.

Roback, Jennifer. 1982. "Wages, Rents, and the Quality of Life." *Journal of Political Economy* 90 (6): 1257–78.

Rosen, Sherwin. 1974. "Hedonic Prices and Implicit Markets: Product Differentiation in Pure Competition." *Journal of Political Economy* 82 (1): 34–55.

Sieg, Holger, V. Kerry Smith, H. Spencer Banzhaf, and Randy Walsh. 2004. "Estimating the General Equilibrium Benefits of Large Changes in Spatially Delineated Public Goods." *International Economic Review* 45 (4): 1047–77.

Smith, Brent C. 2006. "The Impact of Tax Increment Finance Districts on Localized Real Estate: Evidence from Chicago's Multifamily Markets." *Journal of Housing Economics* 15 (1): 21–37.

Smith, Lawrence B., Kenneth T. Rosen, and George Fallis. 1988. "Recent Developments in Economic Models of Housing Markets." *Journal of Economic Literature* 26 (1): 29–64.

Smith, V. Kerry, Holger Sieg, H. Spencer Banzhaf, and Randall P. Walsh. 2004. "General Equilibrium Benefits for Environmental Improvements: Projected Ozone Reductions under EPA's Prospective Analysis for the Los Angeles Air Basin." *Journal of Environmental Economics and Management* 47 (3): 559–84.

Weber, Rachel, Saurav Dev Bhatta, and David Merriman. 2003. "Does Tax Increment Financing Raise Urban Industrial Property Values?" *Urban Studies* 40 (10): 2001–21.

———. 2007. "Spillovers from Tax Increment Financing Districts: Implications for Housing Price Discrimination." *Regional Science and Urban Economics* 37 (2): 259–81.

Woolard, Cathy. 2003. "Make a Beeline for the BeltLine." *Atlanta Journal-Constitution*, February 14, 2003.

III
The Behavior of Polluting Firms

THE SIMPLEST EXPLANATION for the observed environmental justice correlations is that polluting firms locate in communities with a greater concentration of minorities and the poor. (This explanation is in direct contrast to the "coming to the nuisance" hypothesis whereby firm location is taken as given and households migrate ex post.) If firms do locate in such areas, it may be because of "pure discrimination" in which they are indulging discriminatory tastes rather than merely maximizing profits (the first hypothesis discussed in Chapter 1). Or it may be because, in the pursuit of profits, they locate in areas with features that are associated with poor populations, either directly or indirectly, through some other social process (the fifth hypothesis discussed in Chapter 1). Examples might be cheaper land prices, lower wages, access to transportation corridors, access to other (polluting) industries, and so on.

In important earlier work, Been (1994, 1997); Pastor, Sadd, and Hipp (2001); and Baden and Coursey (2002) investigated these questions by regressing the presence of a polluting facility on various demographic factors *at the time of siting*, finding mixed results. This body of work effectively treats a census tract or other geographic entity as the unit of analysis for explaining the locational decision-making process. In this short section, Ann Wolverton offers a significant methodological advance on this earlier literature. In particular, she directly models the behavior of firms, looking at their choice of *where* to site a polluting facility. Given a firm's decision to establish a facility somewhere, Wolverton models the firm's choice of location among all the possible locations. She explains their choice patterns as a function of demographics, prices, transportation options, and so forth. She offers convincing evidence that these choices are driven more by profits than by pure discrimination.

References

Baden, Brett M., and Don L. Coursey. 2002. "The Locality of Waste Sites within the City of Chicago: A Demographic, Social, and Economic Analysis." *Resource and Energy Economics* 24 (1–2): 53–93.

Been, Vicki. 1994. "Locally Undesirable Land Uses in Minority Neighborhoods: Disproportionate Siting or Market Dynamics?" *Yale Law Journal* 103:1383–1422.

Been, Vicki, with Francis Gupta. 1997. "Coming to the Nuisance or Going to the Barrios? A Longitudinal Analysis of Environmental Justice Claims." *Ecology Law Quarterly* 24 (1): 1–56.

Pastor, Manuel, Jim Sadd, and John Hipp. 2001. "Which Came First? Toxic Facilities, Minority Move-In, and Environmental Justice." *Journal of Urban Affairs* 23 (1): 1–21.

8 The Role of Demographic and Cost-Related Factors in Determining Where Plants Locate

A Tale of Two Texas Cities

Ann Wolverton

Introduction

It is fairly common in the environmental justice literature to focus on the relationship between contemporaneous socioeconomic characteristics and site or plant location for the purposes of investigating disproportionate impacts. The studies that have examined whether socioeconomic factors contribute to location decisions at the time of siting often exclude variables recognized in the firm location literature as important determinants of location choice, for instance, the costs of land, labor, and transportation. In this chapter, I use a similar approach to Wolverton (2009): I examine plant location decisions at the time of siting but incorporate variables recognized as important in both the firm location and the environmental justice literatures into a single analysis. While most environmental justice studies that model location choice use a binary response model, I allow for multiple location alternatives to more closely approximate a firm's evaluation of potential substitute sites to the location chosen.

Unlike Wolverton (2009), this chapter examines the potential influence of geographic scope on the analytic results. Studies in the environmental justice literature report mixed results with regard to the relevance of race, ethnicity, poverty, and income to location decisions. Bryant and Mohai (1992) point out that one possible reason for such a mix of findings may be that the scope of the analysis differs so widely by study—some focus on a particular urban area or region, while others are national in scope.[1] Results from city-specific analyses cannot be easily generalized to other geographic contexts. However, more aggregate studies—those on the state or national level—may mask the importance of socioeconomic factors in firm decision making. This chapter examines factors related to a polluting plant's decision of where to locate within two large Texas cities, Dallas–Fort Worth and Houston, at the time of siting between 1978 and 1985, using a conditional logit framework. It then compares these results to those for the state of Texas while using consistent methodology and sets of variables.

The Environmental Justice Literature

Early studies that match site location to contemporaneous socioeconomic characteristics often rely on simple statistical techniques and tend to find strong evidence of a relationship between race and poverty variables and site location.[2] Later studies that examine similar relationships often use more sophisticated techniques and therefore tend to be more careful in the interpretation of results. Scope varies widely across these studies—some focus on a particular urban area or region, while others are national in scope.[3]

Zimmerman (1993) finds that a greater percentage of minorities lives near inactive hazardous waste sites that appear on the National Priority List but that the population living in poverty does not differ significantly from the national average. This trend is found to hold at the regional level as well. Baden, Noonan, and Turaga (2007) find that race and ethnicity are correlated with the presence of a Superfund site at the national level, but they conclude that this relationship is sensitive to changes in both geographic scope and scale (i.e., how the neighborhood is defined). On the other hand, Anderton et al. (1994) find only limited evidence of disproportionate numbers of hazardous waste facilities located in minority or poor neighborhoods. This result is also found to hold at a more disaggregated level when the country is divided into 10 regions.[4]

There are a handful of studies that examine the relationship between neighborhood characteristics and facility location decisions at the time of siting. These studies also find a mixed record with regard to the importance of socioeconomic variables to plant location decisions. Unlike studies that match site location to contemporaneous socioeconomic characteristics, however, they rarely examine how results change with the scope of the analysis. Been (1997) obtains mixed evidence that race played a role at the time of siting for active commercial hazardous waste treatment, storage, and disposal facilities (TSDFs) in the United States. While waste disposal sites are correlated with certain 1990 socioeconomic characteristics such as race and income, neither the percentage of the poor nor the percentage of African Americans in a neighborhood is significant at the time of siting. The percentage of Hispanics does remain significant at the time of siting. Pastor, Sadd, and Hipp (2001) examine the location of TSDF sites in Los Angeles County, California, and find greater evidence of disproportionate siting in established Latino and African American communities than minority move-in after the TSDF establishment. Baden and Coursey (2002) examine the location of Superfund sites in Chicago, Illinois, and find that sites were disproportionately located in poor neighborhoods in the 1960s but not in the 1990s. However, they find little evidence for disproportionate exposure of African Americans either currently or at the time of siting. Jenkins, Maguire, and Morgan (2004) study compensation to communities in exchange for hosting municipal solid waste landfills. Controlling for tipping fees paid from the landfill to the community, they find that socioeconomic characteristics such as income and race do not matter at the city level but do appear to matter at the county level.[5] Finally, Wolverton (2009) examines the siting decisions of Toxics Release Inventory (TRI) plants in the 1980s and 1990s in the state of Texas and finds that input-related cost factors are consistently more important than determinants related to the socioeconomic characteristics of the surrounding neighborhood. Race and ethnicity are not related to plant location decisions, while poverty appears to act as a deterrent.

The Firm Location Literature

In the economics literature, a firm is assumed to evaluate potential locations for a new plant based on the principle of profit maximization. In doing so, the firm takes into account many location-specific attributes related to production and transportation costs that may affect potential profits in each potential location. Production costs include costs related to relatively immobile inputs such as land, labor, and housing, and costs related to operation such as taxes, public utility fees, and environmental regulations. Transportation costs include freight rates, distance to input markets, and distance to output markets. Most studies of new plant location do not have measures for all production and transportation costs because of limitations in the data but do usually include measures of labor costs, land costs, transportation costs, energy costs, and level of taxation.[6] It is also important to consider any offsetting location benefits from agglomeration economies such as a shared infrastructure or labor pool.

Some environmental justice studies include variables to serve as proxies for land and labor costs but rarely include other variables associated with firm location (e.g., Davidson and Anderton 2000). Kriesel, Centner, and Keeler (1996), while focusing on the incidence of emissions rather than on plant location, is a notable exception within the environmental justice literature. Along with land and labor costs, they include proximity to an interstate highway and find that the inclusion of these factors renders race and poverty insignificant. This finding points to the importance of including such variables in any study of site location decisions. Wolverton (2009) includes measures of labor costs, land costs, distance to major highways and rail, and possible agglomeration economies. She also finds that traditional firm location variables dominate in importance and render race variables insignificant.

As discussed in Chapter 1 of this volume, Hamilton (1995) offers three additional hypotheses as to why a plant may locate in a poor or minority neighborhood. The first hypothesis stems from Coase (1960): a plant is established where residents' valuation of environmental quality, and therefore the potential compensation by the firm to the neighborhood residents, is lowest. Since local willingness to pay for environmental quality is positively correlated with income, firms will tend to locate plants in poorer neighborhoods to minimize the costs of compensation.[7] The second hypothesis as to why plants may locate in poor or minority neighborhoods is that firms locate polluting plants where the likelihood of a community engaging in collective activities is relatively low. In this case, a firm owes less to the community in the form of compensation not because the neighborhood values the externality any less than other communities but because the transaction costs of collective action are high. Hamilton's final hypothesis is that firm owners or managers trade off profits in favor of discriminating against a particular demographic group by locating a heavily polluting plant in that community. Since it is easier and therefore less costly to discriminate in neighborhoods with a substantial minority population, plants tend to be located in these neighborhoods.

Empirical Model and Approach

I adopt the empirical model of firm location decisions first developed by Levinson (1996) and then adapted by Wolverton (2009) for the purposes of incorporating Hamilton's additional hypotheses related to firm location. Levinson (1996) assumes that each firm has an unobserved profit function for each possible location that depends on location-specific variables such as factor prices, fixed inputs (land, labor), and the stringency of environmental regulation. Wolverton (2009) includes the cost of discrimination in the form of foregone profits and the cost of required compensation, which is a function of the value placed on environmental amenities in the neighborhood and the propensity of the neighborhood to engage in collective action. Based on the assumption that firms are motivated by a desire to maximize their profits, a firm then chooses to locate a plant in the neighborhood that yields the highest potential profit. An increase in the cost of a location—because of an increase in input prices, the cost of discrimination, or the level of compensation required—implies a decrease in profits. An increase in the availability of inputs implies an increase in profits.

Most environmental justice studies that model location choice use a binary response model.[8] Allowing for multiple location alternatives seems more appropriate, since firms typically choose from a spectrum of competitive locations when deciding where to site a plant. Following Wolverton (2009), I use a conditional logit model to represent the choice of a particular location from a set of many neighborhoods. Assume that firm i faces J possible plant location alternatives and that these J choices are independently and identically distributed. The firm will choose location j when its profits π_{ij} are maximized in that particular location compared to all other possible choices. It is possible to write firm i's profits as follows:

$$\pi_{ij} = \beta' z_{ij} + e_{ij}, \tag{8.1}$$

where z_{ij} is defined as the set of observed characteristics specific to location j and plant i. Assume that the error term e_{ij} has a Weibull distribution. If the firm's underlying production function is assumed to be Cobb-Douglas, then profits will be log-linear.

Conditional on the decision to open a new plant, the probability that firm i will choose a particular location k can be written as

$$\Pr(ik) = \frac{e^{\beta' z_{ik}}}{\sum_{j=1}^{J} e^{\beta' z_{ij}}}. \tag{8.2}$$

Because of the limited number of observations in the Dallas–Fort Worth and Houston areas, a firm is modeled as selecting a location for its plant from the actual location and nine randomly selected alternatives drawn from the full choice set for a given metropolitan area. This technique has been shown to yield consistent estimates and has the added advantage that the likelihood function is identical to that used for estimating a conditional logit with the full choice set (McFadden 1978).

Data

In this chapter, I focus on location decisions in two urban areas of Texas: Dallas–Fort Worth and Houston.[9] These are two of the largest cities in Texas, and both rank within the top 10 largest cities in the United States by population. These two metropolitan areas differ in a number of interesting ways that may influence plant location decisions. For instance, Houston has a much more concentrated industry profile than Dallas–Fort Worth, with the majority of its industry engaged in chemical manufacturing. Houston also does not limit land use through zoning restrictions, while Dallas–Fort Worth does. This implies that industry in the Houston area faces fewer constraints on its location decisions, all else equal, in comparison to those that choose to locate in Dallas–Fort Worth. This could increase the likelihood that facilities in Houston are located closer to existing residential areas.

I examine the location decisions of manufacturing plants sited between 1976 and 1985 in the Houston and Dallas–Fort Worth areas that reported to the TRI. Each TRI plant in Texas is matched to the census tract in which it is located. Any plant that appears in the TRI at least once is eligible for inclusion.[10] The location of the plants is matched to the appropriate census tract and socioeconomic characteristics from the 1980 US Census of Population and Housing. A total of 106 census tracts have one or more plants locating in the Dallas–Fort Worth area, and 56 census tracts have one or more plants locating in the Houston-Galveston area during this time period.[11] Data are also drawn from the US Census of Manufactures, the County and City Data Books, and several directories of manufacturers for the state of Texas.[12]

Variable Definitions

I use variables associated with each of the four relevant considerations for plant location decisions that were outlined previously: profit maximization,[13] willingness to pay for environmental amenities, propensity to engage in collective action, and opportunities to discriminate.

I capture differences in the cost of land, labor, and transportation, all of which enter into a firm's calculation of potential profits, through the use of the average property value of owner-occupied housing in a neighborhood, $PROPERTY_j$;[14] the average wage of a production worker in manufacturing at the county level, $WAGE_j$; and the average distance of a given neighborhood from the nearest railroad, $RAIL_j$.[15] To control for potential differences in the costs of environmental regulation, I also include the percentage of years for which a county was out of attainment for ozone and total suspended particulates over the years studied, $NATTN_j$.[16] This is a potentially relevant factor since it is arguably more difficult to locate a polluting plant in a county already out of attainment with existing regulations. Following Arora and Cason (1998), I also include the percentage of the population employed in manufacturing, $MANUF_{ij}$, to capture the potential trade-off between jobs and environment. To account for the role that zoning or agglomeration economies may play, the number of preexisting TRI facilities in the same census tract, $OLDSITE_j$, is included. Finally, a variable measuring the percentage of the population living in an urbanized area, $URBAN_j$, is also included in the analysis. More urbanized areas may offer more immediate access to large labor pools, better infrastructure, and easy access to public services. However, they also tend to have higher taxes, more traffic, and more crime.[17]

The potential compensation a firm pays to a neighborhood depends on the neighborhood's willingness to pay for environmental quality and its propensity for collective action. Residents' willingness to pay for environmental amenities is most closely associated with income levels, $INCOME_j$. The percentage of households living below the poverty line, $POVERTY_j$, is also included as a variable. If a firm compensates each member of the neighborhood, then the more densely populated a neighborhood, $POPDENS_j$, the more costly it is to the firm and the less likely it will be to locate a plant in that neighborhood.[18] Following Arora and Cason (1998), I also include variables that affect a population's "stake" in the neighborhood as well as their desire to free ride: the average number of children per household, $CHILD_j$; the percentage of the population over the age of 65, $AGE65_j$; and the percentage of households that are renters, $RENTER_j$.[19]

Two variables are included to represent the possibility that firms seek out neighborhoods where it is easier to discriminate on the basis of race or ethnicity: the percentage of the population who are nonwhite, $NONWHT_j$, and the percentage who are foreign-born, $FOREIGN_j$.[20]

Multicollinearity

A few of the independent variables described in the previous section are highly correlated. For instance, use of property values in the same regression as income is potentially problematic since they have a correlation coefficient above 80 percent. Likewise, the percentage of the population living in poverty is highly correlated with income and the percentage of the population who are nonwhite. Because the traditional environmental justice literature includes these variables indiscriminately, I include one specification that ignores these multicollinearity problems. However, I also explore an alternate specification: I use $PBUILT70_j$, the percentage of housing in a neighborhood that was built prior to 1970, as a proxy for land value. This measure is expected to be a rather imperfect substitute since it is related to the housing stock and therefore more closely associated with property values than with land value, but it allows me to explore the robustness of the results. I also use $NOPHON_j$, the percentage of households without a phone in their home, as a proxy for the poverty rate. This measure is fairly highly correlated with poverty (67 percent) but is far less correlated with the income and race variables.

Matching of All Plants Regardless of When They Are Established

The focus of much of the environmental justice literature is on the correlation between plant location and socioeconomic characteristics without accounting for the timing of the siting decision. To ensure our sample is consistent with previous studies, I match all plants from the TRI, for which establishment data are available, that have been sited in the Houston-Galveston and Dallas–Fort Worth areas earlier than 1986 to socioeconomic characteristics from the 1990 US Census. A total of 150 census tracts have one or more plants from the data set being established in the Dallas–Fort Worth area and 134 census tracts have one or more plants being established in the Houston-Galveston area prior to 1986.

I find that for both the Dallas–Fort Worth and the Houston-Galveston areas, the summary statistics show that neighborhoods with a plant generally have, on average, lower incomes (17 percent lower in Houston and 25 percent in Dallas), higher percentages of nonwhite (5 percentage points more in Dallas) and foreign-born (1–3 percentage points across cities), higher percentage living in poverty (2 percentage points), and a greater percentage of renters (2–4 percentage points).[21] Such a finding is consistent with the correlations observed in the literature when all plants are matched to contemporaneous neighborhood characteristics regardless of the time of siting. Figures 8.1 to 8.4 further illustrate the broad correlation between the location of older TRI plants and two socioeconomic characteristics, percentage nonwhite and per capita income in 1990. This correlation is less evident for the subset of plants sited between 1976 and 1985.

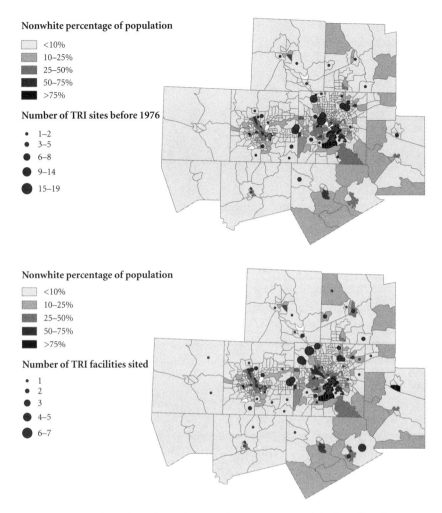

Nonwhite percentage of population

- [ ] <10%
- [ ] 10–25%
- [ ] 25–50%
- [ ] 50–75%
- [ ] >75%

Number of TRI sites before 1976

- · 1–2
- · 3–5
- ● 6–8
- ● 9–14
- ● 15–19

Nonwhite percentage of population

- [ ] <10%
- [ ] 10–25%
- [ ] 25–50%
- [ ] 50–75%
- [ ] >75%

Number of TRI facilities sited

- · 1
- · 2
- ● 3
- ● 4–5
- ● 6–7

Figure 8.1 Map of number of TRI plants and percentage nonwhite in Dallas–Fort Worth, before 1976 and 1976–1986, respectively

Summary Statistics for 1980 Established Plants Only

For the time period studied, plants are concentrated in only a few two-digit Standard Industrial Classifications (SICs) in the two metropolitan statistical areas (MSAs). Dallas–Fort Worth appears somewhat more diverse than Houston-Galveston in this regard. In Houston-Galveston, almost half of the plants are in the chemicals and allied products (SIC 28) industry. Another 26 percent are in fabricated metal products (SIC 34), and 9 percent are in the rubber and

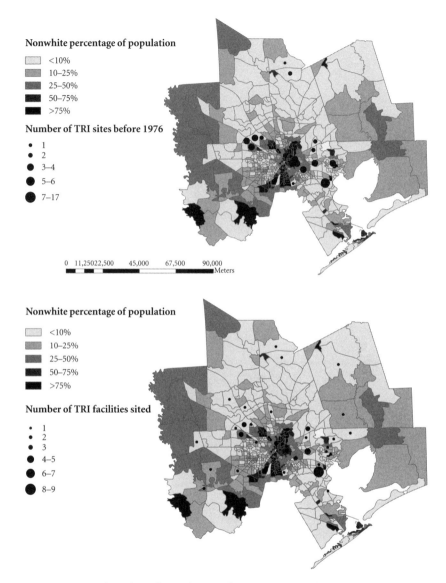

Figure 8.2 Map of number of TRI plants and percentage nonwhite in Houston-Galveston, before 1976 and 1976–1986, respectively

miscellaneous plastics (SIC 30) industry. In Dallas–Fort Worth, most plants are spread across five main industries: 24 percent of manufacturing plants are in the chemicals and allied products (SIC 28) industry, 15 percent are in fabricated metal products (SIC 34), another 15 percent are in electronic and other

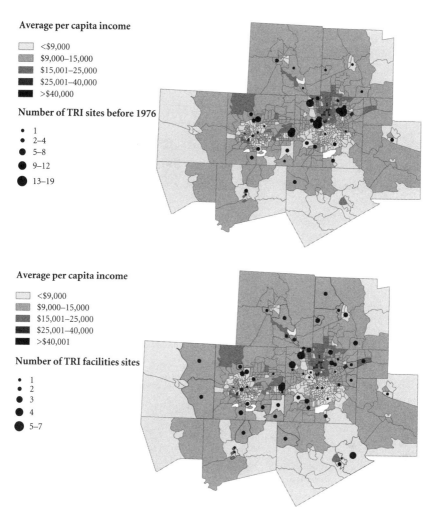

Average per capita income

- ☐ <$9,000
- ▨ $9,000–15,000
- ▨ $15,001–25,000
- ■ $25,001–40,000
- ■ >$40,000

Number of TRI sites before 1976

- • 1
- • 2–4
- • 5–8
- ● 9–12
- ● 13–19

Average per capita income

- ☐ <$9,000
- ▨ $9,000–15,000
- ▨ $15,001–25,000
- ■ $25,001–40,000
- ■ >$40,001

Number of TRI facilities sites

- • 1
- • 2
- • 3
- ● 4
- ● 5–7

Figure 8.3 Map of number of TRI plants and per capita income in Dallas–Fort Worth, before 1976 and 1976–1986, respectively

electrical equipment (SIC 36), 13 percent are in rubber and miscellaneous plastics (SIC 30), and 8 percent are in the industrial/commercial machinery and computer equipment (SIC 35) industry.

Several characteristics differ between Houston area tracts with a TRI plant established between 1976 and 1985 and Houston area tracts without a TRI plant established during this same time period (see Table 8.1). While the summary statistics generally adhere to expectations with regard to input-related costs,

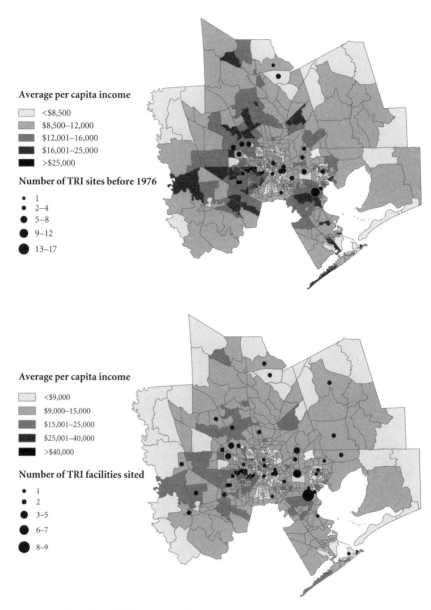

Average per capita income

☐ <$8,500
☐ $8,500–12,000
☐ $12,001–16,000
☐ $16,001–25,000
☐ >$25,000

Number of TRI sites before 1976

- 1
- 2–4
- 5–8
- 9–12
- 13–17

Average per capita income

☐ <$9,000
☐ $9,000–15,000
☐ $15,001–25,000
☐ $25,001–40,000
☐ >$40,000

Number of TRI facilities sited

- 1
- 2
- 3–5
- 6–7
- 8–9

Figure 8.4 Number of TRI plants and per capita income in Houston-Galveston, before 1976 and 1976–1986, respectively

Table 8.1 Houston-Galveston and Dallas–Fort Worth summary statistics—plants established between 1976 and 1985 matched to 1980 characteristics

Variable	Houston-Galveston MSA		Dallas–Fort Worth MSA	
	Tracts with plant (n = 56)	Tracts without plant (n = 584)	Tracts with plant (n = 106)	Tracts without plant (n = 529)
Nonwhite	0.21 (0.28)	0.29 (0.31)	0.21 (0.25)	0.23 (0.30)
Foreign-born	0.06 (0.07)	0.07 (0.07)	0.04 (0.04)	0.05 (0.06)
Poverty	0.09 (0.09)	0.11 (0.09)	0.11 (0.10)	0.11 (0.11)
Average income	10,064.69 (3,944.61)	11,334.16 (4,961.67)	9,671.05 (2,949.16)	10.982.96 (6,008.98)
Population density	828.95 (1,068.45)	2,822.44 (2,594.61)	922.16 (1,065.02)	3,278.46 (2,964.74)
Renter	0.26 (0.19)	0.39 (0.24)	0.38 (0.26)	0.38 (0.25)
Percentage with children	0.47 (0.16)	0.41 (0.15)	0.39 (0.14)	0.38 (0.15)
Percentage over the age of 65	0.05 (0.04)	0.07 (0.05)	0.09 (0.07)	0.10 (0.07)
Manufacturing	0.21 (0.08)	0.18 (0.07)	0.27 (0.08)	0.22 (0.07)
Average wage	20,811.34 (1,800.33)	21,110.82 (2,044.82)	15,560.74 (1,773.37)	15,835.02 (1,694.78)
Average property value	36,131.34 (18,588.62)	44,978.37 (27,661.09)	31,163.21 (21,799.31)	45,760.67 (33,426.65)
Nonattainment status	0.84 (0.37)	0.88 (0.32)	0.71 (0.46)	0.80 (0.40)
Distance to rail	1.09 (1.35)	1.32 (1.45)	1.06 (1.43)	1.11 (0.99)
Built prior to 1970	0.49 (0.30)	0.64 (0.31)	0.58 (0.28)	0.71 (0.28)
Number of old TRI sites	4.52 (5.91)	0.23 (0.65)	2.87 (3.96)	0.25 (0.78)
Urban	0.71 (0.43)	0.84 (0.35)	0.66 (0.46)	0.84 (0.36)

Note: Each row shows the mean and standard deviation of the respective variable and location.

this is not always the case for socioeconomic characteristics. Tracts in which a plant locates tend to have a higher percentage employed in manufacturing, lower property values, and a greater number of preexisting TRI facilities. They also tend to be less urban, closer to a rail line, and have lower population densities. With regard to socioeconomic characteristics that are often the focus of the environmental justice literature, tracts in which a plant locates tend to have lower incomes but fewer nonwhite households and less poverty. There is little difference in the percentage of foreign-born residents, on average. Contrary to expectations, they also tend to have fewer renters, fewer older homes, and more children. To examine whether socioeconomic characteristics in these communities show closer adherence to the environmental justice story in the subsequent decade, I also examine 1990 socioeconomic characteristics for tracts with and without a plant established in the 1980s. I find a story consistent with the summary statistics presented in Table 8.1: while average income is higher in census tracts without a plant, the percentages nonwhite, foreign, in poverty, and renters are all lower in neighborhoods where a plant was established a decade previously. Thus, a large part of the environmental justice story when contemporaneous socioeconomic characteristics are matched to plant location appears to be driven by the existence of older plants.

While many variables for Dallas–Fort Worth look similar to those for Houston, there are a number of differences across the two MSAs worth noting. In Dallas–Fort Worth, tracts in which plants locate between 1976 and 1985 appear to have similar percentages of minority populations to those without plants. This is not the case in Houston, where tracts in which plants locate have, on average, a noticeably lower percentage of minority populations. Likewise, Houston appears to have fewer households with children living in the neighborhoods in which plants locate, while there is little difference in the percentage of children living in neighborhoods with or without a new plant in Dallas–Fort Worth. Houston also appears to have a much higher percentage of renters residing in tracts without plants than in tracts in which they locate. In Dallas–Fort Worth, there is little difference in the proportion of residents who are renters. As is the case with the Houston area, 1990 socioeconomic characteristics for tracts with and without a plant established in the 1980s are consistent with the summary statistics presented in Table 8.1 for the main socioeconomic characteristics of interest.

Finally, note that the number of preexisting TRI sites is far greater in tracts in which plants locate than in tracts where they do not across the two time periods and the two cities. However, while tracts without plants appear to have a similar average incidence of preexisting sites across the two cities, Houston appears to have a noticeably greater average number of preexisting sites in tracts with plants than Dallas–Fort Worth.

Results

Columns 2–5 of Table 8.2 report the results of conditional logit regressions for Dallas–Fort Worth and Houston-Galveston; the last two columns contain results for the entire state of Texas using the same set of variables.[22] Two specifications are presented for each geographic region: the first uses alternate measures of poverty and property values—percentage of households without a phone and percentage of housing built prior to 1970—to better account for multicollinearity between these variables and the race and income variables; the second specification ignores the multicollinearity problem and presents the variables typically used in the environmental justice literature—race, income, poverty, and property values. It is worth noting that the fit of the three regressions varies—the best fit is for the Houston-Galveston regression (54 to 55 percent), followed by Texas as a whole (39 percent) and then Dallas–Forth Worth (28 to 29 percent).

Contrary to results cited in the environmental justice literature, there is little evidence to support the hypothesis that firms discriminate on the basis of race or ethnicity, controlling for other location-relevant factors. The results are remarkably consistent in this regard in spite of variation in the scope of the analysis across the three sets of regressions.[23]

With regard to income and poverty, variables related to a neighborhood's willingness to pay for environmental amenities, geographic scope appears to have some influence on the results. Neither income nor poverty (or its proxy) is significant for either of the two sets of MSA-level regressions. Income is also not significant at the state level. However, at the state level, depending on the specification, poverty is significant and negatively related to location choice. Note that the sign on the poverty variable is opposite of what has been posited in the environmental justice literature.

Of the variables associated with collective action by the community, only population density is consistently significant across the three geographic areas I examine. The more densely populated an area, the less likely it is that a polluting plant locates there. The percentages of renters and children are not significant for any of the three geographic areas. The percentage over the age of 65 is significant for Texas as a whole but for only one of the two specifications presented. It is not significant for either Dallas–Fort Worth or Houston-Galveston.

Variables traditionally considered in the firm location literature but often omitted from environmental justice studies—those associated with

Table 8.2 Conditional logit regression results

Variable	Dallas–Fort Worth (for 58 plants)		Houston-Galveston (for 138 plants)		All of Texas (for 362 plants)	
	Model I	Model II	Model I	Model II	Model I	Model II
Nonwhite	0.11	0.48	0.28	−0.08	0.32	0.52
	(0.76)	(0.80)	(0.93)	(1.14)	(0.37)	(0.39)
Foreign-born	−4.52	−3.21	0.57	0.15	−0.23	0.43
	(3.46)	(3.28)	(3.02)	(3.00)	(1.09)	(1.00)
Income	−0.51	−0.04	−0.08	−0.73	−0.02	0.02
	(0.62)	(0.53)	(0.24)	(0.81)	(0.05)	(0.05)
No phone	−1.35		1.91		−0.73	
	(2.12)		(3.18)		(1.00)	
Poverty		−3.37		1.63		−2.58**
		(2.67)		(4.72)		(1.07)
Population density	−0.18*	−0.23**	−0.47**	−0.55**	−0.28***	−0.28***
	(0.11)	(0.97)	(0.22)	(0.24)	(0.05)	(0.05)
Renter	0.79	0.88	−0.16	0.11	0.42	0.18
	(0.87)	(0.91)	(1.74)	(1.73)	(0.32)	(0.35)
Children	−0.26	0.33	3.30	3.25	0.87	0.83
	(1.51)	(1.46)	(2.88)	(2.93)	(0.63)	(0.59)
Over 65 years old	−0.68	−4.42	2.64	0.68	−2.44	−4.66**
	(3.17)	(2.71)	(10.05)	(8.57)	(2.06)	(1.84)
Manufacturing	6.93***	6.45***	5.39**	5.90**	3.00***	2.82***
	(1.93)	(1.88)	(2.72)	(2.79)	(0.71)	(0.68)
Wage	−0.78	−0.68	1.97	1.53	−0.63*	−0.96**
	(1.57)	(1.52)	(2.15)	(2.09)	(0.38)	(0.39)
Distance to rail	−0.10	−0.13	−0.41**	−0.41**	−0.25***	−0.23***
	(0.10)	(0.10)	(0.17)	(0.16)	(0.05)	(0.05)
Nonattainment	1.35**	1.17**	−0.61	−0.53	0.06	0.002
	(0.56)	(0.59)	(0.80)	(0.80)	(0.25)	(0.02)
Built before 1970	−1.94***		−0.59		−1.13***	
	(0.57)		(1.19)		(0.33)	
Property value		−0.05		0.62		−0.03
		(0.04)		(0.68)		(0.03)
Urban	−1.81***	−1.86***	−0.04	0.03	−0.49**	−0.61**
	(0.54)	(0.58)	(0.91)	(0.93)	(0.25)	(0.26)
Old TRI sites	0.19***	0.18***	0.49***	0.50***	0.22***	0.22***
	(0.06)	(0.05)	(0.16)	(0.16)	(0.04)	(0.03)
Old × SIC 28	0.25*	0.20*			0.08	0.09
	(0.14)	(0.12)			(0.06)	(0.06)
Old × SIC 30	0.22*	0.17			0.01	0.004
	(0.13)	(0.11)			(0.08)	(0.08)
Old × SIC 34			0.49*	−0.51*	0.28**	0.28**
			(0.30)	(0.29)	(0.14)	(0.14)
Log-likelihood	−171.52	−173.94	−63.40	−63.12	−832.77	−834.49
Pseudo R^2	0.30	0.29	0.51	0.51	0.40	0.40

Note: Standard errors are shown in parentheses.

*Significant at 10% level; **significant at 5% level; ***significant at 1% level.

production and transportation costs—are significant. This finding is consistent with Wolverton (2009); what appears to matter most to a plant's location decision, regardless of geographic scope, are the variables emphasized in the firm location literature. Without these variables the pseudo R^2 falls to 7 percent for Dallas–Fort Worth, 18 percent for Houston-Galveston, and 31 percent for Texas as a whole.

What is perhaps most interesting is that there are differences in the specific profit maximization variables that are significant across the three sets of regressions. County-level wage rate is significant and of the expected sign (negative) for Texas as a whole but is insignificant at the MSA level. Distance to a major railroad is significant and negatively related to plant location for Houston-Galveston and Texas, but it does not appear to matter to location decisions in the Dallas–Fort Worth area. County-level attainment status for traditional air pollutants is important to plant location decisions in the Dallas–Fort Worth area but not for Houston-Galveston or Texas as a whole.[24] Property value is not significantly correlated with plant location for any of the geographic areas. However, the alternative measure of land value, average age of housing, is significant and negatively correlated with plant location in Dallas–Fort Worth and Texas as a whole. However, its sign indicates that it may be capturing factors other than property values, to the extent homes in older neighborhoods are less expensive. The percentage of the population residing in urban areas also follows this pattern: it is significant in Dallas–Fort Worth and Texas as a whole but not in Houston-Galveston.

Two variables are consistently significant across all geographic areas and specifications: the percentage employed in manufacturing and the presence of one or more preexisting TRI sites. The greater the percentage employed in manufacturing, the more likely it is that a plant will locate in that neighborhood. Likewise, once an older site is located in a particular neighborhood, it is more likely for an additional plant to locate there. This may be due to agglomeration economies or factors not controlled for in these regressions such as taxes and zoning.

Given the importance of preexisting TRI sites in the regressions, I also examine whether the significance of the main race and income variables changes when this variable is dropped. For the MSA-level regressions, percentage nonwhite and percentage foreign remain insignificant. However, income is now significant in three of the four MSA-level regressions. The percentage of the population living in poverty becomes significant at the 10 percent level for Dallas–Fort Worth but is still negatively related to plant location: the higher the poverty rate, the less likely a plant is located in that neighborhood. It remains insignificant for Houston-Galveston. Finally, the percentage of households without a phone is now significant for both MSA-level regressions and continues to be positively related to plant location. When preexisting TRI sites are dropped from the regressions for all plants sited in Texas over this time period, the results remain unchanged for all race and income variables with one notable exception. Percentage foreign is now significant in both specifications at the 1 percent level. This result runs counter to what was found in Wolverton (2009) but points to the importance of preexisting sites to the main finding and highlights an area for continued future research.

Conclusion

In the environmental justice literature, evidence of disproportionate siting in poor or minority neighborhoods is decidedly mixed. Some allege this is because of the difference in whether the study looks at evidence at the national, state, or city level. Here, I compare results from two of the largest cities in Texas—Dallas–Fort Worth and Houston-Galveston—to results for the state overall to discern whether important demographic or other differences are evident at the city level that may be masked at a more aggregate level of analysis.

I examine whether results associated with four possible hypotheses for why plants may locate in poor or minority neighborhoods remain consistent across geographic scope. I find remarkably consistent results for most hypotheses. Variables associated with profit maximization appear to contribute most to the overall fit of the regressions, both at the city and the state level. Variables associated with possible discrimination or collective action on the part of the community appear to be largely insignificant across specifications and geographic scope, with the exception of population density. It is worth noting, however, that I include relatively indirect measures of collective action compared to other studies. Variables associated with willingness to pay for environmental amenities appear to be the exception: poverty is sometimes significant at the state level but is never significant at the level of the city. Thus, I find that in most cases, geographic scope does not play a major role in determining the importance of either demographic or cost variables in plant location decisions.

Notes

For their helpful comments and suggestions, I thank Spencer Banzhaf, two reviewers, and the participants of the 2008 Markets for Land and Pollution: Implications for Environmental Justice workshop. I also thank Emma Roach for her superior GIS skills. The views expressed in this chapter are those of the author and do not necessarily represent those of the US Environmental Protection Agency. This chapter has not been subjected to EPA's review process and therefore does not represent official policy or views.

1. Other reasons for differences in results include variation in neighborhood definition, empirical technique, control variables, and type of facility examined.

2. For instance, see Bullard (1983), US Government Accounting Office (GAO; 1983), and United Church of Christ (1987).

3. Ringquist (2005) presents the results of a meta-analysis with regard to environmental equity studies. He finds that studies that are national in scope tend to result in smaller estimates of race-based inequities than studies at a more disaggregated level. However, Ringquist lumps together studies at the time of siting with those that examine characteristics after the fact and does not include this as a relevant factor for explaining differences across studies included in his meta-analysis.

4. Bowen et al. (1995) do not examine site location, instead focusing on how releases of toxic chemicals vary with study scope. They find that releases and minority populations are highly spatially correlated at the state level but that this relationship disappears when the study scope is limited to the metropolitan area. The authors posit that a state-level analysis is less appropriate in this instance since both industry and minority populations are concentrated in the metropolitan area in their sample.

5. Lambert and Boerner (1995) examine site location at the time of establishment in the context of changing socioeconomic dynamics. They do not find large initial differences in the percentage of poor and minority residents between neighborhoods with and without waste sites. However, housing values grew less rapidly in neighborhoods with waste sites, and minority populations moved into these neighborhoods at a faster rate. Hersh (1995) conducts a historical analysis of the change in racial and industrial dynamics for firms reporting to the Toxics Release Inventory (TRI). He finds that, in general, industries and blue-collar neighborhoods located near each other for job-related reasons. Also, he notes that both white and rich residents took flight to cleaner parts of the city after firms located in a particular neighborhood and that there was an eventual movement of minorities into more polluted areas. Krieg (1995) finds that race is associated with the number of waste sites in areas with a long history of industrial activity and that class is more closely associated with the number of waste sites in areas with more recent industrial activity. Noonan (Chapter 7) examines how environmental quality is capitalized into property values when both residents and environmental quality are changing over time.

6. See Carlton (1983), Bartik (1985), Beckman and Thisse (1986), Lee and Wasylenko (1987), McConnell and Schwab (1990), Finney (1994), Harrington and Warf (1995), and Levinson (1996).

7. Compensation can be thought of as both monetary and in-kind (e.g., free access to certain services, the building of a community park) forms of remuneration given by the firm to the community to offset the perceived risks of an increase in pollution because of the location of a new plant in the area.

8. See, for example, Pastor, Sadd, and Hipp (2001); Davidson and Anderton (2000); Been (1997); Boer et al. (1997); and Anderton et al. (1994).

9. The urban areas are based on the definitions of the metropolitan statistical areas used in 1980 by the US Census Bureau.

10. Plants that use more than 10,000 pounds or manufacture more than 25,000 pounds of the 329 listed toxic chemicals are required to report how much of each chemical is released into air, land, or water.

11. I do not include plant decisions that occur later in time—between 1986 and 1993—because the data set becomes too small to include a reasonable number of control variables and alternate locations before running out of degrees of freedom. I have data on only 32 plant locations in the Dallas–Fort Worth area and 26 plant locations in the Houston-Galveston area for this time period.

12. The establishment date for each plant is collected from the Bureau of Business Research Directory of Texas Manufacturers: Volume I (1990–1993), the Harris Texas Manufacturers Directory (1995), the Texas High Technology Directory (1995), and the Texas Manufacturers Register (1994).

13. A number of other variables are potentially important to location decisions, for instance, differences in energy costs and property taxes. Unfortunately, no information is available on the cost of electricity by location during the 1980s. Property tax rates by county in Texas are only available beginning in 1991. Because they fluctuate across time, it seems inappropriate to use 1991 tax rates as a proxy unless the relative difference in rates stays roughly constant across counties over time. That said, when the 1991 tax rate is included, it is insignificant.

14. Both property values and household income are adjusted to 1980 dollars. The consumer price index for the southern region of the United States is used to make this adjustment. Property values act as a proxy for land values (which are unavailable at the census tract level in 1980) faced by firms when making location decisions.

15. I also explore a variable measuring the average distance to a major highway. It was not significant in any of the regressions and did not change the sign or significance of other variables.

16. Shadbegian and Gray (Chapter 9) speak to potential differences in regulatory costs in the environmental justice context: they examine whether regulators focus more regulatory attention on plants in rich, white neighborhoods than on plants in poor, minority neighborhoods.

17. Average plant size is a significant explanatory variable in Wolverton (2009). In that article, I used an MSA-level definition. It is not included here because of the inability to access 1982 census data.

18. Since census tracts vary in size, we include population density instead of population.

19. The percentage who voted in the presidential election was used in Wolverton (2009) to represent the propensity to engage in collective action. It was significant. However, this variable does not have enough variation at the county level to allow for inclusion here.

20. Because Hispanics are included in both percentage nonwhite and percentage white in the US Census, using percentage Hispanic directly in the regression is problematic. In Texas, the percentage foreign-born is strongly correlated with the percentage Hispanic.

21. The table of summary statistics when plants are matched to 1990 socioeconomic characteristics is presented in Table A.8.1 in the online appendix at http://www.sup.org/environmentaljustice.

22. The Texas-level regressions are similar to those in Wolverton (2009), including the actual location and 49 alternatives. Here, I improve on previously published results by using population density instead of just population, taking into account whether a county is in attainment, and including interaction dummies between preexisting TRI sites and SIC codes. As in Wolverton (2009), I also include geographic dummies for the Houston-Galveston and Dallas–Fort Worth areas, though neither is significant.

23. As an alternative, a count regression model is used to examine what variables are associated with the number of facilities located in a particular neighborhood. The results for the race, ethnicity, poverty, and income variables appear to be robust to the regression technique.

24. I also explored the significance of nonattainment status interacted with industry-related variables such as percentage manufacturing, county wage, or SIC dummy variables. None of these interaction terms were significant for plant location decisions in the Houston-Galveston area. In the Dallas–Fort Worth area, only one interaction term was significant: between nonattainment status and percentage manufacturing. However, when the interaction term is significant, nonattainment status alone is no longer significant.

References

Anderton, Douglas, Andy Anderson, John Michael Oakes, and Michael Fraser. 1994. "Environmental Equity: The Demographics of Dumping." *Demography* 31 (2): 229–48.

Arora, Seema, and Timothy N. Cason. 1998. "Do Community Characteristics Influence Environmental Outcomes? Evidence from the Toxics Release Inventory." *Journal of Applied Economics* 1 (2): 413–53.

Baden, Brett M., and Don L. Coursey. 2002. "The Locality of Waste Sites within the City of Chicago: A Demographic, Social, and Economic Analysis." *Resource and Energy Economics* 24 (1–2): 53–93.

Baden, Brett M., Douglas S. Noonan, and Rama Mohana R. Turaga. 2007. "Scales of Justice: Is There a Geographic Bias in Environmental Equity Analysis?" *Journal of Environmental Planning and Management* 50 (2): 163–85.

Bartik, Timothy. 1985. "Business Location Decisions in the United States: Estimates of the Effects of Unionization, Taxes, and Other Characteristics of States." *Journal of Business and Economic Statistics* 3 (1): 14–22.

Beckman, Martin, and Jacques Thisse. 1986. "The Location of Production Activities." In *Handbook of Regional and Urban Economics*, vol. 1, edited by P. Nijkamp. Amsterdam: North-Holland.

Been, Vicki, with Francis Gupta. 1997. "Coming to the Nuisance or Going to the Barrios? A Longitudinal Analysis of Environmental Justice Claims." *Ecology Law Quarterly* 24 (1): 1–56.

Boer, J. Tom, Manuel Pastor Jr., James L. Sadd, and Lori D. Snyder. 1997. "Is There Environmental Racism? The Demographics of Hazardous Waste in Los Angeles County." *Social Science Quarterly* 78 (4): 793–810.

Bowen, William, Mark Salling, Kingsley Haynes, and Ellen Cyran. 1995. "Toward Environmental Justice: Spatial Equity in Ohio and Cleveland." *Annals of the Association of American Geographers* 85 (4): 641–63.

Bryant, Bunyan, and Paul Mohai, eds. 1992. *Race and the Incidence of Environmental Hazards*. Boulder, CO: Westview Press.

Bullard, Robert D. 1983. "Solid Waste Sites and the Black Houston Community." *Sociological Inquiry* 53 (2–3): 273–88.

Carlton, Dennis. 1983. "The Location and Employment Choices of New Firms: An Econometric Model with Discrete and Continuous Endogenous Variables." *Review of Economics and Statistics* 65 (3): 440–49.

Coase, Ronald H. 1960. "The Problem of Social Cost." *Journal of Law and Economics* 3 (1): 1–44.

Davidson, Pamela, and Douglas Anderton. 2000. "Demographics of Dumping II: A National Environmental Equity Survey and the Distribution of Hazardous Materials Handlers." *Demography* 37 (4): 461–66.

Finney, Miles. 1994. "Property Tax Effects on Intrametropolitan Firm Location: Further Evidence." *Applied Economic Letters* 1 (2): 29–31.

Hamilton, James T. 1995. "Testing for Environmental Racism: Prejudice, Profits, Political Power?" *Journal of Policy Analysis and Management* 14 (1): 107–32.

Harrington, James, and Barney Warf. 1995. *Industrial Location: Principles, Practice, and Policy*. New York: Routledge.

Hersh, Robert. 1995. "Race and Industrial Hazards: An Historical Geography of the Pittsburgh Region, 1900–1990." Discussion Paper 95-18, Resources for the Future, Washington, DC.

Jenkins, Robin R., Kelly B. Maguire, and Cynthia L. Morgan. 2004. "Host Community Compensation and Municipal Solid Waste Landfills." *Land Economics* 80 (4): 513–28.

Krieg, Eric. 1995. "A Socio-Historical Interpretation of Toxic Waste Sites: The Case of Greater Boston." *American Journal of Economics and Sociology* 54 (1): 1–14.

Kriesel, Warren, Terence J. Centner, and Andrew G. Keeler. 1996. "Neighborhood Exposure to Toxic Releases: Are There Racial Inequities?" *Growth and Change* 27 (4): 479–99.

Lambert, Thomas, and Christopher Boerner. 1995. *Environmental Inequity: Economic Causes, Economic Solutions.* St. Louis: Center for the Study of American Business.

Lee, Haeduck, and Michael Wasylenko. 1987. "A Comment on the Appropriate Estimation of Intrametropolitan Firm Location Models." *Land Economics* 63 (3): 306–9.

Levinson, Arik. 1996. "Environmental Regulations and Manufacturers' Location Choices: Evidence from the Census of Manufactures." *Journal of Public Economics* 62 (1–2): 5–29.

McConnell, Virginia, and Robert Schwab. 1990. "The Impact of Environmental Regulation on Industry Location Decisions: The Motor Vehicle Industry." *Land Economics* 66 (1): 67–81.

McFadden, Daniel. 1978. "Modeling the Choice of Residential Location." In *Spatial Interaction Theory and Residential Location*, edited by A. Karlquist. Amsterdam: North-Holland.

Pastor, Manuel, Jim Sadd, and John Hipp. 2001. "Which Came First? Toxic Facilities, Minority Move-In, and Environmental Justice." *Journal of Urban Affairs* 23 (1): 1–21.

Ringquist, Evan. 2005. "Assessing Evidence of Environmental Inequities: A Meta-Analysis." *Journal of Policy Analysis and Management* 24 (2): 223–47.

United Church of Christ. 1987. *Toxic Wastes and Race in the United States: A National Report on the Racial and Socio-Economic Characteristics of Communities with Hazardous Waste Sites.* New York: Public Data Access.

US General Accounting Office (GAO). 1983. *Siting of Hazardous Waste Landfills and Their Correlation with Racial and Economic Status of Surrounding Communities.* Washington, DC: GAO.

Wolverton, Ann. 2009. "Effects of Socio-Economic and Input-Related Factors on Polluting Plants' Location Decisions." *Berkeley Electronic Journal of Economic Analysis and Policy, Advances* 9 (1). http://www.bepress.com/bejeap/vol9/iss1/art14.

Zimmerman, Rae. 1993. "Social Equity and Environmental Risk." *Risk Analysis* 13 (6): 649–66.

IV Government Regulation and Enforcement

WHEREAS THE FIRST TWO sections of this volume focus on household behavior and the third on firm behavior, this final section turns to the behavior of governments. As discussed in Chapter 1, the observed environmental justice correlations might arise if governments are discriminatory in their enforcement of environmental regulations. For example, they might give applications for operating permits less scrutiny in poor/minority areas or be less rigorous when monitoring firms' compliance with environmental regulations in these areas. (This is the sixth and final hypothesis considered in Chapter 1.)

If present, such governmental behavior might arise from many of the other motivations considered for other agents. It might arise, for example, from pure discrimination among bureaucrats or among elected representatives. Or it might represent governmental agencies whose objective function includes avoiding political backlash. That is, it may be that the "squeaky wheel gets the grease." In this case, agencies might be particularly careful to enforce regulations in areas that have a higher willingness to pay to avoid pollution. As Becker (1983) emphasizes, this might be economically efficient, with the "lobbying market" serving the same role as Tiebout's land markets or Coasian bargaining. But it might also be that governmental agents are particularly careful to enforce regulations in areas that are more politically connected. In the language of transaction costs, some groups may have lower barriers to organizing and communicating with those in power. Such groups may find it easier to overcome those barriers and gain access, even if pollution is less costly for them to bear than for others. This would have a very different implication for efficiency indeed.

The two chapters in this section consider the behavior of two different branches of government. In Chapter 9, Ronald Shadbegian and Wayne Gray consider the behavior of regulators in the executive branch of state governments, looking at enforcement activities taking place in different locations. They look at how intensively regulators monitor and enforce regulations at individual facilities as a function of the people who live near those facilities. In Chapter 10, Robin Jenkins and Kelly Maguire look at the legislative branch of government. They look at the disposal fees that states charge for disposing both hazardous waste and municipal waste. They then look at the interstate patterns of those fees based on the statewide demographics as well as the demographics around the waste sites.

Neither chapter finds much support for the hypothesis that governments are discriminating in their behavior toward pollution policy. Although a negative result, eliminating the importance of government behavior as a source of the observed environmental correlations is as useful as confirming the importance of household behavior and firm behavior.

Reference

Becker, Gary S. 1983. "A Theory of Competition among Pressure Groups for Political Influence." *Quarterly Journal of Economics* 98 (3): 371–400.

9 Spatial Patterns in Regulatory Enforcement

Local Tests of Environmental Justice

Ronald J. Shadbegian and Wayne B. Gray

Introduction

This chapter examines the allocation of environmental regulatory activity, testing a key potential explanation for "environmental justice" concerns.[1] In the United States, environmental policy making is carried out under a federalist system. The US Environmental Protection Agency (EPA) sets national air and water quality standards for particular pollutants, while state regulatory agencies have the primary responsibility to implement and enforce those regulations. The power of the states to implement and enforce regulations affords them a substantial amount of discretion (e.g., setting a plant's permitted level of air and water pollution emissions or allocating inspections across different facilities). We might expect regulators to direct more enforcement activity at plants located in areas that receive greater benefits (or face lower costs) from pollution abatement. Regulators could also respond to political pressure, directing more activity at plants in rich, white neighborhoods and less activity at plants in poor, minority neighborhoods, which could result in poorer environmental conditions in less privileged areas, creating a potential for environmental injustice. Of course, this implicitly assumes that the affected neighborhoods prefer to receive more regulatory activity; if regulatory actions result in plant closings or job loss, however, the community might prefer less regulatory activity.

We study regulatory activity at 1,616 manufacturing plants located near four large US cities: Los Angeles, California; Boston, Massachusetts; Columbus, Ohio; and Houston, Texas. We use plant-level information from the US Census Bureau's confidential establishment-level Longitudinal Research Database

(LRD). The LRD contains annual information on individual manufacturing plants, including total value of shipments, labor productivity, capital stock, fuel use, and age of the plant; we use data for 2002, originally collected in the 2002 Census of Manufactures.

We measure the regulatory stringency directed toward a particular plant in terms of the number of air pollution inspections and enforcement actions directed at that plant from 2000 to 2002, using data taken from the EPA's Integrated Data for Enforcement Analysis (IDEA) database. We find evidence, as expected, that plant characteristics significantly affect the amount of regulatory activity directed at a plant. In particular, we find that bigger plants and plants with higher fuel consumption face significantly more regulatory activity, as do plants in single-plant firms (i.e., firms that own a single manufacturing facility).

We find that nearby political activity significantly affects the amount of regulatory activity directed at a plant. Plants surrounded by politically active populations (measured by voter turnout) and more liberal populations (measured by the percentage voting for the Democratic candidate for president) receive more regulatory attention. These results are broadly consistent with the results of prior research. For example, Hamilton (1995) finds that the capacity expansion decisions of commercial hazardous waste facilities are negatively correlated with political activity. Viscusi and Hamilton (1999) find that Superfund sites located in more pro-environmental areas and with greater political activity have more stringent environmental cleanup targets for cancer risk, while Sigman (2001) finds that the EPA processes Superfund sites faster in communities with more political activity. These results show that community activism is an important factor affecting the EPA's bureaucratic priorities. In Chapter 10, Jenkins and Maguire find that more politically active states set higher hazardous waste taxes, providing a greater deterrent to waste disposal. However, Becker (2004) does not find any statistical evidence that community political activity raises air pollution abatement expenditures of US manufacturing facilities. Furthermore, Wolverton (2009; see also Chapter 8) finds that the location of polluting plants in two large cities in Texas is not significantly influenced by the level of community political activity.

The focus of our analysis is on how the demographic characteristics of the nearby populations influence the amount of regulatory activity faced by our plants. We examine two sets of demographic variables: one representing groups expected to have relatively high sensitivity to air pollution (children and elders), and the other representing disadvantaged groups (the poor and minorities). We find some of the expected relationships but relatively little statistical significance. In terms of the more sensitive groups, we find that plants with more elders nearby do face more inspections (though not more enforcement), but this effect is only significant when we exclude the other control variables from our model. Plants with more children nearby do not show a clear pattern, although areas with more children appear to receive more regulation in models without other control variables. These findings are consistent with those of Gray and Shadbegian (2004), who examined US pulp and paper mills.

In terms of our environmental justice analysis, we also find relatively little statistical evidence that regulatory activity is less intense in plants near disadvantaged demographic groups. Plants located in minority neighborhoods, as expected, are inspected less often and face fewer enforcement actions, but both these effects are insignificant in models with a full set of controls, and plants located in poor neighborhoods tend to face (unexpectedly) more regulatory activity.[2] Some models (without a full set of control variables) find significantly fewer inspections at plants near minority populations. Most of our results are consistent with previous research by Hamilton (1995), Been (1997), Arora and Cason (1999), Gray and Shadbegian (2004), and Wolverton (2009; see also Chapter 8), which all find in various ways that minorities and the poor are not consistently exposed to more pollution, in models that control for other socioeconomic pathways that might influence exposures. It's important to note that our results do not eliminate all potential environmental justice concerns. In fact, plants located near minority communities do seem to receive somewhat less regulatory attention, but this is not a "pure discrimination" effect, since it can be explained by other pathways, such as lower voter turnout in those communities.

However, our results are less consistent with some studies that find evidence supporting possible environmental justice concerns. Sigman (2001) finds that the EPA processes Superfund sites more quickly in communities with higher median income. Jenkins, Maguire, and Morgan (2004) find that communities with relatively more minorities receive lower "host" fees for the siting of landfills, while richer communities receive higher "host" fees. These different results may reflect actual differences in the regulatory decisions being studied (e.g., landfill siting versus air pollution inspections). They may also reflect differences in the statistical models being used (we are comparing regulatory activity across neighborhoods within four cities, rather than comparing activity across communities throughout the country). In results similar to ours, Jenkins and Maguire (Chapter 10) find that states with larger minority populations living near waste sites do not set hazardous waste taxes any higher than other states.

This chapter outlines a simple model of pollution abatement in a federalist system, describes our data and our empirical methodology, details our results, and presents some concluding remarks and possible extensions.

Model of Pollution Abatement Regulation under Federalism

Why do profit-maximizing plants allocate resources to pollution abatement? If pollution were a pure externality, only negatively affecting people who live downwind or downstream of the emitting source, we would not expect to observe any profit-maximizing plant allocating any resources to pollution abatement. Thus, there must be some "external" pressure on the firm to provide an incentive for pollution abatement. Many sources of such external pressure exist. Some of these are market-based, such as consumer demand for products manufactured with "green/clean" technologies, which allows firms doing more pollution abatement to charge higher prices. The threat of civil lawsuits or the possibility of Coasian bargaining could provide additional incentives. If the firm's managers have a taste for "good citizenship" (and the flexibility to spend the firm's funds on pollution abatement), that could also "internalize" the externality, from the perspective of the firm's decision making.

However, we believe that the main incentive for reducing pollution emissions in the United States is external governmental regulatory activity, especially for the air pollutants we examine in this chapter.[3] Therefore, it is important to understand the determinants of the amount of regulatory pressure faced by a plant. A large part of that regulatory pressure comes from routine inspections to identify noncompliance and from enforcement actions designed to force changes at noncompliant plants, and the allocation of those inspections and enforcement actions is the focus of our analysis.

As noted above, the United States conducts environmental policy making under a federal system, in which the EPA sets national standards and each individual state has its own environmental regulatory agency that is responsible for implementing and enforcing regulations to meet those standards. The responsibility of the states to implement and enforce regulations affords them considerable flexibility to apply varying degrees of regulatory pressure on polluting plants, in spite of the fact that their activities are monitored at the federal level by the EPA. In fact, state regulators have the responsibility and authority to write the State Implementation Plans that identify permitted air emissions at individual facilities, in order to meet ambient air quality requirements. In addition, the vast majority of air pollution inspections and enforcement actions are performed by state, not federal, regulators. The importance of state-level decisions makes it more likely that local political pressures could influence regulatory activity (as compared to a centralized system where all the important decisions are being made in Washington, DC, far from local political influence). This means that regulatory actions are more likely to respond to local benefits and costs but may also be more open to other political pressures, including discrimination.

Optimal regulations would maximize social welfare by setting the marginal benefit from pollution abatement equal to the marginal cost of abatement. In Equation (9.1), optimal abatement values, A_i^*, differ for each plant, based on factors that affect the marginal benefits and marginal costs of abatement. The marginal benefits of pollution abatement differ across plants depending mainly on the number (and characteristics) of the people who live near the plant and who are exposed to the pollution. On the other hand, the marginal costs of abatement differ across plants based mainly on their production technology, size, and age. Making the standard assumption that the marginal cost of pollution abatement increases with abatement intensity (or at least intersects the marginal benefits curve from below), plants with higher marginal benefits (or lower marginal costs) should perform more abatement. If A^* is the optimal abatement level, we have $dA_i^*/dPLANT_i < 0$ for plant characteristics that increase marginal costs and $dA_i^*/dPEOPLE_i > 0$ for people characteristics that increase marginal benefits. Thus, optimal regulations meet the condition

$$MC(PLANT_i, A_i^*) = MB(PEOPLE_i, A_i^*). \tag{9.1}$$

Our study focuses on the differences across plants in the marginal benefits of pollution abatement (MB_i), while also controlling for plant characteristics affecting marginal abatement costs (e.g., size, fuel use, etc.). We model the marginal benefit function as aggregating up the individual marginal benefits from pollution reductions for all people living around a plant, as shown in Equation (9.2). The locations of the people are indexed by x and y. The marginal benefits MB_i from pollution abatement at a given plant depend largely on the number of people in the area (measured by ρ_{xy}, the population density at a given point) and the emissions to which they are exposed (E_{xy}).[4] We measure differences in people's health susceptibility to pollution exposure by S_{xy}.[5] Finally, we allow for the possibility that the benefits accruing to different population groups are given different weights, through the use of the α_{xy} term:

$$MB = \iint_{xy} \alpha_{xy} S_{xy} E_{xy} \rho_{xy} dx dy. \tag{9.2}$$

Note that differences in α_{xy} across groups of people (e.g., by race or socio-economic status) could be associated with "environmental justice concerns," since people with lower α_{xy} are likely to be exposed to higher pollution levels (cleaning up the pollution affecting those groups would receive a "lower benefit" in the $MB = MC$ calculation, resulting in less cleanup). Where could these differences in α_{xy} come from? This depends in large part on how the marginal benefits are assumed to be affecting the firm's decision about how much pollution to abate. If pollution abatement comes from the firm's managers deciding to "do good" for the community, they may be more sympathetic to neighborhoods whose demographic composition is similar to their own. If it comes from threats of legal action or Coasian bargaining, homogeneous neighborhoods with powerful community connections may receive greater weight, because they cooperate better in collective action. Note that all these examples assume that the affected neighborhoods receive the benefits from pollution abatement without paying the costs (so more abatement is better for them). If abatement pressures are expected to result in plant closings or job loss, the community might in some circumstances prefer to have less pollution abatement.

The possibility that we focus on here is that state regulators are choosing their regulatory stringency (especially the frequency of inspections and enforcement actions) in order to maximize net political support for their regulatory activities (Stigler 1971; Peltzman 1976; Deily and Gray 1991). McCubbins and Schwartz (1984) argue that legislative oversight of regulatory agencies usually responds to complaints brought by individual constituents with political influence ("fire alarms") rather than by conducting systematic reviews ("police patrols"). We expect that regulators' decisions would be designed to avoid triggering those "fire alarms." Socioeconomic groups with less political clout (e.g., the poor or minorities) would be given less weight (assigned a smaller value of α_{xy}) in the agency's calculations. On the other hand, politically active people, especially those who strongly favor environmental issues, may apply extra pressure on regulators to increase the regulatory stringency applied to nearby plants, effectively giving those people a larger value of α_{xy}, resulting in more regulatory activity and more pollution abatement.

Data and Empirical Methodology

Our analysis uses cross-sectional data on environmental regulatory activity in 2000–2002 for 1,616 manufacturing plants located near four large US cities: Los Angeles, Boston, Columbus, and Houston. We included four cities in four different states to allow us to test whether the allocation process differs between cities in higher- and lower-regulation states.[6] Those tests (results are available from the authors upon request) have not shown any systematic differences in the allocation process across the four individual cities, so they are not presented here. We gathered data from EPA databases for all plants located within 50 miles of any of the cities. Plant location information (latitude and longitude) came from the EPA's Facility Registry System (FRS) database. The final sample of 1,616 plants came from a merger of plant-level census data and EPA data that required each plant to be present in both the census and the EPA data sets.

Our regulatory enforcement data come from the EPA's Envirofacts and IDEA databases, focusing on air pollution regulation (primarily for criteria air pollutants). These data sets allow us to differentiate between two different types of regulatory pressures faced by each plant—enforcement actions (*ENFORCE*) and inspection-type actions (*INSP*)—directed at the plant between 2000 and 2002. Enforcement actions include notices of violation, penalties, and follow-up phone calls, while inspection-type actions include on-site inspections, emissions monitoring, and stack tests. Based on discussions with regulators, the number of enforcement actions is more likely to be associated with problems at the plant, while the number of inspections is connected with the size of the plant.

Harrington (1988) illustrates that, in a repeated game, a regulator could increase the expected long-term penalty for noncompliance considerably by establishing two classes of regulated plants—good and bad. The good plants are assumed to cooperate with regulators and are inspected only rarely. The bad plants are assumed to be uncooperative with regulators and face much greater inspection and enforcement activity. To control for this effect, we include a lagged measure of past violations of environmental standards (*VIOL_97*), indicating whether the plant was out of compliance at any point in 1997.[7]

We estimate four different versions of Equation (9.3) for the dependent variables measuring regulatory stringency. We measure stringency as the number of inspections (*INSP*) and enforcement actions (*ENFORCE*) a plant receives over the 2000–2002 period (using three years of data to provide more variation in the dependent variables). Since both *INSP* and *ENFORCE* are often 0 and are otherwise relatively small integers, we estimate the equations using a negative binomial model (as well as a simpler Poisson model).[8] Each dependent variable Y_{it} is a function of *PLANT* and *PEOPLE* characteristics, as well as *STATE* and *COUNTY* variables and *CITY* dummy variables:

$$Y_{it} = F(PLANT_{it}, PEOPLE_{it}, STATE_{it}, COUNTRY_{it}, CITY_i) \qquad (9.3)$$

where Y_{it} is one of the two dependent variables in our analysis: air pollution inspections and enforcement actions.

Prior to discussing the expected impacts of our neighborhood-level socioeconomic and demographic variables, we first detail the plant-, state-, and county-level control variables included in each model. Our plant-level control variables include plant size, capital stock, fuel use, productivity, plant age, and corporate structure from the Census Bureau's confidential plant-level LRD. The LRD contains annual information on individual manufacturing plants, including total value of shipments, labor productivity, capital stock, fuel use, and age of the plant. These data are collected in the Census of Manufactures and the Annual Survey of Manufacturers (for a more detailed description of the LRD data, see McGuckin and Pascoe 1988).[9] From the LRD, we extract information for 2002, originally collected in the 2002 Census of Manufactures. We use the plant's total value of shipments in log form (*SIZE*) and capital stock in log form (*CAPITAL*) to measure the size of the plant. To control for fuel use, which should be positively correlated with air emissions, we use the log of the cost of purchased fuels. Our control for plant age (*AGE*) is based on the first year the plant appears in the LRD.[10] We control for the plant's efficiency using labor productivity (*LPROD*) measured as real output per employee. Finally, we include a dummy variable (*SINGLE*), which identifies plants that are part of single-plant firms (firms that own no other manufacturing plants) to control for corporate structure. If single plants have less political clout, then we would expect to find them receiving more attention from regulators. Single plants might also be more apt to have paperwork violations, as compared to larger firms, which could take advantage of economies of scale in providing regulatory compliance support from their corporate headquarters.

We use voting information at the county level to characterize the political climate surrounding the plant.[11] The use of voter activity to overcome externalities is discussed in Olson (1965). A positive influence on α_{xy} is expected to come from voter activity, measured using county voter turnout in the 2000 presidential election (*TURNOUT*). We also include *DEMOCRAT*, the fraction of voters in the county voting for the Democratic presidential candidate in 2000, as an indication of voter support for more active regulatory interventions.[12] Both of these variables are expected to result in more regulatory activity at a plant, since they are associated with having more politically active, liberal people living near the plant.[13]

Now consider the variables that are at the heart of our analyses, those related to environmental justice concerns that plants might be treated differently based on the racial, ethnic, or socioeconomic composition of the surrounding population. In our analyses, the "potentially less valued" (low α_{xy}) populations are poor and minorities. Our measure of *POOR* is the percentage of the nearby population living below the poverty line; our measure of *MINORITY* is the percentage of the nearby population who are not non-Hispanic whites. Environmental justice concerns could be raised about regulators' actions if plants near *POOR* and *MINORITY* populations face less regulatory activity. We measure the overall population being affected by pollution from the plant (ρ_{xy}) with *POPDEN*, the population density around the plant, which is expected to be associated with increased regulatory activity. Possible differences in health sensitivity by age group (S_{xy} in Equation [9.2]) are represented by *CHILDREN* (the percentage of the nearby population under the age of 6) and *ELDERS* (the percentage of the nearby population over the age of 65). Since both groups are expected to be more sensitive to pollution, both *CHILDREN* and *ELDERS* should be positively related to regulatory activity.

We create the aforementioned socioeconomic and demographic variables from detailed geographic area (census block groups) data on population characteristics from the 2000 US Census of Population, as compiled in the Census-CD data sets prepared by GeoLytics, Inc. We do not know, a priori, the "optimal" (or even most appropriate) size of a neighborhood to examine the effects of benefits and our socioeconomic and demographic variables on regulatory activity. Therefore, we take advantage of our ability to "construct" neighborhoods of different sizes to see how far the benefit and political effects extend. In particular, we construct four different-sized neighborhoods: one consisting of the closest block group, and three additional neighborhoods based on "circles" around the plant—all block groups that fall within R miles of the plant, where $R = 1, 5,$ or 10. Distances are calculated between each plant and the centroid of each block group to determine which block groups fall within R mile(s) of the plant, and the block group values for each population characteristic are aggregated to obtain the overall value for each plant. As it happens, we did not find perfectly consistent results across different neighborhood sizes (some demographic variables had stronger effects when measured in smaller neighborhoods; others were stronger when measured in larger neighborhoods). We report here the results for 1- and 10-mile circles around the plant (other results are available from the authors upon request).

We also considered alternative demographic measures, based on the heterogeneity of the population surrounding the plant, presuming that a more heterogeneous population will have a more difficult time mobilizing for political action. Researchers have considered the impact of ethnic or linguistic fragmentation as it affects economic growth in developing countries (e.g., Easterly and Levine 1997) or the impact of racial or educational heterogeneity on community activity (e.g., Vigdor 2004; Videras 2007). For our analysis, we constructed two homogeneity indices, each calculated as the sum of squared shares of subgroups within the population. If everyone belongs to one group (perfect homogeneity), the index achieves its maximum value of 1.0; if people are spread evenly across N groups, the index achieves its minimum value of $1/N$. The education homogeneity index (HOM_ED) is based on the percentages of college graduates, high school graduates, and high school dropouts near the plant. The racial homogeneity index (HOM_RACE) is based on the percentages of African Americans, Asians, Native Americans, Hispanics, and non-Hispanic whites near the plant (with the latter group also including "all other" racial groups).

Results

A table of means and standard deviations, along with variable descriptions for all variables used in this study, is available in the online appendix.[14] In our data, the average plant receives roughly twice as many air inspections as enforcement actions (mean $INSP = 0.50$ while mean $ENFORCE = 0.27$). Furthermore, the inspection distribution is skewed, with more than half of the plants receiving no inspections during the 2000–2002 period. We now turn to our key demographic variables, which allow us to test for environmental justice concerns. First, in terms of segments of the population who may be more sensitive to pollution emissions ($CHILDREN$ and $ELDERS$), less than 10 percent of our population is under the age of 6 and roughly 12 percent is over the age of 65. Second, in terms of our variables that measure segments of the population who have less "political clout" ($POOR$ and $MINORITY$), about 14 percent of our population has income below the poverty line and just over 25 percent of our population

Table 9.1 Basic inspection and enforcement models

Variable	INSP		ENFORCE	
	OLS	Negative binomial	OLS	Negative binomial
Constant	−2.537	−3.489	−1.598	−6.166
	(0.428)	(0.506)	(0.237)	(0.838)
BOSTON	0.266	0.106	0.307	1.651
	(0.167)	(0.175)	(0.092)	(0.536)
HOUSTON	1.553	1.089	1.120	3.237
	(0.193)	(0.183)	(0.107)	(0.534)
LOS ANGELES	−0.012	−1.239	0.386	2.059
	(0.174)	(0.220)	(0.096)	(0.534)
SIZE	0.099	0.139	0.044	0.127
	(0.042)	(0.053)	(0.023)	(0.079)
LPROD	0.126	−0.046	0.099	0.052
	(0.055)	(0.065)	(0.030)	(0.093)
CAPITAL	0.003	−0.025	0.012	0.020
	(0.024)	(0.027)	(0.013)	(0.041)
FUELS	0.168	0.233	0.095	0.239
	(0.024)	(0.030)	(0.013)	(0.042)
SINGLE	0.333	0.270	0.203	0.421
	(0.102)	(0.130)	(0.057)	(0.187)
AGE	0.071	0.120	−0.029	−0.204
	(0.083)	(0.107)	(0.046)	(0.138)
VIOL_97	0.960	0.227	0.638	0.335
	(0.257)	(0.216)	(0.143)	(0.335)
R^2	0.206	0.173	0.225	0.175

Note: Standard errors are shown in parentheses. A pseudo R^2 statistic is reported for the negative binomial model.

are minorities. There is much more variation across plants in the POOR and MINORITY variables than in the CHILDREN and ELDERS variables.

Table 9.1 presents the results of the basic model for air pollution regulatory activity. All the results include city fixed effects, although we get qualitatively similar results when we drop the fixed effects (results are available from the authors upon request). Our basic model works quite well, explaining roughly 20 percent of the variation across plants in inspection and enforcement activity. The key control variables have the expected sign in nearly all cases. We find that larger plants, which typically generate more pollution, face more inspections and enforcement activity. Plants that use more fuels, again expected to emit more air pollution, face significantly more regulatory activity. Plants that are owned by single-plant firms (firms that own no other manufacturing plants) also face significantly more regulatory activity. This is consistent with the notion that they may have less political clout or less expertise at complying with regulations. Finally, plants with past violations (*VIOL_97*) face greater regulatory activity, although this effect is only significant in the ordinary least squares (OLS) models. The other control variables (capital intensity, labor productivity, and plant age) have less consistent and generally insignificant effects.

We add three additional variables to our basic model in Table 9.2: *POPDEN*, *TURNOUT*, and *DEMOCRAT*. In general, the key plant-level control variables continue to have the same effect as found in the basic model in Table 9.1. *POPDEN*, our proxy for the marginal benefits from pollution abatement, has an unexpectedly negative effect on the amount of regulatory activity faced by a plant but is only significant in the OLS model for inspections.[15] This implies that regulators are not directing additional regulatory pressure, in the form of more inspections or more enforcement actions, toward potentially high benefit plants. On the other hand, our political variables, *TURNOUT* and *DEMOCRAT*, have the expected positive signs and are generally significant. This provides evidence that regulators respond to pressure from the surrounding population, with more politically active and more liberal populations encouraging more regulatory activity.

In Tables 9.3 and 9.4, we add demographic/socioeconomic variables to our full model, with Table 9.3 focusing on *INSP* and Table 9.4 focusing on *ENFORCE*.[16] Consider first the results in the top panel of each table, for models that include all other control variables. *CHILDREN* and *ELDERS* are two demographic groups who are expected to receive greater health benefits from pollution abatement than the rest of the population. Focusing on the results of the negative binomial models, we see that plants that are near more sensitive population groups (*CHILDREN* and *ELDERS*) face more inspections, as expected. However, this effect is never significant. On the other hand, *ELDERS* and *CHILDREN* show some unexpectedly negative (yet generally insignificant) effects on enforcement activity. Moreover, there are some differences between the OLS and negative binomial results. On the whole, we do not find convincing evidence that regulators put more pressure, in the form of inspections and enforcement activity, on plants located in areas with more sensitive populations. This is a surprise, but it may be the case that our measures of regulatory pressure (simple counts of inspection and enforcement actions) are not really capturing the amount of pressure these plants face. High-benefit plants may face other kinds of pressures (e.g., community action, permit stringency, etc.) that we

Table 9.2 Expanded basic inspection and enforcement models

	INSP		ENFORCE	
Variable	OLS	Negative binomial	OLS	Negative binomial
Constant	−3.596	−4.554	−2.708	−10.624
	(0.969)	(1.130)	(0.539)	(1.760)
BOSTON	0.126	−0.029	0.107	0.809
	(0.234)	(0.289)	(0.130)	(0.612)
HOUSTON	1.820	1.330	1.290	3.871
	(0.231)	(0.233)	(0.128)	(0.588)
LOS ANGELES	0.268	−1.000	0.453	2.207
	(0.207)	(0.266)	(0.115)	(0.582)
SIZE	0.102	0.140	0.045	0.125
	(0.042)	(0.052)	(0.023)	(0.078)
LPROD	0.118	−0.061	0.097	0.040
	(0.055)	(0.066)	(0.030)	(0.093)
CAPITAL	0.002	−0.024	0.013	0.024
	(0.024)	(0.027)	(0.013)	(0.041)
FUELS	0.165	0.232	0.094	0.238
	(0.024)	(0.031)	(0.014)	(0.042)
SINGLE	0.354	0.278	0.209	0.436
	(0.102)	(0.129)	(0.057)	(0.188)
AGE	0.078	0.120	−0.032	−0.214
	(0.083)	(0.107)	(0.046)	(0.137)
VIOL_97	0.868	0.148	0.605	0.330
	(0.258)	(0.219)	(0.143)	(0.327)
TURNOUT	0.024	0.022	0.015	0.056
	(0.011)	(0.013)	(0.006)	(0.021)
DEMOCRAT	0.007	0.006	0.009	0.035
	(0.008)	(0.011)	(0.004)	(0.014)
POPDEN	−0.071	−0.040	−0.007	0.014
	(0.033)	(0.031)	(0.018)	(0.043)
R^2	0.211	0.175	0.229	0.180

Note: Standard errors are shown in parentheses. A pseudo R^2 statistic is reported for the negative binomial model.

cannot observe. If regulators, with limited time to perform regulatory enforcement, know that a plant is facing these other pressures, then they might not feel the need to allocate more inspections and enforcement actions to those plants.

Now we turn to the impact of POOR and MÎNORITY (our potentially disadvantaged populations) on regulatory activity, the focus of our environmental justice analysis. As happened with CHILDREN and ELDERS, we find little

Table 9.3 Inspection models

Model	POOR	MINORITY	ELDERS	CHILDREN	R^2
			Variable		
Full models—each model contains all control variables					
OLS—1 mile	1.689	−0.394	0.957	−4.794	0.217
	(0.639)	(0.344)	(1.188)	(2.166)	
NB—1 mile	1.167	−0.699	0.855	1.913	0.176
	(0.745)	(0.407)	(1.301)	(2.292)	
OLS—10 miles	2.938	−1.875	2.858	−7.569	0.218
	(2.100)	(1.134)	(4.151)	(7.618)	
NB—10 miles	1.720	−1.398	3.206	8.405	0.182
	(2.757)	(1.328)	(4.935)	(8.846)	
Demographic variables only					
OLS—1 mile	0.847	−0.768	0.399	−4.891	0.120
	(0.634)	(0.343)	(1.245)	(2.232)	
NB—1 mile	1.037	−1.035	0.849	−1.009	0.116
	(0.829)	(0.452)	(1.473)	(2.443)	
OLS—10 miles	0.399	−1.612	7.838	7.647	0.210
	(1.934)	(0.816)	(4.141)	(7.389)	
NB—10 miles	0.570	−2.706	11.584	20.597	0.122
	(2.581)	(1.028)	(5.035)	(9.780)	
Demographic variables only—each variable entered separately					
OLS—1 mile	−0.352	−0.642	1.593	−5.275	
	(0.502)	(0.278)	(1.146)	(2.000)	
NB—1 mile	−0.313	−0.703	1.239	−2.262	
	(0.619)	(0.333)	(1.388)	(2.231)	
OLS—10 miles	−1.971	−1.549	6.289	−1.645	
	(1.136)	(0.488)	(3.038)	(5.813)	
NB—10 miles	−3.334	−2.620	5.480	4.070	
	(1.566)	(0.645)	(3.303)	(6.790)	

Note: Standard errors are shown in parentheses. A pseudo R^2 statistic is reported for the negative binomial (NB) model. Top panel: all models contain all the variables listed in Table 9.2. Middle and bottom panels: all models also contain city dummy variables. Bottom panel: each coefficient comes from a separate regression, as inspections and enforcement are regressed on one demographic variable at a time.

evidence that regulators treat poor or minority populations differently than other populations in their allocation of regulatory activity, after controlling for other variables. *MINORITY* has the expected negative effect on regulatory activity, but this effect is insignificant, while the *POOR* coefficient has an unexpectedly positive effect on regulatory activity, although this effect is also generally insignificant.

Table 9.4 Enforcement models

Model	POOR	MINORITY	ELDERS	CHILDREN	R^2
			Variable		
Full models—each model contains all control variables					
OLS—1 mile	0.758	−0.258	0.505	1.429	0.232
	(0.356)	(0.192)	(0.661)	(1.206)	
NB—1 mile	0.533	−0.445	−0.140	8.040	0.185
	(1.012)	(0.565)	(1.932)	(3.273)	
OLS—10 miles	1.854	−0.424	0.280	−2.668	0.233
	(1.169)	(0.632)	(2.312)	(4.243)	
NB—10 miles	4.519	−0.367	−11.245	−4.468	0.184
	(3.751)	(1.896)	(7.893)	(13.538)	
Demographics variables only					
OLS—1 mile	0.399	−0.367	0.159	1.254	0.126
	(0.355)	(0.192)	(0.698)	(1.251)	
NB—1 mile	0.651	−0.763	0.464	5.968	0.106
	(1.108)	(0.611)	(2.136)	(3.366)	
OLS—10 miles	0.456	−0.355	3.225	6.624	0.126
	(1.084)	(0.457)	(2.322)	(4.143)	
NB—10 miles	0.872	−0.664	9.422	27.734	0.106
	(3.574)	(1.472)	(7.598)	(14.431)	
Demographics variables only—each variable entered separately					
OLS—1 mile	0.089	−0.209	−0.061	1.085	
	(0.281)	(0.156)	(0.641)	(1.120)	
NB—1 mile	0.268	−0.256	−0.998	4.962	
	(0.827)	(0.462)	(1.971)	(2.949)	
OLS—10 miles	0.018	−0.228	1.522	2.838	
	(0.635)	(0.273)	(1.700)	(3.249)	
NB—10 miles	0.881	0.061	0.165	14.125	
	(1.911)	(0.816)	(5.081)	(9.745)	

Note: Standard errors are shown in parentheses. A pseudo R^2 statistic is reported for the negative binomial (NB) model. Top panel: all models contain all the variables listed in Table 9.2. Middle and bottom panels: all models also contain city dummy variables. Bottom panel: each coefficient comes from a separate regression, as inspections and enforcement are regressed on one demographic variable at a time.

One possible concern with the results in the top panels is that we are estimating the full model and that some of our control variables may be capturing the mechanisms by which the demographic variables might influence regulatory activity. For example, poor and minority neighborhoods have lower voter turnout, so the significant *TURNOUT* effect in the model might leave little to be explained by *POOR* and *MINORITY*.[17] We tested several variations of our models, including different combinations of the demographic variables or excluding some control variables (such as lagged violations and political activism). The remaining panels consider progressively simpler models. The middle panels include our four key demographic variables and city dummies, but no other control variables, while the bottom panels include only one demographic variable at a time along with city dummies. It's worth noting that dropping the other control variables results in considerably less explanatory power (lower R^2) in these analyses, as compared to those in the top panels.

There is a tendency, most noticeable in the middle panels, for the coefficients on the demographic variables to become more consistent in sign—and occasionally significant—when the other control variables are dropped from the model. *ELDERS* and *CHILDREN* are more consistently positive than in the full model, and they are both significant in the 10-mile-circle negative binomial inspection model. *POOR* is consistently positive (but insignificant), while *MINORITY* remains negative and is significant for the negative binomial inspection equations. In the bottom panels, where the demographic variables enter separately, the coefficients on *ELDERS* and *CHILDREN* are less consistently positive, but we now see significantly negative (negative binomial) results for *POOR* and *MINORITY*, with fewer inspections at plants in poor and minority neighborhoods.

In Table 9.5, we consider the possibility that the homogeneity of the surrounding population might influence their ability to mobilize support for greater regulatory activity. We test homogeneity in educational attainment as well as in racial composition. We should find positive coefficients, if (as expected) more homogeneous neighborhoods are able to exert more effective pressure on regulators. We find the expected results for educational homogeneity, where we find positive effects that are usually significant, but not for racial homogeneity, where the coefficients are negative (and generally insignificant).

Given these initial results, we concentrate our attention on educational homogeneity in the remainder of Table 9.5 (we carried out similar analyses for racial homogeneity, without finding much of significance). We first consider a decomposition of the educational homogeneity index into its three components, the squared shares of the three educational subcategories. These components usually show positive effects on regulatory activity, consistent with the *HOM_ED* coefficients; the dropout share is more often negative than the others, but the differences between the components are not generally significant. We then test whether homogeneity matters differently for different populations

Table 9.5 Inspection and enforcement models including homogeneity measures ($N = 1,616$)

Model:	OLS	NB	OLS	NB	OLS	NB	OLS	NB	OLS	NB
Dependent variable:	INSP	INSP	INSP	INSP	ENFORCE	ENFORCE	ENFORCE	ENFORCE	ENFORCE	ENFORCE
Distance:	1 mile	1 mile	10 miles	10 miles	1 mile	1 mile	10 miles	10 miles	10 miles	10 miles
Race homogeneity										
HOM_RACE	−0.414	−0.283	−1.952	−1.070	−0.135	−0.224	−1.090	−1.165		
	(0.305)	(0.367)	(0.803)	(0.990)	(0.170)	(0.472)	(0.447)	(1.418)		
Education homogeneity										
HOM_ED	2.784	2.241	6.172	2.991	1.810	2.705	2.725	−0.637		
	(0.896)	(0.959)	(1.630)	(1.748)	(0.499)	(1.387)	(0.909)	(2.433)		
Education homogeneity decomposition										
DROPOUT2	5.007	3.081	−9.978	−10.648	0.705	1.524	−5.429	−17.371		
	(2.540)	(2.844)	(7.553)	(8.814)	(1.413)	(3.997)	(4.214)	(13.406)		
HSGRAD2	3.214	2.304	5.289	1.403	1.762	2.164	2.197	−3.904		
	(0.982)	(1.053)	(1.821)	(1.982)	(0.546)	(1.566)	(1.016)	(2.961)		
COLLEGE2	3.889	2.354	4.016	−1.320	1.713	1.133	1.406	−9.798		
	(1.385)	(1.492)	(2.749)	(3.129)	(0.770)	(2.455)	(1.534)	(5.352)		

(continued)

Table 9.5 (*Continued*)

Model:	OLS	NB	OLS	NB	OLS	NB	OLS	NB
Dependent variable:	INSP	INSP	INSP	INSP	ENFORCE	ENFORCE	ENFORCE	ENFORCE
Distance:	1 mile	1 mile	10 miles	10 miles	1 mile	1 mile	10 miles	10 miles
Education homogeneity interacted with POOR								
HOM_ED	2.186	2.921	0.770	5.425	1.230	5.467	0.269	7.510
	(1.514)	(1.552)	(3.332)	(3.652)	(0.842)	(2.295)	(1.859)	(6.059)
HOM_ED × POOR	4.479	−5.257	39.210	−17.647	4.339	−19.505	17.822	−53.338
	(9.136)	(9.404)	(21.098)	(23.264)	(5.080)	(12.796)	(11.774)	(36.465)
Education homogeneity interacted with MINORITY								
HOM_ED	4.185	3.021	3.923	4.948	1.872	3.194	1.686	2.418
	(1.264)	(1.286)	(2.518)	(2.751)	(0.703)	(2.003)	(1.405)	(4.938)
HOM_ED × MINORITY	−5.981	−4.169	7.682	−6.996	−0.268	−2.038	3.549	−8.821
	(3.804)	(4.518)	(6.557)	(7.592)	(2.117)	(5.971)	(3.658)	(12.451)
Education homogeneity interacted with TURNOUT								
HOM_ED	6.687	−1.391	2.669	−9.987	7.087	7.820	2.865	−4.542
	(4.832)	(5.317)	(6.525)	(7.289)	(2.685)	(7.998)	(3.640)	(11.668)
HOM_ED × TURNOUT	−0.081	0.075	0.076	0.279	−0.109	−0.112	−0.003	0.089
	(0.098)	(0.109)	(0.136)	(0.152)	(0.055)	(0.173)	(0.076)	(0.259)

Note: Standard errors are shown in parentheses. All models in this table contain all the variables listed in Table 9.2, plus the four demographic variables.

by interacting *HOM_ED* with other variables: *TURNOUT*, *POOR*, and *MINORITY*. None of the interactions are significant, but we do find negative coefficients on *POOR* and *MINORITY*, suggesting that the advantages of homogeneity are less effective in poor or minority neighborhoods.

Conclusion

In this chapter, we use a plant-level data set consisting of 1,616 manufacturing plants in four large US cities—Los Angeles, Boston, Columbus, and Houston— to test whether regulators treat different segments of the population differently when allocating regulatory activity. A key potential explanation for environmental justice concerns is that regulators might direct more regulatory activity at plants in rich, white neighborhoods and less in poor, minority neighborhoods, resulting in poorer environmental conditions in less privileged areas. We focus on differences across plants in the benefit side of the $MB = MC$ equation, but our use of confidential census plant-level data allows us to control for a variety of plant characteristics (size, age, productivity, capital intensity, and energy intensity), which could affect marginal abatement costs as well.

Our basic model for air pollution regulatory activity works quite well, explaining roughly 20 percent of the variation in inspection and enforcement activity, and our key control variables generally have the expected sign. One exception to this is the population density near the plant, which should increase the benefits of pollution reductions but, if anything, seems to have a negative effect on regulatory enforcement (though significant in only one model).

Examining the characteristics of the nearby population, we find that, as expected, plants in areas with more politically active (*TURNOUT*) and more liberal (*DEMOCRAT*) populations face significantly more regulatory pressure. For the demographic characteristics, the results are much weaker. We expect *CHILDREN* and *ELDERS* to be more sensitive to pollution emissions, but their coefficients are not always positive and rarely significant.

Our measures of disadvantaged populations also show limited effects. We expect plants with more poor and minorities nearby to face less regulatory pressure. We find the expected sign for *MINORITY*, but these impacts are insignificant, while we find (unexpected) positive signs for *POOR*. Thus, we find relatively little statistical evidence that regulators are less active at plants near poor or minority populations—when other explanatory variables, such as political activity, are included in the model. When these other variables are excluded from the model, the negative *MINORITY* effect is significant for inspections (but the *POOR* effect remains surprisingly positive).

We also test for the impact of population homogeneity near the plant, using measures of educational attainment and racial diversity. We find the expected impact for diversity in educational attainment (more homogeneous neighborhoods seem to have greater political clout in terms of receiving more regulatory attention) but no impact of racial diversity on regulatory activity. Interactions of educational diversity with other demographic variables are generally insignificant.

The generally insignificant results for *POOR* and *MINORITY* in the complete model do not necessarily rule out the presence of environmental justice concerns in the allocation of regulatory activity across plants. Differences in regulatory pressure may arise through other avenues than the simple numeric count of inspections or enforcement actions. A politically well connected population could intervene in permit renewals, organize community action against the plant, or encourage regulators to pursue qualitatively different avenues (e.g., the use of criminal penalties for violations) that we cannot observe in our data.

In the final analysis, it is striking that, although there is some evidence that regulatory actions occur less often in minority communities, this relationship diminishes substantially and loses its statistical significance once other variables are taken into account. This suggests that any shortfall in government regulatory activity in these communities is not because of "pure discrimination" based solely on their demographic characteristics but can instead be explained by differences in political activity and other characteristics included in the complete model.

Notes

1. According to the EPA's Office of Environmental Justice, environmental justice exists when "no group of people, including racial, ethnic, or socioeconomic group, ... bear[s] a disproportionate share of the negative environmental consequences resulting from industrial, municipal, and commercial operations."

2. Gray and Shadbegian (2004) find little significant evidence of diminished regulatory activity near poor and minority populations.

3. The compliance-enforcement literature contains numerous studies that show the effectiveness of EPA enforcement, including Magat and Viscusi (1990), Gray and Deily (1996), Laplante and Rilstone (1996), Nadeau (1997), Helland (1998), Shadbegian and Gray (2003), and Gray and Shadbegian (2005, 2007).

4. Our only direct measure of the overall benefits from pollution abatement at a particular plant is population density. This implicitly assumes equal exposures E_{xy} for everyone included in Equation (9.2), although we do test different-sized neighborhoods around the plants, which could allow for some diminution of impact with distance.

5. Our interpretation focuses on health benefits from pollution abatement, but if people differ in the utility they assign to pollution reductions, those differences could also translate into different values of S_{xy}.

6. According to Hall and Kerr's (1991) "Green Policies" index, designed to measure the stringency of state environmental regulations, Los Angeles and Boston are in higher-regulation states than Columbus and Houston (scores of 0.8, 1.4, 2.0, and 2.7, respectively, where a lower score reflects stricter regulation). The scope of the sample we created for this project (i.e., analyzing only four cities) was limited by the considerable effort required to gather, merge, and clean the multiple EPA and census data sets needed for the analysis.

7. It would be interesting to know whether these violations are related to paperwork violations or actual emissions violations, but, unfortunately, this information is not provided in the air pollution compliance data used here.

8. Both models are appropriate in cases when the dependent variable is a count (small integer), such as the number of inspections and enforcement actions. The Poisson distribution assumes that the dependent variable's mean is equal to its variance, but in many cases, count data exhibit overdispersion (a variance greater than its mean). In these cases, a model that allows for overdispersion, such as the negative binomial model used here, is more appropriate. (Our negative binomial results show significant overdispersion in our data.) We also estimate each model with OLS, to test the robustness of the coefficient results.

9. The establishment-level data in the LRD are collected and protected under Title 13 of the US Code. Restricted access to these data can be arranged through the US Census Bureau's Center for Economic Studies (CES). See http://www.census.gov/ces for details.

10. We would like to thank John Haltiwanger for providing us with our plant's age and capital stock, which were calculated based on establishment-level census data.

11. Unfortunately, voting data at finer levels of geographic detail (e.g., precinct-level data) cannot be used, because they are not collected in similar ways across these four states.

12. We tried using League of Conservation Voters data on pro-environmental voting in Congress, which did get the expected positive coefficient but was consistently insignificant, perhaps because of limited geographic variability, being measured at the congressional district level (results are available from the authors on request).

13. Politically active Republicans might be expected to push for less regulatory activity on ideological grounds. The political clout of Democrats might be expected to depend on the party affiliation of the state's governor, but during our sample period, only California had a Democratic governor, so we had no variation to test that hypothesis.

14. See Table A.9.1 in the online appendix at http://www.sup.org/environmental justice.

15. Gray and Shadbegian (2004) find similarly odd results, using much more sophisticated measures of the marginal benefit of pollution abatement. We also tried including measures of plant density (the number of other plants in our data within a given radius of the plant), to test whether areas with many plants received fewer inspections per plant (possibly explaining the negative *POPDEN* results), but plant density was generally insignificant, and its inclusion in the model didn't affect the *POPDEN* coefficient's sign (results are available from the authors on request).

16. We only provide the newly estimated coefficients in Tables 9.3 and 9.4, but, in general, the other variables have the same qualitative effects shown in Tables 9.1 and 9.2.

17. Indeed, in our data set, the correlations of *POOR* and *MINORITY* with *TURNOUT* are about −0.7.

References

Arora, Seema, and Timothy N. Cason. 1999. "Do Community Characteristics Influence Environmental Outcomes? Evidence from the Toxics Release Inventory." *Southern Economic Journal* 65 (4): 691–716.

Becker, Randy A. 2004. "Pollution Abatement Expenditure by U.S. Manufacturing Plants: Do Community Characteristics Matter?" *Contributions to Economic Analysis and Policy* 3 (2). http://www.bepress.com/bejeap/contributions/vol3/iss2/art6.

Been, Vicki, with Francis Gupta. 1997. "Coming to the Nuisance or Going to the Barrios? A Longitudinal Analysis of Environmental Justice Claims." *Ecology Law Quarterly* 24 (1): 1–56.

Deily, Mary E., and Wayne B. Gray. 1991. "Enforcement of Pollution Regulations in a Declining Industry." *Journal of Environmental Economics and Management* 21 (3): 260–74.

Easterly, William, and Ross Levine. 1997. "Africa's Growth Tragedy: Policies and Ethnic Divisions." *Quarterly Journal of Economics* 112 (4): 1203–50.

Gray, Wayne B., and Mary E. Deily. 1996. "Compliance and Enforcement: Air Pollution Regulation in the U.S. Steel Industry." *Journal of Environmental Economics and Management* 31 (1): 96–111.

Gray, Wayne B., and Ronald J. Shadbegian. 2004. "'Optimal' Pollution Abatement—Whose Benefits Matter, and How Much." *Journal of Environmental Economics and Management* 47 (3): 510–34.

———. 2005. "When and Why Do Plants Comply? Paper Mills in the 1980s." *Law and Policy* 27 (2): 238–61.

———. 2007. "The Environmental Performance of Polluting Plants: A Spatial Analysis." *Journal of Regional Science* 47 (1): 63–84.

Hall, Bob, and Mary Lee Kerr. 1991. *Green Index: A State-by-State Guide to the Nation's Environmental Health.* Washington, DC: Island Press.

Hamilton, James T. 1995. "Testing for Environmental Racism: Prejudice, Profits, Political Power?" *Journal of Policy Analysis and Management* 14 (1): 107–32.

Harrington, Winston. 1988. "Enforcement Leverage When Penalties Are Restricted." *Journal of Public Economics* 37 (1): 29–53.

Helland, Eric. 1998. "The Enforcement of Pollution Control Laws: Inspections, Violations, and Self-Reporting." *Review of Economics and Statistics* 80 (1): 141–53.

Jenkins, Robin R., Kelly B. Maguire, and Cynthia L. Morgan. 2004. "Host Community Compensation and Municipal Solid Waste Landfills." *Land Economics* 80 (4): 513–28.

Laplante, Benoit, and Paul Rilstone. 1996. "Environmental Inspections and Emissions of the Pulp and Paper Industry in Quebec." *Journal of Environmental Economics and Management* 31 (1): 19–36.

Magat, Wesley, and W. Kip. Viscusi. 1990. "Effectiveness of the EPA's Regulatory Enforcement: The Case of Industrial Effluent Standards." *Journal of Law and Economics* 33 (2): 331–60.

McCubbins, Matthew D., and Thomas Schwartz. 1984. "Congressional Oversight Overlooked: Police Patrols versus Fire Alarms." *American Journal of Political Science* 28 (1): 165–79.

McGuckin, Robert H., and George A. Pascoe. 1988. "The Longitudinal Research Database: Status and Research Possibilities." *Survey of Current Business* 68 (11): 30–37.

Nadeau, Louis W. 1997. "EPA Effectiveness at Reducing the Duration of Plant-Level Noncompliance." *Journal of Environmental Economics and Management* 34 (1): 54–78.

Olson, Mancur. 1965. *The Logic of Collective Action.* Cambridge, MA: Harvard University Press.

Peltzman, Sam. 1976. "Toward a More General Theory of Regulation." *Journal of Law and Economics* 19 (2): 211–40.

Shadbegian, Ronald J., and Wayne B. Gray. 2003. "What Determines the Environmental Performance of Paper Mills? The Roles of Abatement Spending, Regulation, and Efficiency." *Topics in Economic Analysis and Policy* 3 (1). http://www.bepress.com/bejeap/topics/vol3/iss1/art15.

Sigman, Hilary. 2001. "The Pace of Progress at Superfund Sites: Policy Goals and Interest Group Influence." *Journal of Law and Economics* 44 (1): 315–44.

Stigler, George J. 1971. "The Theory of Economic Regulation." *Bell Journal of Economics and Management Science* 2 (1): 3–21.

Videras, Julio. 2007. "The Effects of Diversity on Revealed Preferences for Environmental Goods." Unpublished manuscript, Hamilton College, Clinton, NY.

Vigdor, Jacob. 2004. "Community Composition and Collective Action: Analyzing Initial Mail Response to the 2000 Census." *Review of Economics and Statistics* 86 (1): 303–12.

Viscusi, W. Kip, and James T. Hamilton. 1999. "Are Risk Regulators Rational? Evidence from Hazardous Waste Cleanup Decisions." *American Economic Review* 89 (4): 1010–27.

Wolverton, Ann. 2009. "Effects of Socio-Economic and Input-Related Factors on Polluting Plants' Location Decisions." *Berkeley Electronic Journal of Economic Analysis and Policy, Advances* 9 (1). http://www.bepress.com/bejeap/vol9/iss1/art14.

10 An Examination of the Correlation between Race and State Hazardous and Solid Waste Taxes

Robin R. Jenkins and Kelly B. Maguire

Introduction

Waste facilities, especially those handling hazardous waste, have long been a focus of investigation in the environmental justice literature. Early findings of socioeconomic disparities in areas hosting these facilities (US General Accounting Office 1983; Bullard 1983; United Church of Christ 1987) have been confirmed repeatedly (see Chapter 1 for additional citations).[1] Siting that varies by community income levels can be partially understood as a trade-off by residents between affordable housing and environmental risk. While this is cause for concern, our focus in this chapter is on disparities that arise because of race, a more puzzling outcome. Specifically, this chapter aims to better understand the correlation between race and environmental taxes levied on waste quantities.

The latest empirical literature continues to report significant racial disparities in waste facility locations. Perhaps most recently, in 2007 the United Church of Christ Commission for Racial Justice updated its 20-year-old landmark investigation into the correlation between race and the locations of hazardous waste disposal facilities (Bullard et al. 2007). The update concludes that neighborhoods surrounding hazardous waste facilities continue to have higher proportions of people of color (56 percent) than nonhost neighborhoods (30 percent).[2]

While there are many potential explanations as to why waste facilities are disproportionately located in communities of color, one contributing factor might be that governments treat waste facilities differently, depending on the racial makeup of the facilities' host communities. One can postulate a variety of motivations for differential treatment that may or may not be intentional, including policy makers' perceptions of different levels of political engagement, or discriminatory attitudes (Hamilton 1995). Putting aside the motivations, disproportionate siting could be the outcome if the inclination of policy makers to give disincentives to waste facilities depends on the racial makeup of host neighborhoods.

On a larger scale, policies might also vary according to the racial makeup of entire constituencies, not just of host communities. Policy makers might treat waste facilities differently, depending on the racial consistency of their entire districts. Again, there could be a variety of motivations including perceptions of constituent preferences that vary according to racial consistency.

The purpose of this chapter is to examine one tool—taxation—that is increasingly used by state policy makers and whose implementation, ceteris paribus, should serve as a deterrent to waste facilities. Specifically, we examine the determinants of state taxes charged per unit of solid and hazardous waste managed. Across states, these taxes are highly variable and are sometimes set to vary with the type of solid or hazardous waste, the management method (e.g., disposal or incineration), the size of the facility, and a variety of other factors. This variation has the potential to improve efficiency as states provide disincentives for the categories of waste or the waste management methods that their constituents find most objectionable. Alternatively, or additionally, these taxes might reflect the motivations described above that lead, whether intentionally or not, to racially disparate outcomes. We explore whether the race of host neighborhoods and the race of the overall state are potential determinants of waste taxes. If such taxes are set differently depending on race, this could contribute to disproportionate siting of waste facilities. In this sense, our analysis of waste taxes parallels the analysis by Shadbegian and Gray (see Chapter 9) of enforcement activity but for a different policy tool and a different branch of government.

Of course, there are many factors other than race that might influence state policy makers' decisions regarding waste taxes. While we are unaware of any studies that have examined the determinants of *solid* waste taxes, there are two studies that have explored the determinants of state *hazardous* waste taxes, although neither focused on questions of environmental justice. Levinson (2003) used a multiyear data set and found evidence that taxes are set competitively among jurisdictions that are engaged in a "race to the top" in environmental quality. Sigman (2003) studied taxes for a single year, 1997, and considered interjurisdictional competition but emphasized, and found partial support for, environmental costs as a potential determinant of hazardous waste tax rates.

We examine taxes levied by states on the quantity of hazardous waste managed and the amount of solid waste landfilled. Like Levinson (2003) and Sigman (2003), we also consider interjurisdictional competition and external costs as factors affecting the variability in state waste taxes. However, we build on these studies by examining a larger set of factors that might be determining state tax rates. In particular, we add consideration of factors important to environmental justice. We explore the importance to state tax rates of racial makeup at two scales—the overall state and the specific communities that host waste facilities. We also consider the importance of alternative sources of revenue in the state (i.e., sales and income taxes)[3] and the interplay between state and local government policy. In addition to examining a more comprehensive set of factors that influence hazardous waste taxes, as a contrast we also examine the determinants of municipal solid waste tax rates.

The chapter begins with a discussion of the reasons behind solid and hazardous waste facility siting problems and the increasing prevalence of waste taxes. We then explain alternative frameworks for understanding the variability in tax rates across states. We describe our data set and present the results of two econometric models—one for hazardous waste taxes and a second for municipal solid waste taxes. We conclude with a brief discussion.

Background

The Resource Conservation and Recovery Act of 1976 (RCRA) changed the institutions that manage hazardous and solid waste in the United States. RCRA Subtitle C established a cradle-to-grave hazardous waste management process that led to the creation of a new type of industry consisting of firms that treat, store, and dispose of hazardous waste (Jenkins, Kopits, and Simpson 2009).[4] These facilities are often considered undesirable because of their association with environmental risks, and many communities are opposed to hosting them. Similarly, RCRA Subtitle D, which targets municipal solid waste, required capital-intensive technologies, such as landfill liners and methane extraction systems, which led to a consolidation in the landfill industry. Small local landfills were replaced by large regional ones that faced greater opposition by potential host communities (Jenkins, Kopits, and Simpson 2009). Thus, siting difficulties developed for both hazardous and solid waste facilities as an unintentional consequence of RCRA.[5]

The opposition to hosting waste facilities rests at least in part on environmental risk. A significant number of hazardous waste management facilities have been designated RCRA corrective action sites in need of cleanup action. Old solid waste dumps make up a significant proportion of Superfund sites.[6] Landfills are also associated with truck traffic, odors, and other potential declines in quality of life. Both types of facilities can stigmatize a community. Presumably at least partly in response to their undesirability, states began taxing waste facilities.

Over time, waste taxes have become increasingly common. For hazardous waste, most states introduced taxes during the 1980s. Hazardous waste fees were unknown prior to RCRA. But, as of 1987, 22 states taxed hazardous waste; by 1990, 31 states did; by 2005, our data suggest the number had inched up to 33 (Sigman 1996; Levinson 1999a). The US Environmental Protection Agency (EPA) developed the rules for municipal solid waste management more slowly than the rules for hazardous waste. This is reflected by the gradual move toward large facilities to which communities were opposed. It is also reflected in the evolution of state-mandated waste taxes for solid waste landfills. In 1996, for a sample of 24 states, Jenkins, Maguire, and Morgan (2004) identified only 3 states, or 12 percent, that had mandated solid waste taxes. At present, our data suggest 30 states, or 60 percent, do.

Frameworks for Understanding Tax Variability

We posit five frameworks for understanding waste tax variability. The first is concerned with environmental justice. Hamilton (1995) hypothesizes that discriminatory attitudes might affect environmental policy. He offers two additional hypotheses—variations in a population's willingness to pay and differences in their ability to undertake collective action. Hamilton studies expansion decisions by hazardous waste facilities and finds that household income and a community's propensity to engage in collective action, as measured by the percentage of the population who votes, are significant determinants. He finds that the percentage of the population who is nonwhite is not significant when collective action variables are included in the model. We examine how these variables affect waste tax rates.

A second framework is explored by Sigman (2003), who focuses on the possibility that taxes are correlated with the negative externalities associated with hazardous waste facilities. The variation in state tax rates might simply reflect different external costs. Oates and Portney (2003) review both theoretical and empirical approaches developed by economists to improve our understanding of environmental policy choices. The standard normative theory is for the policy to internalize the external costs of pollution and an option to accomplish this is to tax polluting activities at a rate equal to marginal social damages. In practice, policies diverge from this ideal. One positive model to explain actual environmental policy is the median-voter model in which the policy choice reflects the median of the most preferred outcomes of the individuals represented by government. Under certain restrictive conditions, this model predicts a policy outcome that coincides with the normative theory. In the case of hazardous waste disposal facilities and solid waste landfills, the normative and median-voter models suggest that we should expect waste taxes that vary according to the marginal social damages caused by the facilities.

A different argument, not directly related to justice questions but one that also suggests a wedge between environmental policy choice and welfare costs, is offered by Sigman (1996) in a study of the impact of taxes on industrial solvent wastes. Sigman offers the straightforward suggestion that hazardous waste tax rates are determined based on state revenue needs.[7] It is also possible that states are attempting to acquire a share of waste firms' monopoly profits. To examine these potential motivations, we test the correlation between taxes and firm profitability.

Potentially relevant to any state policy decision is a fourth framework that has evolved to explain interjurisdictional tax competition and strategic environmental policy making among states. Levinson (1999b) highlights two distinct possibilities. On the one hand, states might compete to attract polluting firms by lowering environmental standards in a "race to the bottom." A state may engage in such a policy because of the revenue raised by taxing such a facility. On the other hand, states might compete to deter polluting activity by raising environmental standards in a "race to the top," thereby attracting residents by being "clean." Oates (2001) reviews the limited empirical evidence and concludes that, in terms of environmental regulation, there is more evidence for a race to the top. This is supported by Fredriksson and Millimet (2002), who find that states do incorporate the stringency of environmental policies in neighboring states into their own policies.

Finally, the interplay between state and local levels of government is potentially important. Multiple levels of taxing authority can result in inefficiently high tax rates (Sobel 1997). Jenkins, Maguire, and Morgan (2004) find that county and city government host fees for solid waste services are positively correlated with whether a state had a mandated tax; states with mandated taxes had higher local government host fees. Jenkins, Maguire, and Morgan suggest that a state mandate might signal to local governments that payment from a landfill is indeed a practical possibility. This might work both ways with local government fees serving as a signal to state governments so that the latter are more inclined to tax waste. Or the opposite might be more accurate—that state governments try to avoid overtaxation by backing off in the presence of local taxes.

To begin to understand which of these alternative frameworks might shed insight on the determinants of waste taxes, we turn to an empirical model suggested by Oates and Portney (2003) and developed by Aidt (1998). In the model, negative externalities are efficiently internalized via regulation as a consequence of competition among interest groups, typically including both environmental advocacy groups and potentially regulated parties. Aidt's model hypothesizes that governments seek to maximize political contributions and the general well-being of the electorate. If interest groups truly represent the interests of their own constituencies, policy choices will be efficient.

We apply Aidt's model and assume the affected parties include the general population, environmental interest groups, and industry lobby groups. We include additional variables to test the alternative frameworks for understanding environmental tax policy. Measures of race, income, and voting behavior are used to gain insight into justice questions. Measures of groundwater use illustrate the importance of negative externalities.[8] We explore the possibility that a state's need for income or its targeting of waste firms' profits might influence waste tax rates by including state revenues garnered from other sources and the profitability of disposal facilities. We examine the response of state tax rates to the rates charged by neighboring states to determine any possible correlation; however, our data are for a single year, and thus our ability to explore interjurisdictional reactions is limited. Finally, we examine the interplay between state and local tax setting by accounting for whether facilities are publicly or privately owned. State governments might partially avoid overlap with local government finances by avoiding taxes when facilities are publicly owned. This measure is less than ideal but gives us some sense of how state and local governments interact with regard to waste policy.

Data Description

In order to estimate the determinants of state waste tax policy, we gathered data for each state on the variables just described as well as on the taxes levied on hazardous waste management and municipal solid waste landfills.[9]

State Waste Taxes

The foundation of our state hazardous waste tax data is a 2005 report by the US Army Corps of Engineers (USACE) on state hazardous waste management taxes. The report presents detailed tax data gathered via state websites and phone interviews with state officials. There are a variety of ways in which states tax hazardous waste (e.g., by type of waste or management method). Based on these raw data, we calculate a weighted average tax rate per ton of hazardous waste for each state, where the weights are the tons of waste associated with a particular tax as reported in the 2005 Biennial Reporting System (BRS). This measure of taxes more accurately reflects the rate a state receives than the un-weighted average tax rate used in previous studies.

We were unable to locate a comprehensive report of taxes levied on municipal solid waste landfills at the state level, so we used the same approach as the authors of the USACE report in order to create a data set of solid waste taxes. We examined state websites for environmental statutes regarding municipal solid waste taxes. In some cases, particularly if no state tax was found, we confirmed the information using alternative search methods (e.g., Google) for newspaper articles or other information that might point to a state municipal solid waste landfill tax. When solid waste taxes are levied, they are applied uniformly to all solid waste generated in the state; therefore, it was unnecessary to calculate a weighted tax.

Taxes are levied on hazardous waste by 69 percent of the states and on solid waste by 60 percent of the states. Twenty-one states tax both hazardous and solid waste, and eight states do not tax either waste stream. As expected, the average tax is significantly higher for hazardous waste than for solid waste: $19.84 per ton versus $1.34 per ton, respectively. The average hazardous waste tax for the 33 states that charge a positive amount is $28.86 per ton. For the 29 states that charge a solid waste tax, the average is $2.21 per ton.[10] This is the first evidence that the taxes are in some way compensating for negative externalities, given that the risks associated with hazardous waste are typically greater than those associated with municipal solid waste.

Alternative Frameworks

The remaining variables provide insight into the alternative frameworks to explain variation in taxes across states. To examine the importance of justice issues, we include race variables at two levels of aggregation: state and local. We measure the percentage of the state who identifies as black, 11 percent on average, and Hispanic, 9 percent on average. The 20-year update of the landmark United Church of Christ Commission for Racial Justice study (Bullard et al. 2007) provides us with our host community race information. It examines demographic information for the year 2000 for the 3-kilometer area surrounding 413 hazardous waste management facilities across the United States. We adopt its state averages for these 3-kilometer "host" areas for the percentages of blacks and Hispanics. Across states, on average, 20 percent of the residents hosting hazardous waste sites are black and 13 percent are Hispanic. We were unable to locate host community demographics for solid waste landfills.

Apart from race, taxes may vary according to the willingness to pay for environmental protection. If so, states with higher household income will have higher taxes. Finally, justice issues may arise because individuals in the state are less likely to participate in the decision-making process. We measure the percentage of the population who voted in the 2006 presidential election and predict that the higher the voting percentage, the higher the waste taxes in the state.

To account for efficiency factors, we include four categories of variables: socioeconomics, environmental interest groups, industry lobby groups, and risk. To account for preferences of the general electorate, we include two socioeconomic measures—state income levels and age distribution. The strength of environmental interest groups is measured by each state's per capita contributions to environmental organizations in 2001.[11] States in which the waste industry is more concentrated might do a better job at lobbying against higher taxes. To measure this, we include the percentage of total tons of waste managed by the three largest facilities in the state to reflect oligopoly power.[12] Risk is measured by the gallons of groundwater withdrawn in the state, as reported by the US Geological Survey (USGS) for the year 2000. On average, states withdrew 8.41 trillion gallons of water in 2000. This variable ranges in value from 0.43 to 51.2. We posit that the more groundwater withdrawn in a state, the greater potential risk posed by a landfill and therefore the higher the tax rates.

In order to capture the degree to which the state may need or want to raise revenue by taxing waste, we use an indicator variable to denote whether the state has an income tax and the value of the state sales tax rate. Our hypothesis is that these taxes would be substitutes for waste taxes and therefore we expect a negative relationship between the income and sales tax variables and the waste tax.

States may tax waste as a means to get a share of firm profits. Thus, tax rates may depend in part on waste quantities or the number of waste managers. Several earlier studies examine the effect of hazardous waste taxes on the quantity of waste managed (Sigman 1996; Levinson 1999a, 1999b). An intuitive hypothesis is that there is feedback between tax rates and quantities of waste managed.[13] We rely again on the 2005 BRS to estimate quantities of hazardous waste. The 2004 *BioCycle* survey is the source for our estimates of quantities of landfilled municipal solid waste (Simmons et al. 2006). Much more solid waste is managed than hazardous waste, as expected, although the average number of managers per state is approximately the same for both waste streams—between 32 and 36. Tipping fees are also an indication of firm profits, although we have this information for municipal solid waste landfills only. The average solid waste tipping fee is almost $38 per ton, with a range of $17 to almost $100 per ton.

We construct two variables to measure interjurisdictional competition. One is an indicator variable equal to 0 if all adjacent states do not have a tax law and 1 if any adjacent state has such a law. We also include the unweighted average tax charged by adjacent states.

Finally, to get a sense of the interplay between state and local governments, for solid waste landfills only, we used the Chartwell database to determine the percentage of landfills that are privately owned. This is about 30 percent, on average, but with variation between 0 and 90 percent. The measure does not take into account the quantity of waste accepted by these landfills. We expect state taxes to vary directly with the percentage of privately owned landfills.

Econometric Results

To accommodate the censored dependent variable, we use a Tobit model to estimate the determinants of state taxes. A concern is the potential feedback between several of our regressors and the tax. Our first potentially endogenous variable is the quantity of waste managed, although the direction of the relationship is unclear. A positive relationship suggests that the larger tax base presents an opportunity for greater revenue or that greater waste is associated with higher externalities and perhaps justifies the effort to pass a tax. However, quantities may be lower in the presence of the tax than they would otherwise be. Alternatively, the tax might be set lower with larger quantities because a high tax is not needed to raise as much revenue. In addition, firms might respond to the taxes by shifting waste disposal activities to other lower-tax states. Regardless, the quantity of waste managed could be endogenous, or characteristics of states that are correlated with both the tax rate and the quantity of waste managed could have been omitted. We use instrumental variables to test for endogeneity; specifically, we use the size of the state, as measured by the number of acres, and the population of the state. Both variables are likely to affect the quantity of waste managed in the state but not the state tax. Tests reveal that the quantity of waste managed is endogenous but only in the model with regional controls. We correct for this in the results presented in Table 10.1.

Our second and third potentially endogenous variables measure interjurisdictional competition, specifically, whether adjacent states have a waste tax and the value of that tax. In both cases, home states may set their taxes in response to neighbor behavior, which presents the opportunity for feedback between the waste tax variable and these regressors because of a "race to the top/bottom" as discussed earlier. We instrument for the first interjurisdictional variable—the indicator for whether any adjacent states have a waste tax—with two variables. One is a measure of how "green" the congressional voting patterns are in the adjacent states based on the League of Conservation Voters Green Index. The second is an indicator for the presence in the adjacent states of an income tax. "Greener" states may be more likely to have a waste tax to discourage waste disposal in the state; a state income tax may be a substitute revenue source for waste taxes. However, neither variable is likely to affect the value of the waste tax in the state of interest. The indicator variable for whether any adjacent states have a waste tax is endogenous in the solid waste tax model without regional controls.

Finally, we instrument for the value of adjacent state waste taxes with the value of adjacent states' sales tax rates and their average household income. A higher sales tax may substitute for a higher waste tax. The relationship between household income and a state's waste tax is uncertain. A positive relationship suggests more revenue; a negative relationship suggests a lower tax is needed to maintain a particular revenue stream. In either case, neither variable is likely to affect the neighboring state's waste tax. This variable is endogenous in both of the solid waste tax models, with and without regional controls.

In none of our tests are these variables endogenous in the hazardous waste models, a finding that differs from that of Levinson (1999b). One possibility

Table 10.1 Results

Variable	Hazardous waste models		Solid waste models	
	No regional controls	Regional controls	No regional controls	Regional controls
SOUTHEAST		58.78		0.24
		(0.17)		(0.91)
MIDWEST		20.15		1.37
		(0.60)		(0.48)
NORTH		−48.03		−1.07
		(0.34)		(0.70)
SOUTH		67.77		−1.66
		(0.17)		(0.53)
WEST		181.35***		−1.28
		(0.003)		(0.61)

Environmental justice variables

Variable	No regional controls	Regional controls	No regional controls	Regional controls
BLACK_STATE	−268.02	−311.93**	−12.52**	−25.25***
	(0.19)	(0.05)	(0.018)	(0.001)
HISPANIC_STATE	17.83	−80.79	−11.20*	12.69
	(0.95)	(0.73)	(0.08)	(0.19)
BLACK_HOST AREA	122.23	11.07	n/a	n/a
	(0.25)	(0.90)		
HISPANIC_HOST AREA	57.99	−117.01	n/a	n/a
	(0.77)	(0.49)		
INCOME	−1.65	1.43	0.03	−0.07
	(0.41)	(0.42)	(0.68)	(0.43)
VOTE	371.25*	299.99*	−6.48	−14.01
	(0.08)	(0.09)	(0.29)	(0.11)

Efficiency variables

Socioeconomics

Variable	No regional controls	Regional controls	No regional controls	Regional controls
INCOME	See above	See above	See above	See above
AGE	2,284.01	2,769.93	28.51	−187.39
	(0.20)	(0.13)	(0.70)	(0.16)

Environmental interest groups

ENVIRO DONATIONS	5.48	5.45	0.11	0.13
	(0.22)	(0.11)	(0.49)	(0.51)

Industry lobby groups

OLIGOPOLY	32.60	33.98	−5.27*	3.32
	(0.62)	(0.44)	(0.09)	(0.37)

Risk

GROUNDWATER	−0.99	0.02	−0.10	−0.16
	(0.64)	(0.99)	(0.35)	(0.24)

(*continued*)

Table 10.1 (*Continued*)

Variable	Hazardous waste models		Solid waste models	
	No regional controls	*Regional controls*	*No regional controls*	*Regional controls*
Revenue-seeking variables				
Other sources of income				
INCOME TAX DUMMY	44.90	−1.17	2.12	3.18
	(0.30)	(0.97)	(0.13)	(0.11)
SALES TAX RATE	−19.02***	−13.67**	0.19	0.79**
	(0.01)	(0.03)	(0.43)	(0.04)
Profitability of firms				
TONS MANAGED	0.06	−0.02	0.001	−0.003
	(0.92)	(0.97)	(0.98)	(0.93)
NUMBER MANAGERS	0.67	0.51*	0.04	0.04
	(0.13)	(0.09)	(0.13)	(0.24)
TIPPING FEE	n/a	n/a	0.08*	−0.03
			(0.10)	(0.54)
Interjurisdictional competition				
NEIGHBOR TAX DUMMY	−55.39	−46.64	2.53	−16.90***
	(0.31)	(0.30)	(0.38)	(0.01)
AVG NEIGHBOR TAX	−0.13	−1.17***	−0.81	4.72**
	(0.68)	(0.00)	(0.32)	(0.02)
State and local tax interaction				
PRIVATE	n/a	n/a	1.64	1.08
			(0.50)	(0.71)
Constant	−216.35	−302.78*	−2.81	17.16*
	(0.30)	(0.07)	(0.70)	(0.07)
Log-likelihood	−185.54	−170.03	−71.37	−65.31

Note: p values are shown in parentheses.

*Significant at 10% level; **significant at 5% level; ***significant at 1% level.

is that our models omit state characteristics that result in more or less waste managed (e.g., geologic features). We are unable to include state fixed effects because we have only 48 total observations for each waste stream. However, we can include regional controls under the assumption that omitted variables are likely to be similar across a particular region in the United States.

Table 10.1 provides results for both the hazardous waste models and the solid waste models, with and without regional controls. For the hazardous waste model without regional controls, we find that voting participation and revenue seeking drive the results. However, the model with regional controls is much more robust. For it, the same categories are important, as well as interjurisdictional competition. We find that the more politically active the population, as measured by voting behavior, the higher are the taxes. And, importantly, we find that the more blacks in the state, the lower are the hazardous waste tax rates. This holds, even though we find no relationship between taxes and the characteristics of the population hosting the sites.[14] This suggests that tax rates are not set to discriminate against host communities but rather that policies vary with the socioeconomics of the entire state constituency. Perhaps policy makers perceive different preferences among constituents depending on the racial mix of the state.

In terms of revenue seeking, our results show that sales taxes substitute for waste taxes. In states generating more revenue from sales taxes, the hazardous waste taxes are lower. And, in the model with regional controls, we find that the more waste managers in the state, the higher are the tax rates (perhaps this is an effort by states to gain a share of profits).

We find that state waste tax policy is also affected by interjurisdictional competition. Home state taxes move in the opposite direction of the neighbor's taxes. That is, when neighbors have a high tax, the home state has a lower tax and vice versa. This coefficient is difficult to interpret given the cross-sectional nature of the data, but it does suggest that states consider neighbors' taxes when setting their rates.

Turning to the models of municipal solid waste taxes, the variation in the dependent variable is much smaller than in the hazardous waste tax variable; thus, the estimation is not as robust. Similar to the hazardous waste models, we find evidence that environmental justice factors, revenue-seeking behavior, and interjurisdictional competition affect tax rates. Like the hazardous waste tax model with regional controls, the more blacks in the state, the lower are the tax rates; we also find that the more Hispanics in the state, the lower are the tax rates for the solid waste model without regional controls. Again, this may indicate a difference in how preferences of constituents are perceived, depending on the demographics in the state. We have no information on host community demographics and therefore are unable to assess a correlation with state solid waste taxes. Unlike the hazardous waste models, the percentage of the population who voted is not significant. We also find that the more concentrated the industry is, the lower is the tax in the model without regional controls. This could indicate greater lobbying efforts on the part of the larger facilities.

Finally, we find some evidence that there could be complementarity in taxes. The higher the tipping fee or sales tax in our solid waste models, without and with regional controls, respectively, the higher are the taxes. We find interesting results with regard to interjurisdictional competition: the more likely it is that neighbors have a tax, the lower the tax rate, however the higher the neighbor's tax, the higher the tax rate.

Conclusion

We find that hazardous waste taxes vary positively with constituents' past voting behavior but that solid waste taxes do not. Hazardous waste is associated with greater risk, and there is perhaps a higher aversion to hosting its disposal facilities compared to solid waste landfills. This might explain why state policy makers seem more sensitive to public preferences and the public's inclination toward collective action when setting hazardous waste taxes.

Unlike the results in Hamilton (1995), even controlling for voting behavior, the percentage of blacks at the state level persists as significantly correlated with lower hazardous and solid waste taxes. We find no evidence that policy makers consider the racial makeup of the community immediately surrounding the waste facilities when setting taxes. At least for hazardous waste, taxes do not vary according to the race of the host community. Thus, state waste taxes do not seem to be directly contributing to the differential siting of waste facilities identified time and again in the environmental justice literature. The more aggregate finding that tax rates vary according to state racial consistency, however, could potentially contribute to racial disparity in siting. The importance of race at the state level is difficult to interpret but might suggest that policy makers seem to attribute, rightly or wrongly, different preferences depending on race.

Our results are consistent with those of Shadbegian and Gray (see Chapter 9), who set out to discover whether state environmental enforcement activity is correlated with the demographics of neighborhoods hosting plants. Their results show little evidence of disparities in enforcement. Thus, two state policy mechanisms—environmental enforcement and waste taxes—are uncorrelated with environmental justice variables at the neighborhood level.

Unlike Sigman (2003), we do not find that greater dependence on groundwater leads to higher waste taxes. However, we find some evidence that states rely on waste taxes as a revenue source, and, like Levinson (2003), we find that neighboring state's policy choices are important.

In addition to exploring the factors that are important to waste tax rates, our findings also lend insight into the larger question of what determines state policies that impose environmental requirements that exceed federal mandates.

In some sense, waste taxes can be viewed as stringency in environmental policy beyond what is required by federal legislation through RCRA. We find that the stringency of at least this one environmental policy does not depend on the race of the community directly shouldering the negative externalities. We do find, however, that it varies according to the racial makeup of the entire state and that the state's race matters even after accounting for voting behavior and income.

Further research might investigate the factors that influence preferences by citizens regarding waste taxes and other environmental issues. One consideration might be how consumers experience the tax burden of waste taxes. We suspect the impact of such taxes is fairly diffuse. Often, hazardous waste generators are in the chemicals and petroleum sectors producing intermediate inputs. By the time the tax is passed along to consumers, it is likely to be diffused throughout many different products.[15] At first glance, the connection between solid waste taxes and the consumer might seem more direct, but most households pay for waste services through flat fees or indirectly through property taxes. Thus, the much smaller solid waste tax is also not typically directly experienced by consumers. How, then, do consumers perceive the desirability of waste taxes in particular and environmental taxes generally? Does this perception vary by race? Perhaps future research addressing this question can lend insight into our own findings.

Notes

The views expressed in this chapter are those of the authors and do not necessarily represent those of the US Environmental Protection Agency. No official agency endorsement should be inferred. The authors appreciate the conscientious research assistance by Tristan Harris, Emma Roach, and Rebecca Toseland.

1. Ringquist (2005) systematically assesses the correlation between race and environmental risk by conducting a meta-analysis of 49 environmental justice studies. He concludes there is "ubiquitous evidence of environmental inequities based upon race." However, Wolverton (Chapter 8) finds no evidence of discrimination at the time of siting.

2. The differences in race are more pronounced after narrowing the host area studied to a small 3-kilometer circle, as opposed to examining the host census tract without regard to the tract's size or boundary in relation to the waste facility's location (Bullard et al. 2007).

3. Sigman (2003) considers a specific state revenue need by exploring the impact the number of state Superfund sites has on hazardous tax rates and hypothesizes that

states with more sites will have a greater need for funding. However, she finds no association between the number of sites and hazardous waste tax rates.

4. Not all hazardous waste is managed by treatment, storage, and disposal facilities; most is managed by the waste generators themselves.

5. Presumably siting difficulties were also unanticipated as evidenced by the sparse guidance in RCRA for handling them.

6. The cleanup activities usually target contamination that occurred prior to the safeguards put in place by RCRA.

7. Slightly different but along the same vein is the possibility that state governments levy taxes to recoup the costs of their waste management efforts. However, virtually all states impose licensing and registration fees on waste facilities with the explicit purpose of recouping these costs.

8. This is one measure that Sigman (2003) found to be significant to state hazardous waste tax rates.

9. We exclude Alaska and Hawaii from the analysis because of their unique locations. Alaska taxes neither hazardous nor municipal waste; Hawaii taxes municipal waste only.

10. Variable definitions and descriptive statistics are presented in Tables A.10.1 and A.10.2, respectively, in the online appendix at http://www.sup.org/environmentaljustice.

11. Contributions are measured by each state's per-capita contributions in the United States to environmental organizations between 1988 and 2001, as collected by the National Center for Charitable Statistics/GuideStar National Nonprofit Database. We also have each state's share of the total membership in the Sierra Club, but found that the variable measuring contributions was more robust.

12. To gauge the degree of concentration for hazardous waste, we rely on the 2005 Biennial Reporting System (BRS). On average, the three firms managing the greatest quantities of hazardous waste are handling 84 percent of total hazardous waste managed in a state. For solid waste landfills, we estimate concentration based on data from the 2003 Chartwell database. The three landfills accepting the highest quantities of solid waste, on average, manage 39 percent of total municipal waste disposed of in a state

13. We address the endogeneity problem in the "Econometric Results" section.

14. We estimated the models excluding the state race variables but including the race of the host areas, and the latter remained insignificant.

15. Fullerton (1996) provides evidence that environmental taxes have diffuse effects. He examines the effect of nine separate environmental taxes on 41 outputs and finds that only two output prices are affected by more than 1 percent.

References

Aidt, Toke S. 1998. "Political Internalization of Economic Externalities and Environmental Policy." *Journal of Public Economics* 69 (1): 1–16.

Bullard, Robert D. 1983. "Solid Waste Sites and the Black Houston Community." *Sociological Inquiry* 53 (2–3): 273–88.

Bullard, Robert D., Paul Mohai, Robin Saha, and Beverly Wright. 2007. *Toxic Wastes and Race at Twenty: 1987–2007*. Report prepared for the United Church of Christ Justice and Witness Ministries, Cleveland, OH. http://www.ucc.org/assets/pdfs/toxic20.pdf.

Fredriksson, Per G., and Daniel L. Millimet. 2002. "Strategic Interaction and the Determination of Environmental Policy across U.S. States." *Journal of Urban Economics* 51 (1): 101–22.

Fullerton, Don. 1996. "Why Have Separate Environmental Taxes?" In *Tax Policy and the Economy*, edited by James M. Poterba, 33–70. Cambridge, MA: MIT Press.

Hamilton, James T. 1995. "Testing for Environmental Racism: Prejudice, Profits, Political Power?" *Journal of Policy Analysis and Management* 14 (1): 107–32.

Jenkins, Robin R., Elizabeth Kopits, and David Simpson. 2009. "The Evolution of Solid and Hazardous Waste Regulation in the United States." *Review of Environmental Economics and Policy* 3 (1): 104–20.

Jenkins, Robin R., Kelly B. Maguire, and Cynthia L. Morgan. 2004. "Host Community Compensation and Municipal Solid Waste Landfills." *Land Economics* 80 (4): 513–28.

Levinson, Arik. 1999a. "NIMBY Taxes Matter: The Case of State Hazardous Waste Disposal Taxes." *Journal of Public Economics* 74 (1): 31–51.

———. 1999b. "State Taxes and Interstate Hazardous Waste Shipments." *American Economic Review* 89 (3): 666–77.

———. 2003. "Environmental Regulatory Competition: A Status Report and Some New Evidence." *National Tax Journal* 56 (1): 91–106.

Oates, Wallace E. 2001. "A Reconsideration of Environmental Federalism." Discussion Paper 01-54, Resources for the Future, Washington, DC.

Oates, Wallace E., and Paul R. Portney. 2003. "The Political Economy of Environmental Policy." In *The Handbook of Environmental Economics*, edited by Karl-Göran Mäler and Jeffrey R. Vincent, 325–54. Cheltenham, UK: Edward Elgar.

Ringquist, Evan. 2005. "Assessing Evidence of Environmental Inequities: A Meta-Analysis." *Journal of Policy Analysis and Management* 24 (2): 223–47.

Sigman, Hilary. 1996. "The Effects of Hazardous Waste Taxes on Waste Generation and Disposal." *Journal of Environmental Economics and Management* 30 (2): 199–217.

———. 2003. "Taxing Hazardous Waste: The U.S. Experience." *Public Finance and Management* 3 (1): 12–33.

Simmons, Phil, Nora Goldstein, Scott M. Kaufman, Nickolas J. Themelis, and James Thompson Jr. 2006. "The State of Garbage in America." *BioCycle* 47 (4): 26–43.

Sobel, Russell S. 1997. "Optimal Taxation in a Federal System of Governments." *Southern Economic Journal* 64 (2): 468–85.

United Church of Christ. 1987. *Toxic Wastes and Race in the United States: A National Report on the Racial and Socio-Economic Characteristics of Communities with Hazardous Waste Sites.* New York: Public Data Access.

US Army Corps of Engineers (USACE). 2005. *Report on Treatment, Storage and Disposal Facilities (TSDF) for Hazardous, Toxic, and Radioactive Waste, 2006 Update.* http://www.environmental.usace.army.mil/TSDF/tsdf.htm.

US General Accounting Office (GAO). 1983. *Siting of Hazardous Waste Landfills and Their Correlation with Racial and Economic Status of Surrounding Communities.* Washington, DC: GAO.

Postscript

Who Owns the Environment?

Terry L. Anderson

ALL ENVIRONMENTAL issues ultimately boil down to property rights issues. Because of scarcity, people compete for the use of resources—land, water, and air—and, in the process, create opportunity costs for those resources. The question therefore is who bears those opportunity costs. The answer to this question is confused by the concept of externality (see Anderson 2004), which implicitly assumes a set of property rights and therefore determines who bears what costs. In his seminal article "The Problem of Social Cost," Coase (1960) taught us that conflicting uses result in reciprocal costs. One use of a resource—housing—results in foregoing the use of the resource in another use—effluent disposal.[1]

Given scarcity, the question is not whether there are opportunity costs but who bears them. This is determined by who has what property rights. If property rights are clearly defined and enforced, whether they can or will be bargained over in the marketplace is a function of transaction costs.

Environmental justice or injustice is no different; it is a property rights issue. Does the landowner have the right to build houses on her land free of effluent or does the effluent producer have the right to dump effluent on the land?[2] In general, do people living in a certain location have a property right to their environment? Even if the rights are not clearly defined and enforced, will transaction costs allow market adjustments to reflect the cost of resource use?

For the most part, economics has steered clear of environmental justice issues on the grounds that they are normative and therefore outside the scope of positive economics. As this volume illustrates, however, the property rights lens provides a positive framework for analyzing the distributional and efficiency implications of different property rights assignments. Indeed, even if property rights seem unclear or unenforced, they may be bundled to assets like land which do have strong property rights. The chapters in Section I of this volume show that asset price adjustments implicitly account for costs and that those asset price adjustments generate distributional consequences. Moreover, in cases where the environmental property rights reside with the resource owner, bargaining can and does occur. In some cases, this bargaining results in resource owners trading lower environmental quality for other valuable goods or services in their consumption bundle.

Because the assignment of property rights, whether explicit or implicit or whether formal or informal, does have distributional consequences, a normative response is to redistribute those rights in favor of the "disadvantaged." However, given the empirical evidence presented in this volume, the property rights lens raises questions about whether this can be done without efficiency implications.

This postscript uses the property rights lens to put the empirical evidence into the context of four important property rights questions regarding environmental justice:

1. Do the owners of land have the right to control the use of their land for effluent disposal? Does this right extend to water and air on or around their land?
2. Do people renting—as opposed to owning—housing have a property right to their environment?
3. Even if the rights are not clearly defined and enforced, will market adjustments reflect the cost of resource use?
4. Can property rights be clarified or redistributed, ex post, in the name of environmental justice without affecting resource allocation, including rent seeking, to obtain the rights?

Landowner Rights

If we begin to analyze environmental injustice with the assumption that the landowner holds the right to not have his property (including land, water, and air) used as an effluent dump, the potential for a Coasean bargain is in place. The only constraint is transaction costs,[3] including the costs of monitoring the amount of effluent, identifying its source, measuring its impact on the property rights, and establishing a price for it.[4] If these transaction costs are sufficiently low to allow bargaining, the resource value will reflect the environmental value. Either the resource owner will be compensated for having the effluent dumped and will utilize the property for lower-valued uses, or he will not allow the dumping, foregoing compensation and putting the resource to a higher-valued use with a cleaner environment.

Either result could be taken as evidence of environmental injustice. If the property is used as a dump with commensurate lower environmental quality, its lower-valued use could include low-income housing. Rather than the correlation between lower environmental quality and low-income housing being evidence of environmental injustice, however, the property rights lens reveals that the correlation is a market outcome. The gains from trade include gains for the effluent producer who dumps on the property for a price that presumably is lower than alternative disposal methods, gains for the property owner who receives compensation for the dumping, and gains for the low-income person who trades off lower rent for lower environmental quality.

To be sure, the market outcome results from an initial wealth distribution, as do all market outcomes. That initial wealth distribution might be unjust as measured by some normative standard, but the combination of lower environmental quality and low-income housing are not prima facie evidence of environmental injustice.

Renter Rights

The previous discussion assumes that the resource owner holds the rights to be free from effluent dumping, but what if the renter of the resource holds the right? Suppose that a resource renter has rented the resource for a long time and become accustomed to having the resource free of effluent. For example, in the following scenario used by Coase, party A might rent a building for use as a laundry from party B. If party C, subsequent to the initial rental agreement, begins emitting effluent into the air, which dirties the laundry, party A, the renter, might have a claim against party B if the owner of the building claimed it was free from the effluent or against party C for dirtying the laundry.[5] In other words, the renter could have a property right to be free from the effluent.

If the renter had such a property right, she would be in a position to bargain with the building owner for lower rent or with the effluent dumper for compensation. In either case, transaction costs would condition the bargaining result. If the transaction costs are sufficiently low to allow bargaining, the market will reflect the values. Of course, instead of accepting lower rent or compensation for the dirty laundry, the laundry owner might install mechanical dryers as opposed to using a clothes line or she might refuse compensation entirely and force the emitter to cease emissions.

Returning to the case of housing, if the renter has a right to be free from effluent (this could be dirty air or noise) and accepts the effluent in return for compensation, the evidence might suggest environmental injustice with low-income renters having lower environmental quality. The compensation in return for accepting the effluent, however, suggests otherwise. Whether it is a direct cash payment or an agreement from the emitter to build a school or hospital, the correlation between low-income housing and effluent is not prima facie evidence of environmental injustice. Because the amount of the compensation will be a function of the bargaining power of the parties, it may well be that low-income renters will get what appears to be an unjust price, however measured, but this would reflect a potential injustice in the distribution of bargaining power, not environmental injustice per se.

Voting with Your Feet

Charles Tiebout (1956) pointed out that the value of a public good can be captured by immobile resource owners and paid for by the people who value them if people move to places where there is relatively more of the public good. This is known as the "Tiebout effect," and it results from people "voting with their feet." When people move to places with more public goods, they bid up the price of immobile resources such as land and houses. The increased price of such assets is capitalized into asset values and paid for by newcomers.

In the opposite direction, "public bads" such as environmental degradation can reduce immobile asset values and encourage people willing to trade off lower-priced land and housing for lower environmental quality to move to the bad. If these people are lower-income minorities, their proximity to the environmental degradation may appear to be environmental injustice when, in fact, it is another example of market equilibration.

In essence, the Tiebout effect illustrates how property rights and markets internalize externalities, positive or negative, through assets that are location-specific. Because immobile asset values will be higher in the presence of public goods or lower in the presence of public bads, people purchasing these assets, or their services, will pay for the good or will be compensated for the bad. In the case of improved environmental quality, higher real estate values may cause poorer people to move out of the area; in the case of reduced environmental quality, lower real estate values may cause wealthier people to exit. Evidence of the former can be construed as environmental injustice when, in fact, it is a reflection of income disparities. Attempting to offset income disparities by providing environmental public goods will induce people to vote with their feet again—the poor will move away and the rich will move in—and will allow the property owners to capture the value.

Efficiency versus Injustice

The final question regarding environmental justice focuses on the rent seeking that results if property rights are redistributed, ex post, in an effort to correct apparent environmental justice. Suppose, for example, that rent controls are put in place to prevent real estate owners from increasing the price of apartments when environmental quality is improved. In essence, rent controls redistribute a portion of asset values to those occupying apartments at the time controls are imposed. If the rent controls are unanticipated, those occupying apartments will be made better off at the expense of those who pay for the environmental improvements. On the other hand, if the rent controls are anticipated, people will race to capture those values. The time and effort put into the race use resources with alternative productive uses. In the extreme, this rent-seeking effort will dissipate the value of the environmental improvement. As a result, the value of that improvement will be paid for by the rent seekers but will not be captured by the asset owners or by the providers of the public good. In short, the price of achieving environmental justice by redistributing property rights is the efficiency loss associated with rent seeking.

It's Hard to Keep a Good Market Down

Coase had it right; conflicts over resource use create the potential for rent dissipation, but the potential for rent dissipation creates an incentive for bargaining. For bargaining to happen, there must be property rights. Whether the rights evolve through formal legal processes or evolve from first possession,[6] they impart value to the owner. If the environment associated with the property is improved, the asset value will reflect the improvement, and people purchasing the property or services therefrom will pay for the environmental quality. To the extent that income is not evenly distributed, those who value environmental quality will outbid those who do not. Given that environmental quality is typically a normal good (meaning more of it is consumed as incomes rise), income inequality will result in differential environmental consumption. In other words, poorer people will purchase less environmental quality than richer people. Trying to eliminate this disparity by increasing environmental quality for poorer people will most likely increase property values. Assuming that poorer people do not own the property, the higher value will be captured by the owner, and the increased environmental quality will be enjoyed by wealthier people who move to the amenity.

The important take-away from viewing environmental justice through a Coasean lens is that apparent environmental injustice is a reflection of income inequality. Hence, if individuals or society wish to correct the injustice, they will do better to focus on the root cause—income inequality—rather than the effect—environmental quality consumption.

Notes

1. For the purposes of this discussion, effluent includes any alteration of property use that carries over to neighboring property. It could include garbage, fumes, odors, reflected light, and so on.

2. This may seem like an unlikely distribution of property rights, but the legal notion of "coming to the nuisance" can result in precisely this type of property right. For a discussion of coming to the nuisance and how it has been eroded as a common law defense, see Meiners and Yandle (1999).

3. For a discussion of transaction costs in the context of environmental entrepreneurship, see Anderson and McCormick (2004).

4. The last cost can be high if the property owner and the effluent producer are in a bilateral monopoly position. See Libecap (2005) and Brewer and Libecap (2009) for the implications of this problem as it relates to bargaining over water rights.

5. Of course, party B, the building owner, might also have a claim.

6. Note that first possession can also cause rent seeking. See Lueck (2003).

References

Anderson, Terry L. 2004. "Donning Coase-Coloured Glasses: A Property Rights View of Natural Resource Economics." *Australian Journal of Agricultural and Resource Economics* 48 (3): 445–62.

Anderson, Terry L., and Robert E. McCormick. 2004. "The Contractual Nature of the Environment." In *The Elgar Companion to Property Rights*, edited by Enrico Colombatto, 293–309. Cheltenham, UK: Edward Elgar.

Brewer, Jedediah, and Gary D. Libecap. 2009. "Property Rights and the Public Trust Doctrine in Environmental Protection and Natural Resource Conservation." *Australian Journal of Agricultural and Resource Economics* 53 (1): 1–17.

Coase, Ronald H. 1960. "The Problem of Social Cost." *Journal of Law and Economics* 3 (1): 1–44.

Libecap, Gary D. 2005. "Rescuing Water Markets: Lessons from Owens Valley." *PERC Policy Series*, no. 33. Bozeman, MT: Property and Environment Research Center.

Lueck, Dean. 2003. "First Possession as the Basis of Property." In *Property Rights: Cooperation, Conflict, and Law*, edited by Terry L. Anderson and Fred S. McChesney. Princeton, NJ: Princeton University Press.

Meiners, Roger, and Bruce Yandle. 1999. "Common Law and the Conceit of Modern Environmental Policy." *George Mason Law Review* 7 (4): 923–63.

Tiebout, Charles. 1956. "A Pure Theory of Local Expenditures." *Journal of Political Economy* 64 (5): 416–24.

Index